# 𝕾𝖍𝖆𝖐𝖊𝖘𝖕𝖊𝖆𝖗𝖊

## for

# 𝕽𝖊𝖆𝖉𝖊𝖗𝖘' 𝕿𝖍𝖊𝖆𝖙𝖗𝖊

## Volume 1

### *Hamlet*

### *Romeo and Juliet*

### *A Midsummer Night's Dream*

Adapted for Reader's Theatre by

**John Poulsen**

Associate Professor
Drama Education
Faculty of Education
University of Lethbridge

FIVE RIVERS PUBLISHING
NEUSTADT, ONTARIO, CANADA
HTTP://WWW.5RIVERS.ORG

*To Emily. Thanks for your support.*

John Poulsen, PhD, is Associate Professor, Drama Education, Faculty of Education, University of Lethbridge (Alberta, Canada).

Editor: Robert Runté, PhD

Cover Copyright © 2012 by Jeff Minkevics

Interior design: Lorina Stephens

Text set in Adobe Garamond Pro
Headings set in Gill Sans MT
Title set in Old English Text MT

Published by Five Rivers Publishing
Neustadt, Ontario, Canada
www.5rivers.org

Quantity discounts available for educators purchasing class sets.
Contact sales@5rivers.org for details.

Library and Archives Canada Cataloguing in Publication

Poulsen, John Christian S., 1954-
Shakespeare for readers' theatre / adapted for reader's
theatre by John Poulsen.

Includes bibliographical references.
v. 1. Hamlet, Romeo and Juliet, Midsummer night's dream.
Issued also in electronic format.
ISBN 978-1-927400-18-0 (v. 1)

1. Shakespeare, William, 1564-1616--Adaptations.
2. Shakespeare, William, 1564-1616--Dramatic production.
3. Readers' theater. I. Shakespeare, William, 1564-1616 II. Title.

PR3091.P69 2012        822.3'3        C2012-905441-0

# Contents

## Part Two: *Hamlet*

## Part Three: *Romeo and Juliet*

## Part Four: *Midsummer Night's Dream*

To Betty, Kate, and Jason.

## Acknowledgements

The journey of creating this book would have been impossible without my editor, Dr. Robert Runté; thank you, Robert. Thanks are also due to Clem Martini and Cheryl Foggo for their encouragement and advice and to my publisher Lorina Stephens of Five Rivers Publishing. Thanks also to Katherine and Ed Wasiak, the administration of the University of Lethbridge, and the Faculty of Education, without whose support I would not have been able to complete this project.

We are all a product of our past and ongoing upbringing, so I thank my parents for my upbringing, and my immediate and extended family for my continuing development.

# Part One: Introduction

## Chapter 1: Overview

### SHAKESPEARE IS EXTRAORDINARY

That is the premise of this book. Shakespeare's works are delightful and they still speak to us 400 years after being written. His way of saying things resonates right now as being accurate and beautiful. In one fell swoop he can brilliantly catch a concept. "One fell swoop" from *Macbeth* is one of those marvelous phrases that is still used today. Why? Because it is accurate. Because it encapsulates the idea of 'in a single action' or 'suddenly' or 'completely' or 'efficiently' in a wonderfully fresh image. Instead of using a more cumbersome phrase, 'one fell swoop' is clean and slices through ambiguity. It leaves one uplifted.

Here's an example from one of Shakespeare's lesser-known plays, *All's Well that Ends Well*. In Act 2 Shakespeare says, "I have seen a medicine, that's able to breathe life into a stone. Quicken a rock, and make you dance canary." Immediately we are interested. We all want that medicine. Our curiosity is sparked. What is this medicine? What does it taste like? How can I get some? Will it help my lower back?

How does Shakespeare do it? How does he, with just a few words, pique our interest and heighten our senses. It's not easy. The fact that we only have one Shakespeare and he wrote 400 years ago suggests Shakespeares are not created every week.

### LANGUAGE

His language can be difficult. He sometimes uses odd words or uses words in ways that we are not used to seeing. For example, 'dance canary.' We are not sure what the dance would look like, but it has joy in it. First of all, to dance is joyful and then to dance canary sounds like it would be even better, so in this briefly sketched 'dance canary' image he has stirred people's interest. Now, part of us all wants to dance canary, especially after being sick for a period of time.

The poetry is part of what catches us. His way of turning a phrase twigs something in our minds. We have to ponder, "breathe life into a stone." How would you breathe life into a stone? An image of blowing a stone up like a balloon might come to mind. Then it might morph into a stone beginning to expand like a balloon, then arms and legs pop out. Whichever direction individual's minds go, it's good. It is exercise. It is exercise we want. Exercise we crave.

So, why do so many students love him and so many others don't? It might be that some of Shakespeare's language is too obscure; it has been too long since that language has been used in the way that Shakespeare uses it. This text has pared down the number of obsolete terms so that the students are not overwhelmed, while still retaining enough of the original to familiarize students with Shakespearean English.

## ABRIDGEMENT

People have a natural bent toward narration. We love stories. We want to know what happens next. In today's world, TV stories are often told in a succinct 23 minutes or less. It should be no surprise that Shakespeare monologues can feel long, be difficult to understand, and have trouble holding students' attention.

It is routine for productions of Shakespeare's plays to be abridged. Directors will often streamline the play to emphasize those lines and scenes that support the director's interpretation, or simply to shorten it for modern audiences. For the Readers' Theatre abridgements that follow, this routine practice is simply taken much further.

The texts of *Hamlet, Romeo and Juliet,* and *Midsummer Night's Dream* have been pared down to their essentials. The main story remains intact. To achieve this brevity, some characters have been removed. For example, in *Hamlet* Fortinbras is gone, as is his storyline about marching his soldiers across Denmark. However, the gravedigger and Yorick's skull remain. The gravedigger was deemed more important because his examination of life is reflective of Hamlet's own musings. In addition, the gravedigger is funny and his abridged lines still elicit laughter.

Fortinbras could be considered important as a foil to Hamlet. Fortinbras is a man of action, whereas Hamlet can be seen as a man of thought. When reducing these plays, tough decisions had to be made and in the case of *Hamlet*, Fortinbras was removed and the gravedigger was retained.

In cutting some of the minor characters, there are lines that are important to the plot and continuity that have been attributed to other characters. For example, in the play *Hamlet*, lines said by the minor character Marcellus at the top of the play have been given to Bernardo. The words remain

Shakespeare's, but they don't always come out of the original mouths. This may be important to mention so that students are not unduly confused should they read another text and find a different character speaking those lines.

Comedy is sprinkled throughout Shakespeare's plays; however, the speech in some comic sections is often so difficult for modern audiences to understand that the comedy is lost. Fortunately, with a small amount of judicious cutting, the essence of the humour can shine through.

In Act 1 of *Romeo and Juliet,* one of Shakespeare's greatest plays, the Prince gives a 23-line monologue that explains the plot to this point in the play. It runs about one minute and 30 seconds. On the Internet, young people could have surfed through any number of stories in those 90 seconds. There are parts of the speech that are important for understanding the background of the play; however, some of the following lines can be difficult to understand.

**PRINCE**

> Rebellious subjects, enemies to peace,
> Profaners of this neighbour-stained steel,—
> Will they not hear? What, ho! you men, you beasts,
> That quench the fire of your pernicious rage
> With purple fountains issuing from your veins,
> On pain of torture, from those bloody hands
> Throw your mistemper'd weapons to the ground,
> And hear the sentence of your moved prince.
> Three civil brawls, bred of an airy word,
> By thee, old Capulet, and Montague,
> Have thrice disturb'd the quiet of our streets,
> And made Verona's ancient citizens
> Cast by their grave beseeming ornaments,
> To wield old partisans, in hands as old,
> Canker'd with peace, to part your canker'd hate:
> If ever you disturb our streets again,
> Your lives shall pay the forfeit of the peace.
> For this time, all the rest depart away:
> You Capulet; shall go along with me:
> And, Montague, come you this afternoon,
> To know our further pleasure in this case,
> To old Free-town, our common judgment-place.
> Once more, on pain of death, all men depart.

Lines such as these, although important, can be reduced. Some of the poetry is lost, but the gain is brevity that can be attractive to young people. Here is this book's version of the above.

**NARRATOR**

The Prince of Verona enters and stops the fighting.

**PRINCE**

Rebellious subjects, enemies to peace
Will they not hear? What, ho! You men. You beasts.
Three civil brawls, bred of an airy* word (*imagined insult)
By thee old Capulet and Montague
Have thrice disturbed the quiet of our streets.
If ever you disturb our streets again,
Your lives shall pay the forfeit of the peace.
Away, on pain of death, all men depart.

Notice that the shortened version, aside from the Narrator's comment, is all Shakespeare's words. The poetry remains in this abridged version. Yet because of the elimination of 15 lines there is a greater chance that young people will understand. In the above example (from this book), there is enough new and poetic, such as "forfeit of the peace," balanced with the straightforward, "If ever you disturb our streets again," that students are more likely to understand the story and language. Greater understanding increases the probability of enjoyment.

The basic Shakespearean stories are unchanged, and the important and famous lines from each play are retained. This book has carefully abridged Shakespeare, ready for students to grab hold and become energized.

## READERS' THEATRE

Readers' Theatre is also extraordinary. It is an effective form of presentation for a number of reasons. The time from handing out the scripts to presentation can be brief. Students with short attention spans have a greater chance of staying with the process of mounting a Readers' Theatre production than with any other form of presentation. Even poor readers can be successful. If your students mumble when they read and are unable to be heard or understood when the audience is more than 10 feet away, then bring the audience to within nine feet. After the first successful reading of the script, have a rehearsal where reading volume and clarity are the focus. Then for your next performance, move your audience a few feet farther back. The students have a greater chance of working on their reading skill if they have a reason to improve. A successful first presentation of these scripts could be that reason. A scheduled second reading of the script can build on a sense of accomplishment and motivate students to work on their presentation skills.

Whatever else happens, these scripts contain bright stories and fine language. As long as performers can be heard, these stories and this language have proved themselves for more than 400 years. Shakespeare's stories such as *Romeo and Juliet* are so consistently appreciated that the enjoyment of his work seems to be deeply embedded in us.

A Readers' Theatre presentation to their peers can make students engage more, work harder and learn more. Testimonials abound that suggest students who present to an audience work harder than those whose work is only seen by the instructor.

Readers who have performed the work once in front of their peers may be excited about presenting the work to an outside audience. And every time actors present, they read Shakespeare's words with greater understanding. Each time students perform, often a different line 'pops' out at them, taking on new significance, and resonating in a way it may not have before. Shakespearean phrases might even begin to seep into their language. A young woman may describe how, in one fell swoop, she removed her mother's doubt concerning her behavior by bringing home a stellar report card.

Similarly, the concepts behind the poetry of Shakespeare remain. When Juliet asks, "What's in a name? That which we call a rose, by any other name would smell as sweet," she is confronting a concept that young people may not have thought about so clearly. The idea that there can be a disconnect between words and objects that are connected to the words may be new to students. This new idea or a sharpening of the idea, can be exciting and motivating to young people.

## PRESENTATION

This book has reduced the great Shakespearean stories by about 75%. For example, the original *Romeo and Juliet* has about 25,850 words. The version in this book has about 5,535 words or about 21% of the original. The savings in words is partially alleviated by the Readers' Theatre form. The narrator explains, in a much abbreviated fashion, important plot elements. This helps with the pace and playability of these abridgements.

These scripts are ready for Readers' Theatre presentation. With a minimum of rehearsal young people can present Shakespeare using Shakespeare's poetry. A group ranging in number from seven to 15 can present these plays in about 45 minutes. Variable casting can be achieved by some double or even triple casting. It enables a cast to be continually in flux until the curtain opens. The presentation does not depend on everyone being in attendance. A student who is away with the flu or on a school sanctioned off-campus activity does not hold up the show: the part can be given to someone else.

The remaining actors can decide on the new casting, read through the affected sections and shortly thereafter march to their opening positions ready and confident. A performer who has been away for two weeks can be inserted into a minor role with a minimum of preparation or disruption. Organizing a second presentation provides a greater likelihood that everyone will present at some point. That is, the second presentation increases the chances that all class members will read to an audience at least once.

Think your class might be ready for a greater challenge? After only a few classes students can be ready to present Shakespeare to an audience. Scripts given to students on Monday can be performed next class. Providing additional direction and rehearsal time means that those same students could perform with greater skill by the end of the week.

Are you new to this or might you want some suggestions for directing? Recommendations for direction are included in this book. More rehearsal means a greater chance of a better production; more rehearsal that is focused by a director creates an even greater chance of success.

Forty-five minutes too long? Not a problem. The book also has shorter versions that run about 20 minutes. However, there are fewer scenes and fewer of the significant lines. The shorter version could be viewed as a trailer for the play, peeking student interest in seeing or reading the whole thing, just as movie trailers tempt audiences to the cinema. Thanks to its brevity, it can be given to students at the beginning of a 52-minute class and they can perform it before the end of the period.

This book offers two Readers' Theatre versions of each play: *Hamlet, Romeo and Juliet,* and *Midsummer Night's Dream.* The first is a 45-minute abridgement. The second is a 20-minute abridged version of the Shakespearean play, which has a student copy and a teacher's copy.

The teacher's copy is called the *Director's Script.* It has directorial suggestions meant to help create an entertaining and educational presentation. Near the top of *Romeo and Juliet* a quarrel begins the play. At a certain point the combatants begin to quarrel. In Shakespeare's original script there is a simple stage direction (kept here) to bite thumb.

**SAMPSON**

My naked* weapon is out. Quarrel, I will back thee. *(* unsheathed, ready)*

**GREGORY**

I will frown as they pass by, and let them take it as they list*. *(* please)*

**SAMPSON**

Nay as they dare, I will bite my thumb at them, which is a disgrace to them if they bear it (bites thumb).

The above is the student version. Students can see the lines that are to be said in regular text font. The asterisks indicate words or phrases that will be clarified in small italics to help understanding.

In the student script, the above is all the students see. Because it is expected that students keep their own scripts, it is hoped students will highlight their lines and write in their stage directions on their scripts.

In the *Director's Script* there are more detailed suggestions:

**SAMPSON**

My naked* weapon is out. Quarrel, I will back thee. *(* unsheathed, ready)*
**(Roll the script into a sword and show it.)**

**GREGORY**

I will frown as they pass by, and let them take it as they list*. *(* please)*
**(Frown using off stage focus.)**

**SAMPSON**

Nay as they dare, I will bite my thumb at them, which is a disgrace to them if they bear it.
**(Bite thumb in an insulting manner directing the action straight ahead.)**

The actors are using offstage focus that is explained in Chapter 2. This allows them to face the audience at all times so that vocal clarity is not impeded. The directorial recommendations are in bold so they are easy to see.

## READING SKILL

Students cast to read a play can have a range of reading skill. Some students may stumble over even simple words, whereas others read aloud beautifully. Casting stronger readers in the heavier roles can differentiate the workload so that students are challenged, but not swamped. Allow students to take scripts home so they can practice in private. Start each rehearsal with a cacophonous whole cast recitation where readers read their own sections at the same time that other cast members read theirs. Such a warm-up encourages increased volume.

Students do not always realize when they are in a quality production. An audience's response will sway their opinion about the value of the experience. A Shakespearean Readers' Theatre provides a great chance of success. Shakespeare's name carries panache. Although audiences are often fearful that they will not understand Shakespeare's language, they usually respond enthusiastically when they can understand what is being said. The result might be a combination of an exaltation of relief that they can understand, and the genuine joy of comprehending the text.

Giving students and audiences a taste of success through an understandable version of Shakespeare via Readers' Theatre encourages students to work harder. The presenters may, in the performance, get a sense of what has been accomplished. Further, they might get a sense of what can be accomplished with focused work. Through the positive response from the audience, students who have presented a Readers' Theatre play will be motivated to earn that positive response again. They may even be interested in working harder to strengthen the positive audience response. Audiences who have experienced a successful Shakespeare production are more inclined to watch Shakespeare again.

## WRAP-UP

Shakespeare's plays are peopled by wondrous beings and ideas. His was an optimistic view of the world. He had unique thoughts and brilliant ways of expressing those thoughts. The object of this book is that readers will be uplifted, and have a sense that we live in a brave new world, full of hope and expectation. Shakespeare, more than any other, is able to touch an innate hopefulness that resonates in young people. That hopefulness is what this book is about.

## Chapter 2: Readers' Theatre Background and Conventions

### NUTSHELL

Readers' Theatre is a stylized theatre form in which a group "reads" or presents a piece of literature using specific conventions, which are outlined in this chapter. Readers' Theatre can help you and your students by generating the excitement needed to inspire students to work hard, hard work being the best indicator of learning.

### HISTORY

Readers' Theatre traditions can be traced back to Ancient Greece. There is evidence that wondering minstrels called rhapodes read from ancient texts, especially the *Iliad*. The term Readers' Theatre did not arise until 1945 when a professional theatre group in New York called themselves Reader's Theatre, Inc. and produced *Oedipus Rex*. Reader's Theatre Inc., which wanted to present important but seldom produced plays, met with considerable public acclaim.

After the success of Reader's Theatre Inc., a flurry of plays appeared including *Don Juan in Hell* by George Bernard Shaw (1951), Vincent Benét's poem *John Brown's Body* (1952), and in 1967 *You're a Good Man, Charlie Brown* (the first musical presented using this format).

During the 1960s, Readers' Theatre came to classrooms via college and university theatre departments where undergraduate students experimented with the form. These students eventually became teachers who took the form into their classrooms. Readers' Theatre became an efficient method of presenting important literature. Part of its power is that productions could be mounted quickly. Presentations could follow minutes after students were given the scripts. It could also be rehearsed, which increased the theatricality of the presentation. Missing cast members could easily be replaced. Individuals who had trouble memorizing could be helped by the convention of carrying the script. Even poor reading skill was not necessarily a deterrent because poor readers would start with smaller roles and earn larger roles as they developed.

## PRACTICAL READERS' THEATRE

An audience's first encounter with Readers' Theatre usually is a line of chairs or stools on stage. The performers or readers enter shortly thereafter in a stylized fashion, sit, and the play begins.

Readers' Theatre is a group activity involving a cast that "reads" a piece of literature. The term "read" is a misnomer in that performers can read, but more dynamic productions have performers at least partially memorize their lines and say them with more skill.

Reading the play is fine and your audience will appreciate the presentation. Moreover, your performers will gain a deeper understanding of the literature they are presenting as compared to reading the piece of literature on their own. A director, however, can improve the presentation by increasing the vocal and physical skill of the performers. A bit of direction and focused effort can make a Readers' Theatre production more exciting for a variety of audiences.

Issues of clarity and volume can arise with performers who read holding the page down on their laps. Encouraging young performers to enunciate and project can be difficult until the performers become very familiar with the script. Also some audience members relish seeing the faces of performers and gain information about the story from the actors' expressions. A cast that is sufficiently familiar with their scripts that they can speak facing straight forward to the audience improves both understanding and entertainment value.

Ideally, Readers' Theatre performers communicate a piece of literature through vocal and physical suggestion. The more accurate and vivid the vocal and physical suggestion, the better the performance. It follows that the more comfortable performers are with their lines, the more they can engage in characterization. Costumes, props, and sets are not needed, but it is acceptable for an actor to wear minimal costumes such as a hat, scarf, or jacket to suggest a character.

Double casting is not only acceptable in Readers' Theatre, it can be desirable. It can help some performers remain more focused through the entire presentation. If a reader performs the role of Guard at the top of *Hamlet*, she might also be able to perform Ophelia later on. She might wear a helmet as the guard and a scarf as Ophelia. The minor costume pieces help the audience distinguish between the two roles and help the performer develop her characters.

Double casting can also help in performance. An absent performer does not shut down the entire production. The role may be given to another actor and the show goes on.

## CONVENTIONS

A theatrical convention can be described as a shortcut that is understood and accepted by the audience. The intention of a theatrical convention is to enhance audience understanding and enjoyment, and help to illuminate the literature being presented.

There are a series of theatrical conventions that are used in regular theatre production. When the house lights dim, audiences know the show is about to begin. A spotlight on an individual actor while the lights are off in another part of the set suggests the performer is separate from the action in the other part of the stage and cannot be heard by the darkened characters.

Generally there is a separation between audience and actors. Readers' Theatre shares some of these conventions and has some of its own, including stools/chairs. In all Readers' Theatre performers sit for at least a part of the production in a way that makes them easily visible to the audience. Following is an examination of Readers' Theatre theatrical conventions.

### SCRIPT

*Script always On Stage.* Performers arrive on stage with script in hand and usually exit the same way. In between, the script can be used in a variety of ways and even briefly placed on a chair or the floor, if needed. It may even be given temporarily to someone else, but each performer must have a script in hand at the top of the performance.

*Script as a Prop.* A script might be used as a letter that gets ripped up and thrown away. If a character is writing a letter let the script become the paper upon which it is written or even the pen. Rolling up the script turns it into a spyglass or a sword. However, tightly rolled scripts used for sword fights do not usually survive more than one performance.

*Script Memorization.* Memorizing certain parts of the script enables performers to exhibit more interesting blocking and choreography. Fight scenes interrupted by constantly referring to the script may be dangerous. The pace of a show, especially near the climax, is often so tight that students have to memorize this section because reading cannot provide the kind of precision necessary.

Memorization is easier than some actors believe. In some cases, individuals do not realize that just through repetition they have already memorized many of their lines. For example, if the piece begins with "once upon a time," the narrator might be encouraged to look at the audience instead of the page because he or she has probably already memorized that part. Consider setting aside some time for performers to memorize important sections of their scripts.

### STOOLS/CHAIRS

*Back to Audience (BTA).* Stools or chairs are standard in Readers' Theatre. A mix of stools and chairs is preferable; however, just stools or just chairs is fine. Placing the narrators on stools sets these performers higher, making it easier for the audience to see them. Use only armless chairs with no padding. Padding can cause problems when students try to spin away from the audience. In essence, an actor who does not have lines for a certain period of time can turn their back to the audience or BTA Arms on the chairs make the spin impossible.

Turn the chairs so that chair backs are facing stage right or left. That is, turn the chairs so that from the audience's point of view, the chair backs are all to the right or left of the base of the chair. When the students enter they sit on their chair sideways facing the audience. Turning the chair sideways creates greater ease of spinning completely around so that the performers can face away from the audience.

*Preset.* Before the audience arrives have all the chairs and stools set out ready for the performers to enter. Actors should know which seat is theirs and how they will get to their seat. Entering is an important part of the rehearsal process.

Readers' Theatre seats are normally placed in a straight line or in a slight curve, centre stage seating being farther away from the audience. More important characters should sit centre. Narrators often sit at the stage right and stage left ends of the line.

Audience seating should be arranged as well. If the audience is to sit in chairs, then make sure the seating is arranged so all spectators can easily see and hear the performers.

## ENTRANCES AND EXITS

Within the conventions of Readers' Theatre, there are four ways performers can enter and exit. Entering and exiting a scene are important as this indicates to the audience where their attention should be directed. Lines in the following scripts can be short; therefore, it is necessary for audience members to quickly locate the performer who is speaking or they can miss what is happening. Giving clues to the audience so they can find the speaker makes the experience more rewarding.

The various entrances and exits are intended to help audience members find the correct performer, which is usually the one who is speaking. Because actors are sitting for a majority of the performance, it can be difficult to find the one who is speaking.

Exits are deliberate movements that audiences understand means this character is not speaking so ignore him. Entrances indicate non-verbally to audiences to "look at me." Performers can decide which entrance or exit would be best for them at specific points of the scripts. The *Director's Scripts* in this book provide suggestions regarding entrances and exits.

*Offstage to Onstage to Offstage.* The first entrance/exit entails entering onto the stage from offstage. The final entrance/exit involves leaving the stage after having engaged in a curtain call by bowing to the audience. During the first entrance, the group introduces the audience to the play's theme and/or characters. A production's offstage-onstage-offstage entrance and exit ideally "bookend" the performance. If, for example, the script deals with crows, the performers might enter as a murder of crows. They might swoop in cawing as they enter. To bookend the performance, after the curtain call they would exit swooping and cawing as they did upon entering.

Since the Shakespeare plays in this book all deal with royal courts, performers could provide a taste of the royal court and enter as though they are royalty. They might enter speaking in a heightened way so the audience understands the setting of the play.

Or performers might give the audience some foreshadowing of the plot. For *Romeo and Juliet,* the Capulets and the Montagues might enter separately from opposite sides of the stage, glaring at one another as they enter.

The performance may inform the exit. If the performers entered healthy and during the performance the characters became injured, they could exit limping. This still bookends the production and is consistent.

The director may wish to show the audience that the performers are nice people who like one another, unlike many of the characters in *Hamlet*. Actors may enter as themselves chatting about their outside life. As soon as they sit they become their characters and remain so until after the curtain call when they revert back to themselves again to exit. This still could be thematically connected to the play as Shakespeare himself often uses the device of a play within the play.

*Back to Audience (BTA) / Front to Audience (FTA).* The second method of entering and exiting has performers spin 180 degrees on their chairs or stools to face away from or towards the audience. All the scripts in this book require the entire cast to say the title so that each group has to rehearse entering from off-stage, standing in front of their chairs, and sitting on a cue. They also have to determine and rehearse how they say the title, which is said with all performers FTA After stating the title those characters who are not be needed for a page or more exit by turning their backs to the audience (BTA). This convention tells the audience that these performers have left the performance, temporarily.

BTA is a simple technique that enables the audience to focus on the remaining performers. It also helps the unneeded performers to be a bit more relaxed. Where the audience focuses its attention can be important and uninvolved performers who are FTA may accidently distract the audience and impede your production. BTA lowers the chance of this happening.

Narrators do not spin BTA even if they do not have a line for more than a page. The audience accepts the convention that the narrator is on stage, facing the audience for the entire play. Training the narrator to sit still, however, and not to pull focus when they are not reading, is an important part of the rehearsal process.

The BTA performers spin back 180 degrees FTA ready when their next lines are to be delivered. They might spin BTA again if they are not needed for a page or more. However, too much spinning can distract from the performance and negates the FTA/BTA intention, which is to improve the audience's understanding and enjoyment.

*Dropping Head (DH) / Raising Head (RH).* Dropping and raising the head is used when a performer is not required for five or more lines, but less than a page. For example, if the action on stage revolves around three characters. All three actors have their faces up so the audience can easily see them. Should the conversation become centered on only two characters, the third would drop his head and sit still. DH/RH is a fast and efficient way to remove that performer from a scene and enable the audience to understand their focus should go to the narrators and remaining two characters. As soon as the third character raises his head, the audience understands this character is back in the action.

*Freezing.* The final method of exiting and entering is by freezing. When Readers' Theatre performers are not speaking they should remain still so that the audience knows to focus their attention elsewhere. Audiences soon learn that the person who is moving and whose face is animated is where their gaze should go; therefore, when not speaking, all other characters should be still. This also suggests that when speaking a performer should be animated and consider constructing moves that draw the audience's attention.

Narrators generally use the freezing form of entrance and exit. Their lines come so regularly between other characters that they do not have time to spin 180 degrees (BTA/FTA) or even to DH/RH

## FOCUS

Stage focus revolves around the concept of where performers should centre their attention.

*Onstage Focus.* In regular stage acting, performers cheat to the front. That is, even when speaking to someone on stage as though they were on the street and not on stage, instead of facing the other person directly, the performers turn slightly to the audience so that facial expressions can be clearly seen. This cheating is understood by audiences as acceptable and normal behavior. This convention is also used in Readers' Theatre. Facing one another when speaking, but cheating to the front is considered onstage focus. Onstage focus enables performers to look almost directly at one another.

*Offstage Focus.* Offstage focus is where performers blatantly face the audience and speak as though in front of them is another character in the play rather than the audience. Prior to cell phones this could be explained as telephone booth acting. The idea is that there is only one way in and out of a telephone booth. All action in the booth must be out to the front.

Offstage focus requires students to use their peripheral vision to coordinate their action with other actors on stage. Let's use the example of two performers shaking hands on stage. Using onstage focus the performers would simply turn to face one another extend their right arms, clasp hands, and shake. Using offstage focus it would be as though a knife cut the image at the point of contact and turns both performers 90 degrees toward the audience. Now, using offstage focus, performers who are shaking hands would extend their right hands toward the audience and, using their peripheral vision, "grasp" in mime the hand of the performer standing beside them. The grasp of one another's hands should take place at the same time and the shake up and down should be coordinated. Offstage focus can be difficult for younger actors to master; performers facing downstage, however, can increase the audience's enjoyment.

Both onstage and offstage focus are acceptable in Readers' Theatre and directors can use both forms in a single performance. All forms of entrances and exits can be used with onstage or offstage focus.

## CHARACTERIZATION

Characterization refers to creating characters that have strong vocal and physical suggestion. It is not a convention solely within the bounds of Readers' Theatre. Having clear, strong characters applies to many forms of theatre, but this form does not permit complete costumes or great physicality. Readers' Theatre depends on suggestion, although not necessarily always subtle suggestion.

*Foils.* Foils are character opposites. Often when one sort of character is introduced on stage or in literature, an opposite type of character often follows. For example, George (small and quick) and Lennie (huge man with wide sloping shoulders) in *Of Mice and Men*. In theatre it is often pleasing to have different characters inhabit the stage. In Readers' Theatre, character opposites or foils can increase enjoyment for audiences and actors. When working with foils consider looking at simple foils at first, such as fast and slow. Other opposites could be kind and mean, loud and quiet, or grumpy and happy.

*Heightened/Exaggerated.* Heightened or exaggerated refers primarily to how actors feel when presenting these characters. Characters have to be drawn quickly when performing Readers' Theatre scripts. Performers must communicate to the audience who their character is in a quick and efficient manner. As part of the rehearsal process consider having performers create and rehearse strong characters. If a character is a braggart, have students physicalize being an extreme braggart with postures and an accent or vocal quality that enhances their "braggartness." Even a character that is weak or small must be strong within the confines of that character. The actor portraying a weak individual must find a way to make the character extremely weak or small. This might require that the actor expend a great deal of energy or engage in movements that need personal strength. The point is that whatever the character trait, it must be done with performer energy. The character may be lazy, but the performer should have energy.

Consider having performers search for vocal and physical traits that are consistent. A braggart might have a loud voice and extremely erect posture. A sneaky character may have a nasal voice and poor posture, with a head jutting forward. In cases where a single actor must perform two or more different characters, it becomes important for this actor to have two distinctly different postures and voices so the audience recognizes the two different characters.

## ENUNCIATION

Enunciation involves having performers speak clearly and loudly enough so that the audiences can hear and understand the story. Articulation and pronunciation can be developed in performers relatively quickly.

*Clear Endings.* 'Clear endings' refers to a first step in enunciation. Beginning performers are unlikely to have had speech classes. Yet, enunciation is important in Readers' Theatre. Improving students' general enunciation takes concentrated effort over time. There are a great number of factors that play into whether a student speaks clearly.

To begin with, consider defining enunciation in a narrow and observable form of word completion. Enunciation for this performance could be wholly or partially defined as students saying clearly the last sound in each word. This narrow definition can improve the student's enunciation relatively quickly by giving the performer a specific task to complete, which is achievable by most actors.

Slowing some readers down can give their words greater chance of being understood by the audience. Audience appreciation is important. That is, when watching and listening to the performance, an audience will notice word completion. The director's feedback during rehearsals is most helpful when it is specific. Instead of asking performers to enunciate, a director could target a specific word and ask the actor to say the last sound or letter of that word. Greater specificity in direction often provides greater improvement in actors.

*Selective Over-Enunciation.* Over-enunciating important words suggests to the audience that there are words in each speech that are more important than others. This requires some analysis by performers and judgment about which words are most important. It may be that unfamiliar words are important. For example, Hamlet says, "A little more than kin and less than kind." The actor may decide that "kin" is a word that must be over-enunciated, as (1) the word defines his step-father as being a relative, and (2) if audience members do not know the word they can let the word go.

Sometimes audience members fall behind in a production because they are thinking about a word or a phrase that is now past. Part of their falling behind can be questioning whether they heard the word correctly and trying to figure out the meaning. By ensuring that they have clearly heard the word "kin", audience members are more likely to acknowledge that they do or do not know the word and continue to follow the play.

Important words may be identified for other reasons. The word may be significant in understanding the plot or it may introduce an important concept or character. For example, Gertrude says, "All that live must die." The actor might deem "live" as the most important word in that sentence because once an audience member hears and understands "live", there is a greater chance that the rest of the sentence will make sense. Sometimes the first word in a sentence can be the most important, especially when a character first speaks.

Once important words are established, consider having the performers over-enunciate those entire words for emphasis and clarity. Over-enunciation requires that the important words are pronounced with exaggerated clarity, which also moves into the arena of directing the audience's attention. The over-enunciated word indicates to the audience which words and concepts are especially important. So enunciation in this context means the conscious articulating of the ends of all words and the over-enunciation of key words.

Key words can be dictated by the director, who goes through the script and tells the actors which words are key. Greater buy-in from actors might be achieved, however, by having them choose their own key words. Consider indicating to the actors that in each speech there is a key word that must be over-enunciated. A speech can be one line long or 12 lines long. If an actor indicates there are two or more key words in their speech, so much the better.

*Crispness.* Crispness refers to the play's presentation of characterization and speech. It suggests an elevated feel to the play embodied by bright and clear characters and speech. Crispness is required in Readers' Theatre in general and in the scripts in this book in particular. Shakespeare, through Hamlet, has given performers advice about how to speak on stage. He states that actors should "speak the speech…trippingly on the tongue." This suggests a certain liveliness in delivering Shakespeare's phrases. This may impact characterization choices. Choosing a character that mumbles may be less effective than one who over enunciates. The words have to be brightly spoken and easily understood by the audience.

## OVERALL PRODUCTION

The final conventions discussed here deal with the overall look and feel of the show. This section is intended to help direct the production from an overarching point of view.

*Pacing.* Pace refers to the tightness between lines and can be distilled down to making sure there are no dead spots between speeches. Good pace is important in Readers' Theatre because it helps hold audience and performer attention, and builds the production to its climax.

Keeping the gaps between lines to a minimum is necessary for good pace. Once the line has started, performers can slow down and say their lines more slowly and clearly, but it is important to "tighten the Qs."

Tighten the Qs refers to a number of aspects of production, but for these scripts let it stand for having lines butt up to one another. As one performer is finishing her line, let the next performer be starting his. For example, at the introduction of *Midsummers Night's Dream* three readers say the following:

**NARRATOR 2**

The Lovers also include:

**HERMIA**

Hermia, who loves

**LYSANDER**

Lysander, dashingly handsome

The performer reading Hermia should be saying "Hermia" as Narrator 2 is finishing the word, "include." "Hermia" should be dragged out with more volume at the top of the word; if written it might look like, "HEEER-mia." "Hermia" needs more emphasis because, (1) it is an odd word that the audience may not have heard before, (2) it is the name of a main character whom the audience needs to know, (3) it is the beginning of the line so the audience needs a bit of time to locate the character, and (4) this is the first time that this actor speaks, so it is important to let the audience have a bit more time to get use to the actor's voice.

The next performer will start, "Lysander" as Hermia is finishing, "loves." "Lysander", if written, could be said, "LYYYY-sander." The rest of his line could be said more normally, still focusing on ending the words. A good pace requires that the cast has rehearsed enough so that all performers are comfortable and familiar with the script and can jump in when it is their turn to speak.

Having a good pace does not mean saying the lines quickly. An actor may choose to say lines quickly as a character trait, but just as important as strong characters is clarity of speech. The faster a line is said, the greater the chance the words will be unclear. Clarity can be more easily attained with slowing down slightly. Too slow, and clarity may be sacrificed as well; however, it is rare that students speak too slowly.

Consider having performers practice saying their first word or two loudly and slowly so the audience can find the speaker. That is, when a performer starts their line it sometimes takes a moment for the audience to locate them. Once the audience has identified the speaker, then faster speech is acceptable because the audience can gain information from the face and physicality of the performer. This first word should come as the last word of the previous speaker is ending. It means that actors are inhaling on the last few words of the previous sentence so they can start their line briskly as the preceding line ends.

*Shape of Show (Direct Audience's Attention).* The shape of the show refers to clarifying where the audience should focus. Generally in Readers' Theatre, only one reader at a time should command audience attention. That attention may dance between two characters, such as in Romeo and Juliet's balcony scene, but the audience can accommodate this by just moving their eyes. Place interacting performers side-by-side centre so audience focus can slip easily between the two.

The performer who has the audience's focus is called the hub. The hub should do all they can to keep the focus while speaking. Other individuals on stage must help the shape of the show by giving focus to the hub. This is most often accomplished by stopping all action or freezing. Audiences quickly learn that their gaze should follow the action and movement.

*Stage Pictures.* Levels help to create stage pictures that aid understanding and enjoyment of the production. Having one character stand and another sit may help an audience member understand who has dominance in the scene. The act of standing may also help audiences understand an especially passionate moment in the play.

To fully employ levels, use vertical (up and down) and horizontal (side to side, or further and closer to the audience) options. Consider giving the performers a goal that they must all sit at least once and stand at least once during their performance, not necessarily together. That is, after entering and sitting on the chair they must find at least one other part in the script to stand.

Making actors stand and sit at least once, also requires that the performers examine their script. A conversation about build and the climax may help them decide the best time to stand. Students should generally stand nearer the climax as a signal to the audience that this is a more important part of the performance.

*Down Centre (DC).* Down Centre (DC) is the most powerful spot on stage. A stage can be divided into up stage and down stage, which has to do with the "rake" or in essence the angle. Most theatres now rake the audience, which means the front row is below the second row and the third row is higher still. Raked seating provides better sight-lines for audiences than does seating all on one level.

Years ago seating was not raked and audiences were seated on a level floor. The stage was about three feet (one metre) above the floor of the hall. This meant that all audience members would have a good chance of seeing performers standing at the front of the stage, closest to the audience. However, actors standing furthest away from the front of the stage would often be hidden by actors in front of them. To solve the problem theatre designers sloped the stage up, away from the audience. "Upstage" was at the back of the stage farthest from the audience and "Downstage" was closest. Therefore, an actor standing upstage could be seen by the audience, even if there were actors standing down centre.

So downstage was the lowest part of the stage, closest to the audience and upstage was the highest part of the stage farthest from the audience. Stages are rarely raked now: it seems that there were accidents on raked stages of furniture and actors sliding into the audience.

Stage left and stage right are designated from the actor's point of view. Stage left is the left hand side of the stage if one is looking out at the audience. Centre stage is the middle of the stage between left and right. It can also be between Up and Down.

Nine stage areas are created by combining Up and Down with Left and Right plus Centre. U = Up, D = Down, L = Stage Left and R = Stage Right. C = the centre area between Left and Right. UR, UC, and UL stand for up right, up centre, and up left respectively.

| UR | UC | UL |
|----|----|----|
| R | C | L |
| DR | DC | DL |
| Audience | | |

The maxim "DC is the most powerful stage area" means that a performer standing on the middle of the stage closest to the audience is in the most commanding stage area.

An actor standing in Readers' Theatre is a convention that signals to the audience that something special is happening. Actors standing and moving to down centre makes that statement of specialness even stronger. To help clarify the build to the climax in your production, explain to your actors that DC is the most powerful place on the stage. Suggest to your cast that moving forward to the audience increases intensity and helps build the momentum of the production.

It can be awkward to sit after having stood. Moreover, once performers have moved forward toward the audience it can be even more awkward to return to the chair and sit.

Ending DC could be a goal of the productions. For example, Hamlet and Laertes could fight standing facing the audience using offstage focus. Gertrude and Claudius have lines during the fight that could cause them to stand and move slightly downstage of the fighters. The deaths of Gertrude, Claudius, Laertes, and Hamlet could take place downstage, with each death occurring closer to the audience. Because they all die there is no requirement to return to their chairs. At the end of the script they all stand with the other performers, bow and exit.

## WRAP-UP

Readers' Theatre conventions are intended to improve both the viewing and performing experience. Initially, consider using the conventions sparingly. As a director you may find that your students' greater enjoyment of the pieces leads to greater understanding of the texts. It may be that this is your ultimate goal. Please consider that the presentation can be a worthy end in itself.

## Chapter 3: Shakespeare, An Overview

### NUTSHELL

Shakespeare was born in 1564, married in 1582, and exploded onto the London theatre scene in the late 1580s. By1598 he was the most famous playwright of his time. He subsequently became wealthy, thanks to his part ownership of the King's Men theatre company. He died in 1616, having written 37 plays.

### SOURCES OF SHAKESPEARE INFORMATION

Shakespeare has been the subject of hundreds of books. There is much conjecture and few facts known about this important playwright. Information about Shakespeare and his life comes from four sources: his works, records from the time, comments from contemporaries, and hearsay. We will briefly review what can be gleaned from these sources because knowing a bit about the man and the historical environment in which he wrote is important in explaining elements in his plays, and can therefore increase the enjoyment of his work.

#### SHAKESPEARE'S WORK

Arguably a wealth of information about Shakespeare can be found in his works. He has been credited with writing 37 plays, 154 Sonnets, and two narrative poems. Although this range of work should provide a sense of the man, there are inconsistencies. The range of experience suggested in his works indicates a worldly man who travelled much and lived life to the fullest. However, this seems improbable given the sheer volume of the work he created. It is more likely that Shakespeare wrote regularly and gained his worldliness by listening to others and by reading. His brilliance came not from living the worldly life he set down in his work, but rather from being able to incorporate the stories of others into his own writing.

## RECORDS

The primary sources for official written records of the time were the church, court, and register records. The parish register at Stratford-on-Avon provides baptism, marriage and burial information.

The Stationers' Register was an official record book maintained by the Stationers' Company. A royal charter from 1557 underpins its mandate as a trade guild for printers, authors, publishers, and booksellers. By registering his works with the Stationers' Register, Shakespeare was given the right to publish his works and demand that other works written by, but not authorized by, him be destroyed.

The Master of the Revels created a series of documents relating to performances in London and the courts of Queen Elizabeth and King James. These documents dealt primarily with licensing of, fee collection from, payment to, and censorship of theatre companies. These official court records of Queen Elizabeth and King James indicate regular interaction with Shakespeare.

Shakespeare's name can also be found on legal records as witness, plaintiff or defendant. He was in court on November 29, 1596 when a William Wayte testified he feared for his life because of Shakespeare and others. Shakespeare was in court again in 1604 when he sued an apothecary for default on a loan.

In addition, the presentation of his plays left a series of documents including programs, receipts and notes of payment.

## COMMENTS FROM HIS CONTEMPORARIES

In 1592, Robert Greene called Shakespeare an "upstart crow" in a letter published by a friend (Henry Chettle) after Greene's death. Henry Chettle later apologized in print to Shakespeare, calling him "excellent in quality." Others who personally knew Shakespeare mentioned him mostly in references to his plays or characters. For example, Thomas Nash said one of Shakespeare's characters, Talbot, had been seen by "ten thousand spectators." William Camden was another writer who mentioned Shakespeare as one of the 10 best writers of the day. In 1598, Francis Meres published a book titled *Palladis Tamia* in which he included Shakespeare in a list of writers and their publications. Ben Jonson, a prolific writer, often mentioned Shakespeare in his personal writings, calling him a "soul of the age." Thomas Fuller praised Shakespeare's ability and described the wit-combats between Shakespeare and Jonson:

> Many were the wit-combats betwixt him and Ben Jonson, which I behold like a Spanish Great Galleon and an English Man of War: Master Jonson (like the former) was built far higher in learning; solid, but slow in his performances. Shakespeare, with the English Man of War, lesser in bulk but lighter in sailing, could turn with all tides, tack about and take advantage of all winds, by the quickness of his wit and invention.

Phillip Henslowe owned some London theatres and from 1592 to 1602 he wrote a detailed account of the companies that played at his theatres. This important book is known as *Henslowe's Diary*. Henslowe's son-in-law, Edward Alleyn, kept the Diary and bequeathed it along with other papers to the College of God's Gift. This is one of the more important documents that deal with theatre during Shakespeare's time.

## HEARSAY

Hearsay includes material printed after Shakespeare's death that might shed light on his life and work. This includes an introduction to an edited version of Shakespeare's plays that Nicholas Rowe printed in 1709. In his introduction Rowe included some biographical material gained from the actor Thomas Betterton who had traveled to Stratford to gather stories about Shakespeare. This information, though interesting, was gleaned 80 or more years after Shakespeare's death making it unlikely that anyone living in Stratford could have known the bard personally.

John Aubrey wrote a series of biographical sketches between 1669 and 1693 in which he recorded news he had heard about famous people. One of his sources was William Beeston, the son of an actor who had worked with Shakespeare. Included in this category would be traditions and stories that have no other apparent source from Shakespeare's time.

## SHAKESPEARE'S LIFE

Shakespeare was born in 1564 and died in 1616. In between he became the most celebrated playwright of all time. His journey to lasting fame can be examined in five stages: Stratford Early Years (1564 – 1581), The Lost Years (1582 – 1591), Rising Acclaim (1592 -1597), Famous in London (1598 – 1608), and Semi-Retired (1609 – 1616).

### STRATFORD EARLY YEARS (1564-1581)

Shakespeare was born and grew up in Stratford-on-Avon, situated about 100 miles north and west of London. At that time Stratford was a local hub of commerce with a population of about 1,500.

William's baptism took place on April 26, 1564 at Christian Holy Trinity of Stratford-on-Avon church and on April 23, 1616, he was buried at the same church. Probably to keep things simple and permit a sense of symmetry, his birthday is now celebrated on the same day as his death, April 23. His dates of baptism and death are recorded in a document called the Stratford Register. Interestingly, his birth was recorded in Latin and his death in English, which suggests a serious rise in the use and acceptance of English as the official language during Shakespeare's lifetime.

William was the third child born to John and Mary Shakespeare. Mary's maiden name was Arden and her father was a successful farmer. John Shakespeare was a glover, someone who worked with leather to make items such as gloves and purses. He also worked in politics, rising to the role of a bailiff (or mayor) in 1568. In the late 1570s, he encountered some serious financial problems that kept him from attending church regularly. Church records list John Shakespeare as one of many individuals who missed church "for fear of prosecution for debt."

Shakespeare probably attended school as other sons of important men would have done. Boys started at petty school around age 4, then attended grammar school at age 7. In 1575 it was recorded that William's father owned four houses, which suggests that John Shakespeare was probably still an important man in Stratford when William turned 11. Given his father's status, William would have attended a good school at that age. It is speculated that at age 11 William attended King's New Grammar School, based on what other boys of similar parentage did at that time. Boys traditionally went to school until age 15 and then engaged in a trade. Therefore, William probably left school at 15 and worked as an apprentice glover for his father.

### THE LOST YEARS (1582 – 1591)

The lost years are framed by William's marriage in 1582 and a jealous statement by Robert Greene in 1592. No written evidence from the time exists regarding Shakespeare's whereabouts or activities.

A bond certificate states that on November 28, 1582, William (age 18) married Anne Hathaway (age 26), a local farmer's daughter. William was still a minor and required his father's consent to marry. Their first daughter (Susanna) was born six months later (1583), and twins Judith and Hamnet were born in 1585.

William left Stratford and went to London to start acting professionally shortly after the birth of the twins. There are some stories related by Rowe that William had to leave Stratford quickly due to accusations of poaching Sir Thomas Lucy's deer. There is at least one reference to Shakespeare being a teacher. John Aubrey received the news that Shakespeare knew Latin because he had been a "school master in the country."

William's wife and family probably lived permanently in Stratford. He may have only made infrequent trips back to see his family, the more infrequent as his success and fame in London grew.

The London that Shakespeare moved to was expanding rapidly, growing from about 50,000 in 1500 to 200,000 in 1600. This quick growth came with dangerous consequences, as London was rife with crime and disease, due in part to crowded conditions and inadequate sanitation

When first arriving in London, it is probable that Shakespeare attended plays. Comments from the time suggest that theatre in general was considered of low quality, expect for Christopher Marlowe's work. Marlowe was said to have taught everyone who followed how to write blank verse.

There is no mention of Shakespeare until 1592, but he must have been working before that. He probably performed, at least occasionally, with the acting troupe called Strange's Men, that eventually became the Chamberlain's Men, a group in which Shakespeare was a part-owner. It is probable that Shakespeare went to London sporadically between1585 and 1587. By 1588 he was more or less settled in London with regular work as an actor and a writer.

Scholars debate exactly when Shakespeare wrote his plays. Following are nine plays probably created by the end of 1592: *Henry VI Part I, Henry VI Part II, Henry VI Part III, Richard III, Titus Andronicus, Love's Labour Lost, The Two Gentlemen of Verona, The Comedy of Errors,* and *The Taming of the Shrew.*

## RISING ACCLAIM (1592 – 1597)

By 1592 Shakespeare had written and performed in London to some acclaim. He is mentioned in 1592 by a jealous rival playwright, Robert

Greene, as an "upstart crow, beautified with our feathers." Greene's statement suggests that by 1592 Shakespeare was a successful entity in London theatre. Moreover, Greene's complaint implies that Shakespeare was the object of envy for his success as a performer and /or a playwright. The "beautified with our feathers" suggests Shakespeare may have been the object of scorn because he used material, such as story lines, from other playwrights to improve his own plays. It may also mean that as an actor he had become famous by saying the words of others.

Shakespeare was a part-owner of The Lord Chamberlain's Men during their formation in 1594. On December 26 and 27, 1594, The Chamberlain's Men performed two plays for Queen Elizabeth and were paid well. Records show that 20 pounds each were paid to Will Kempe, Richard Burbage, and William Shakespeare. Shakespeare worked as an actor, writer, manager, owner and director for the troupe and focused his attentions on his company. Christopher Beeston said of Shakespeare that he "wouldn't be debauched," suggesting that Shakespeare did not carouse like Christopher Marlowe but focused on his work mounting plays for the Lord Chamberlain's Men.

Theatres often closed because of the plague. Whenever more than 40 people died of the plague in a week, theatres closed, so theatres remained closed most of the time between June 1592 and May 1594. In 1593 alone, more than 11,000 people died of the plague.

Shakespeare was busy during this time. He wrote a couple of long poems dedicated to the Earl of Southampton; *The Rape of Lucrece* and *Venus and Adonis* (entered into the Stationers' Registrar April 18, 1593). This suggests Shakespeare was flirting with the notion of having a patron during this potentially financially difficult time. Taking pains to ensure that they were printed properly, Shakespeare published these poems.

In 1594 as theatres reopened, The Lord Chamberlain's Men were ready. The actors who became The Lord Chamberlain's Men were not idle during the closure of London's theatres. Their flurry of activity after theatres reopened suggests they had been on tour outside London perfecting their new plays. So while other theatres started up slowly after the closure, the Lord Chamberlain's men exploded out of the gates, and in the process became a London favorite with serfs and nobility alike.

It seems reasonable to assume that the actors in The Chamberlain's Men were working constantly because actors were paid only when working. The First Folio printed in 1623 listed 26 members of The Chamberlain's Men ensemble. A troupe of about 15 actors could perform most of Shakespeare's plays. This suggests that as one cast of 15 was performing one play, another cast of 11 was rehearsing the next. A few members of the first play might step in as extra performers if needed in the second play. The Lord Chamberlain's Men seem to have become a well-oiled machine during this time and remained running smoothly until after Shakespeare's death in 1616.

Shakespeare received good and bad news in 1596. His son Hamnet died at age 11 and William Wayte took Shakespeare to court stating that Wayte feared for his life. This was also the year that the College of Heralds approved an application for a Coat of Arms for the family Shakespeare. This enabled Shakespeare to call himself a gentleman and a member of the English gentry.

Scholars suggest that as few as 12 and as many as 22 of Shakespeare's plays were written and successfully presented by late 1597. This is partly substantiated by Shakespeare's purchase in 1597 of The New Place on Chapel Street, touted to be the second largest house in Stratford. The purchase of an expensive item such as a house certainly indicates that money was coming in, probably from successful productions by The Lord Chamberlain's Men. Edward Alleyn, a famous actor during Shakespeare's time, appears to have become wealthy from acting, suggesting that actors made more money than writers. Therefore, out of financial necessity, Shakespeare probably did double duty as a writer and an actor.

The plays that are thought to have been written during this period, before the end of 1597, include: *Romeo and Juliet, A Midsummer Night's Dream, Richard II, King John,* and *The Merchant of Venice.*

### FAMOUS IN LONDON (1598 – 1609)

Beginning in 1598, records about Shakespeare's activities increase. Ben Jonson noted in his 1616 Folio that in 1598 The Lord Chamberlain's Men first performed his play, *Every Man in His Humour.* Jonson mentioned Shakespeare as being a principal comedian along with Burbage, Heminges, Condell, and Kempe. Similarly, in his book *Palladis Tamia,* Francis Meres mentioned Shakespeare and other writers whose publications came out in 1598. Meres praised Shakespeare saying,

> As Plautus and Seneca are accounted the best for Comedy and Tragedy
> among the Latines: so Shakespeare among English is the most excellent
> in both kinds for the stage; for Comedy, witness his *Gentlemen of*

*Verona,* his *Errors,* his *Love Labors Lost,* his *Love Labors Won,* his *Midsummer Night's Dream,* & his *Merchant of Venice;* for tragedy his *Richard the 2, Richard the 3, Henry the 4, King John, Titus Andronicus,* and his *Romeo and Juliet.*"

In 1599, The Lord Chamberlain's Men built a theatre for themselves called The Globe. For actors to own rather than rent, was a bold step. An indicator of how important Shakespeare was becoming came in an inventory of the day, which listed the newly built Globe theatre as belonging to "William Shakespeare and others."

Shakespeare knew his troupe intimately and wrote parts for specific actors, even using their name, such as Will Kempe, when referring to the character. Will Kempe probably left the Chamberlain's Men in 1600 and was replaced by Robert Armin who had a more subtle comic style. Clown roles in Shakespeare's later works reflect this subtle shift.

The Chamberlain's Men changed their name and their benefactor shortly after Queen Elizabeth's death and King James's ascension to the throne in 1603. The newly named "King's Men" was a theatre company on fire. Macbeth may have been written and performed as a form of thanks to the King. Malcolm, who emerges from the carnage of Macbeth as the king, was a forbearer of James. That the King's Men found such an important patron as King James suggests they were the premier theatre company in the country.

Receipts for payment at the royal court demonstrate that the King's Men were well paid. Being well paid attracted other high caliber actors. For a theatre company to be so consistently productive there must have been an excellent working milieu. Though Shakespeare is credited as the author of his plays it is probable that creativity percolated from the group. Although Shakespeare often provided his actors with lines, he probably also recorded bits created by the actors as they performed or rehearsed. There was some back and forth, with Shakespeare writing lines for the actors and using lines provided by them.

In 1608, the King's Men leased Blackfriars Theatre for their exclusive use. Blackfriars was entirely enclosed and suitable for performance under all weather conditions.

That the King's Men had two theatres running signifies more work for the entire troupe and increased revenues. Blackfriars supposedly catered to a wealthier crowd. It was a smaller theatre with higher admission prices.

Documents suggest Blackfriars regularly brought in more money than did the Globe.

The entire time Shakespeare was in London he yearned to return to Stratford. Money made in London regularly made its way back to Stratford. For example, in 1605, with an original investment of 440 pounds, Shakespeare purchased leases on property in Stratford that earned him 60 pounds a year as well as doubling the initial principle value.

The following plays were probably written between 1598 and 1609: *Henry IV Part I, Henry IV Part II, Much Ado About Nothing, Merry Wives of Windsor, As You Like It, Julius Caesar, Henry V, Troilus and Cressida, Hamlet, Twelfth Night, Measure for Measure, All's Well That Ends Well, Othello, King Lear, Macbeth, Timon of Athens, Antony and Cleopatra, Coriolanus,* and *Pericles* (not in the *First Folio*).

## STRATFORD SEMI-RETIREMENT (1610 – 1616)

By 1610 Shakespeare was conducting most of his business in Stratford. Evidence that he settled into the life of a country gentleman includes documentation of him collecting debts in Stratford. Even in Stratford he continued writing for the King's Men and probably made regular trips to London. His departure from London indicates he probably had stopped acting by 1609. His income was still primarily coming from the successful King's Men. Other companies also produced his works, although writers were not particularly well paid during this time.

Shakespeare wrote *Cymbeline, The Winter's Tale,* and *The Tempest* after 1608 and before 1613. His last works, *The Two Noble Kinsmen* and *Henry VIII*, were probably co-written with John Fletcher in 1612/1613. The Globe Theatre burned to the ground during a production of Henry VIII on June 29, 1613. The cause was the firing of a cannon that preceded King Henry's entrance on stage. The contents of the cannon shot, probably some wadding, arched onto the roof catching the straw thatch on fire. The fire consumed the theatre in less than two hours. No one was hurt and the Globe was rebuilt within a year for about 1400 pounds.

In 1607, Shakespeare's oldest daughter, Suzanne, married a successful physician. In 1616, his second daughter, Judith, married a ne'er-do-well, which prompted Shakespeare to revise his will to ensure that Judith was bequeathed money, but her husband received none. In his will, Shakespeare left his wife Anne the second best bed.

Shakespeare died on April 23, 1616. He is buried in the chancel of the same church in which he was baptized. Anne outlived him by seven years and now lies buried beside William. The cause of William's death is unclear, but Reverend John Ward wrote "Shakespeare, Drayton and Ben Jonson had a merie meeting, and it seems drank too hard, for Shakespeare died of a feavour there contracted." This is not consistent with previous descriptions of Shakespeare as temperate but John Ward was a minister and, therefore, believable. Shakespeare's epitaph is a poem asking to be left in peace.

> Good friend, for Jesus' sake forbeare
> To dig the dust enclosed here.
> Blessed be the man that spares these stones,
> And cursed be he that moves my bones.

## SHAKESPEARE IN PRINT

Shakespeare's plays that were published during his lifetime are poorly printed 5x8 inch books called quartos. In stark contrast to these plays, the poems that Shakespeare himself published in 1593 are beautifully done. The *First Folio* that is now what most modern publications use as Shakespeare's plays was published after Shakespeare's death. So Shakespeare himself did not seem to care much about the printing of his plays, probably because he earned most money on the presentation of his plays rather than the texts.

### FOLIOS

Thirty-six of Shakespeare's plays were published in 1623, seven years after his death. Two senior members of Shakespeare's company, John Heminges and Henry Condell, collected and prepared the plays for printing. This collection of plays is now called the *First Folio*. The *First Folio* was printed on 12 x16 inch paper that was folded once so that the size became 12 x 8 inches by about 900 pages. It is the size of paper and the single fold that defines a folio.

The William Droeshout engraving on the cover page of the First Folio was said by Jonson to be an excellent likeness of Shakespeare, with a big forehead and ruffled collar, even though it was created seven years after his death. The second page lists the 26 names of the "Principall Actors in all these plays." The list begins with Shakespeare, Richard Burbadge, John Hemminges, Augustine Phillips, William Kemp, Thomas Poope, George

Bryan, and Henry Condell. That William Kempe was listed as an actor even though he probably left 23 years earlier says a great deal about his importance to the company.

The printing of the plays was done with varying care. Ben Jonson carefully printed his own plays resulting in a thing of beauty. Heminges and Condell's work started well as the first play, *The Tempest* seems to be laid out with elaborate care, but later texts were sent to print with many errors. Sometimes using the character's name in a play, then using the actor's name later in the same play. Because Condell and Heminges were members of Shakespeare's company, it is generally believed that the *First Folio* was based on the prompt books of The King's Men, Shakespeare's own company.

## QUARTOS

Quarto refers to paper that is folded twice into four sections. Each section is about 5 x 8 inches. A page folded in this manner has eight surfaces for printing. They were traditionally called 'six penny pamphlets" and about half of Shakespeare's plays were printed in this way before the 1623 First Folio. The number of pages vary in the quartos from 56 *(Henry V* and *The Merry Wives of Winsor)* to 104 (Hamlet).

Previously quartos were deemed "Bad" or "Good." Bad quartos appear to have been abbreviated versions that were probably illegally copied. Bad Quartos were published first, often shortly after the opening of more popular plays. Good Quartos were often printed some years later with a clarification that this quarto had fixed problems found in the previous quarto. The mention of fixing previous problems suggests that the second quartos were published by Shakespeare himself or at least authorized by him.

Recently academics have suggested that the first quartos might be closer to what Shakespeare actually wrote to put on stage. The names First Quarto and Second Quarto have replaced Bad and Good Quartos because First Quartos are now being touted as more Shakespearean than later versions that probably had more editing.

Questions surrounding the First Quartos are many. Who sent them to print? For what reason? Under whose authority? If it was Shakespeare who sent them to be printed, then these should be the versions closest to what Shakespeare originally wrote. If they were sent to print by an actor who wanted to make money based on pirated versions, then their value lessens, but they still reflect the earliest originals. If the First Quartos are based on audience members jotting down lines they remembered after a recent viewing, then the Quartos are seriously suspect. It seems that the third option is unlikely. There is enough information in the Quartos to suggest they are at least an actor's copy of the play intended for rehearsal. There is evidence that at least some of the Quartos were printed with Shakespeare's blessing, perhaps even his intent.

Profit was probably a motive for printing quartos. At that time playwrights did not have rights to their own plays. Any money made from printing Quartos went to the theatre companies who had paid for the rights and owned the plays. That Shakespeare was an owner of the Lord Chamberlain's Men (later King's Men) meant that he would have eventually received some money from the sale of his plays. Pirated plays may have been more lucrative. Printers would pay cash for a manuscript and then take all proceeds from sales. So someone could earn fast cash by getting hold of a script used in the rehearsal process and taking it to a printer, who hoped to sell enough quartos to make a profit.

It has been argued that Shakespeare took little or no interest in the printing of Quartos, being interested primarily in the plays on stage. The performances were, after all, where he earned the majority of his income as a percentage of the troupe's performance proceeds. The small amounts he could make from publishing his plays were probably not worth the effort. Also, scripts were not seen as literature or works of art; rather they were a practical vehicle that enabled a performance to take place. Shakespeare took care to publish his poem, *Venus and Adonis,* so he knew the process involved, but simply chose not to publish his plays.

Heminges and Condell wrote in the First Folio that some of the quartos were "stolen and surreptitious copies, maimed and deformed by frauds and stealths of injurious imposters." They wrote in their prefix that they wished Shakespeare had published his own plays. They go on to say they did their best regarding the "care and pain to have collected and published them."

## MODERN TEXTS

Modern texts of Shakespeare's plays first published in the *First Folio,* such as *A Winter's Tale,* are relatively easy to deal with compared with plays that had multiple versions from Quartos and the *First Folio,* in that there is only one version of the play that can be printed. Nevertheless, there is still the question of whether the publisher should fix obvious errors or whether errors should be retained as a more faithful rendition of Shakespeare's work.

Plays that have numerous versions in Quarto form and then Folio form are not so easy because questions arise regarding which is the most reliable, entertaining, authoritative, and/or faithful version. With plays that have a number of versions available, the questions expand to include, "Which Shakespeare version do we publish? Would it be best to cobble together a version of the play that includes some from the Folio and some from the Quartos?"

Most modern versions have some editing. The spelling in the *First Folio* was inconsistent, though better than the spelling in Quartos. Modern versions tend to make the words easy to recognize and use contemporary spellings. Although most rely primarily on the *First Folio,* some use Rowe's 1709 edited version, and others take into consideration the quartos.

## WRAP-UP

Robert Browning may have stated it most clearly:
> *As I declare our Poet, him, whose insight makes all others dim.*
> *A thousand poets pried at life, but only one amid the strife*
> *Rose to be Shakespeare.*

Most academics have no doubt that William Shakespeare was a talented playwright and poet who wrote the work attributed to him.

# Part Two: *Hamlet*

## Chapter 4: *Hamlet* Background

### NUTSHELL

*Hamlet* is possibly the most famous play in the world. It is a revenge story that has a mysterious history that includes a *Ur-Hamlet*.

### SYNOPSIS

The basic story of *Hamlet* concerns a young man grieving for his father while faced with the duty to avenge his father's death. A longer explanation is that Prince Hamlet is required by his father's ghost to take revenge on the current King (Hamlet's uncle) who killed Hamlet's father and married the victim's widow, Hamlet's mother, the Queen. Hamlet's complex response to this situation and his agitated relations with others—culminating in his acceptance of his destiny—constitute the play.

### SOURCES

Before there was Shakespeare's *Hamlet* there was another *Hamlet* now named *"Ur-Hamlet."* (The "Ur" is a German prefix that denotes primordial, primitive or original.) The *Ur-Hamlet*, refers to a version of Hamlet that was in existence in the 1580s. This *Ur-Hamlet* could have been written by Thomas Kyd who is credited with writing *The Spanish Tragedy*. It is also possible that *Ur-Hamlet* is a play written by Shakespeare while still in Stratford or on arriving in London. *Ur-Hamlet* was mentioned by Thomas Nashe in 1589 as being a "Senecan tragedy." Seneca was a Roman who wrote plays in the first century CE that had revenge and the supernatural as themes.

*Ur-Hamlet* was probably based on a story from the 13th century. There is historical evidence that in the 1200s there was a Prince Amleth (or Amlethus) who revenged his father the King of Jutland (mainland of Denmark) by killing his uncle King Feng (or Fengo). This story was told in *Historica Danica*, a history of Danes written in Latin by Saxo Grammaticus, towards the end of the 13th century. It was translated into French by François de Belleforest in the 1570s. He embellished on the basic plot, adding Hamlet's introspection.

## PUBLISHING HISTORY

The first official mention of Shakespeare's *Hamlet* is on July 26, 1602 in the Stationers' Register. Shakespeare registered *Hamlet* as an early method of copyright to insure that as the owner he was the only one allowed to publish and profit from the play. This did not mean that Shakespeare did publish the play.

The earliest version that has survived is the 1603 *First Quarto* or *Q1* titled, *The Tragicall Historie of Hamlet*. This was formerly called the *Bad Quarto* because it seems to have been a pirated copy of Shakespeare's play printed without his permission. There are suggestions that it was sold by an actor who played Marcellus. Recently, Q1 is gaining respect because it is touted as a trimmed version of Hamlet meant for performance.

The next version is the *Second Quarto or Q2,* formerly called the *Good Quarto* because it is believed to be printed from Shakespeare's "foul papers," an early draft. Q2 was published in 1604 or 1605 and it is nearly twice as long as the First Quarto. This version is one of Shakespeare's longest plays at 4070 lines and 32,241 words. Q2 acknowledges the previous quartos by stating on the title page that it is "newly imprinted and enlarged to almost as much againe as it was, according to the true and perfect coppie."

The Third (1611), Fourth (1622), and Fifth (1637) Quartos are copies of the Q2. The version in the 1623 *First Folio* was probably from a promptbook for a production of *Hamlet* that came from the King's Men's library.

The difference between the *First Quarto, Second Quarto* and *First Folio* are best exemplified by an examination of the one of Hamlet's soliloquys. The words found in Act I scene ii in most modern versions are: "O that this too too sullied flesh would melt." *Q1* and *Q2* have "sallied" instead of "sullied" and the *First Folio* has "solid."

Most modern texts use "sullied" — as in "contaminated" — as a correction to better fit the speech. "Sullied" suggests *Hamlet* feels that his body and mind are contaminated, unclean and not worthy. "Solid" could suggest that Hamlet is asking to become something other than solid such as a spirit. So "solid" would suggest that Hamlet is contemplating going to the spirit world via suicide. Sallied—meaning sudden attack or charge— may not at first glance seem to make sense. However, Hamlet could be talking about his body and mind being attacked suddenly and often. Using "sallied" would require actors to examine the speech from the point-of-view of Hamlet being mentally and spiritually attacked and injured.

## WHY *HAMLET* IS EXTRAORDINARY

There are two questions here: (1) why is the character Hamlet extraordinary and (2) why is the play *Hamlet* extraordinary? The answer to the first question is Hamlet's complexity. Hamlet is human, full of contradictions and inconsistencies. He struggles with some big issues though constant reflection.

Hamlet continually self-examines. He wonders about the value of continuing on with life. Then he connects sex with life and wonders about the importance of sex. His examination of the role of sex leaves him disgusted by its apparent importance in the life of his mother. He then realizes how life is perpetuated by sex and tells Ophelia to become a nun so she does not have to deal with sex (procreation) and life.

The struggle between good and evil plagues Hamlet. The good is personified in Old Hamlet, his father, and the evil is personified by Claudius, his uncle. At the top of the play Hamlet is an idealist, believing men are as good and noble as himself. As the play progresses, Hamlet becomes more complex seeing evil in others and recognizing the evil in himself. He wonders aloud how both good and evil can coexist in single individuals.

Hamlet condemns people for their inherent dark side. His troubled journey from the marriage of his mother to his uncle through to his own death due to treachery reflects his growing realization of evil in people. He sees the evil within himself, calling himself a rogue and a villain for having thoughts of revenge. He also calls himself a coward for thinking about revenge but being unable to kill his uncle. So, he is irritated at himself for having thoughts about revenge and frustrated that he cannot effect revenge.

Hamlet ponders that vengeance can impede an individual's personal determination. His life as a student is hijacked by the evil act of murder and his father's insistence on revenge. Hamlet's self-determination is swept away in the moment when he swears to avenge his father. Revenge takes on a life of its own, causing Hamlet to act in ways that he does not recognize as his former self, and his punishment for not being himself is death.

A viewer or reader of the play learns to understand Hamlet's motivations. Shakespeare has Hamlet explain himself and his inner thoughts regularly through soliloquies. These wonderfully evocative speeches touch on many of the important issues that most people deal with: the meaning of life versus suicide; the merits versus the flaws of mankind; life after death; and the nature of evil versus nobility.

Accompanying the examination of the big questions in life, Shakespeare adds colour through poetry. One can muse on the importance of life by thinking, "what is life about?" but "To be or not to be" examines life from a point of beauty. By saying "To be or not to be" one has already started to answer the question in the positive. The beauty and value in poetry is one of the reasons to be alive.

## IMPORTANT PRODUCTIONS OF *HAMLET*

### 1600/01

The Chamberlain's Men's first production of *Hamlet*, probably with Richard Burbage in the title role. Will Kempe may have been the Gravedigger and Shakespeare himself is rumored to have played the Ghost.

### 1607

The captain of the ship, *Dragon*, made his crew perform a version of *Hamlet* during a period of inactivity off the coast of Sierra Leone.

### 1661

William Davenant abridged the text of *Hamlet* and directed a production with Thomas Betterton, the best actor of the time, as Hamlet. This production was revived often until Betterton's death in 1710.

### 1734

David Garrick, the foremost actor of his day, performed the brooding Dane often between 1734 and his retirement in 1776.

### 1775

Sarah Siddons was very successful as Ophelia and this year she played Hamlet. Other women followed including Kitty Clive, Charlotte Cushman, Julia Glover, and Sara Bernhardt.

### 1870

Edwin Booth (his brother, John Wilkes, killed Lincoln) has been called the greatest American actor mainly because of his dynamic portrayal of Hamlet.

### 1900

One of the first films ever created had Sarah Bernhardt (The Divine Sarah) performing in a 2-minute black and white film, *Le Duel d'Hamlet*.

**1948**

Laurence Olivier plays Hamlet and directs this black and white classic film. Still worth watching more than half a century later, albeit gloomy. The production was the first British film to win Best Picture at the Oscars. Images of waves crashing against rocks abound as though crashing in Olivier's head.

**1964**

Boris Pasternak created a Russian version that was very dark.

**1990**

Franco Zeffirelli's version of *Hamlet* stars, Glenn Close as Gertrude, Alan Bates as Claudius, and Helena Bonham Carter as Ophelia. This version is uses a heavily cut script focusing more on action. Mel Gibson plays Hamlet as a man of action.

**1996**

Kenneth Branagh adapted, directed and starred in this star studded *Hamlet*. The secondary characters read like a who's who including Judi Dench and John Gielgud as flashback characters, Robin Williams as Osric, a palace courtier involved in the final fencing match, and Billy Crystal as the gravedigger.

**2000**

At least two *Hamlets* arrived in 2000. One from the Hallmark people who make holiday cards. Campbell Scott starred and directed this made for TV movie. Director Michael Almereyda's production stars Ethan Hawke in a modern day New York-based *Hamlet* where the Denmark Corporation is what is rotten.

## WRAP-UP

*Hamlet*, arguably the most popular play ever, is still up-to-date. The play deals with incest, the supernatural, and some of the most important questions people contemplate. Hamlet repeatedly asks what is the purpose and value of life in an unbearable world. He muses about the ambivalence of truth and spirituality. Shakespeare has Hamlet examine action versus thought, with a mind that is passionate, intelligent, and restlessly curious. Rather than this play becoming old and inconsequential it seems to be gaining in poignancy.

# Chapter 5: Hamlet, 45-Minute Readers' Theatre Version

## CASTING SUGGESTIONS

<u>One reader per part</u>

<u>14 readers</u>
    Reader 1: Narrator 1
    Reader 2: Narrator 2
    Reader 3: Hamlet
    Reader 4: Claudius
    Reader : Gertrude
    Reader 6: Polonius
    Reader 7: Laertes
    Reader 8: Ophelia
    Reader 9: Horatio
    Reader 10: Bernardo
    Reader 11: Ghost
    Reader 12: Gravedigger
    Reader 13: Actor King
    Reader 14: Francisco

<u>Using nine readers with some double casting</u>
    Reader 1: Narrator 1
    Reader 2: Narrator 2
    Reader 3: Hamlet
    Reader 4: Claudius, Gravedigger
    Reader 5: Gertrude, Francisco,
    Reader 6: Polonius
    Reader 7: Laertes, Ghost
    Reader 8: Bernardo, Ophelia
    Reader 9: Horatio, Actor King

Using seven readers with some double/triple casting
    Reader 1: Hamlet
    Reader 2: Bernardo, Ophelia
    Reader 3: Horatio, Polonius, Actor King
    Reader 4: Gertrude
    Reader 5: Narrator 1, Narrator 2
    Reader 6: Laertes, Ghost
    Reader 7: Francisco, Claudius, Gravedigger

PART TWO: *HAMLET*

*Hamlet*

## 45-Minute Readers' Theatre Version

**ALL**

    Hamlet Prince of Denmark.

**GHOST**

    By William Shakespeare.

**OPHELIA**

    Adapted by John Poulsen.

**NARRATOR 1**

    The story of Hamlet revolves around…

**HAMLET**

    Prince Hamlet the Dane.

**NARRATOR 2**

    His uncle…

**CLAUDIUS**

    Claudius, the newly married King.

**NARRATOR 1**

    Hamlet's mother…

**GERTRUDE**

    Queen Gertrude. Recently widowed. Recently married.

**NARRATOR 2**

    Hamlet's love.

**OPHELIA**

    Ophelia. The whole castle has been expecting Hamlet and me to get married ever since we could walk.

**NARRATOR 1**

    And Horatio.

**HORATIO**

    Hamlet's good friend.

**NARRATOR 2**

    The story begins in a dark and forbidding castle late on a cold foggy night. Bernardo has come to replace Francisco as the night guard.

**BERNARDO**

Who's there?

**FRANCISCO**

Nay, answer me: stand, and unfold* yourself. *(*show)*

**BERNARDO**

Long live the king!

**FRANCISCO**

Bernardo?

**BERNARDO**

He.

**FRANCISCO**

You come most carefully upon your hour.

**BERNARDO**

Tis now struck twelve; get thee to bed, Francisco.

**FRANCISCO**

For this relief much thanks: 'tis bitter cold, and I am sick at heart.

**BERNARDO**

Have you had quiet guard?

**FRANCISCO**

Not a mouse stirring. Good night.

**NARRATOR 1**

Exit Francisco. Enter Horatio, Hamlet's school companion.

**BERNARDO**

Welcome, Horatio; welcome.

**HORATIO**

What has this thing appeared again tonight?

**BERNARDO**

I have seen nothing.

**HORATIO**

Tush* tush t'will† not appear. *(*no †it will; i.e., no, no, it will not appear)*

**BERNARDO**

Peace break thee off*. Look where it comes again. *(*stop talking)*
Looks it not like the king* that is dead?
*(* the old King Hamlet, Hamlet the younger's father)*

**HORATIO**

Most like:-it harrows* me with fear and wonder. *(* fills)*

**BERNARDO**

Speak to it.

**HORATIO**

By heaven I charge* thee speak. *(*demand)*

**BERNARDO**

Tis here.

**HORATIO**

Tis here.

**BERNARDO**

Tis gone. It was about to speak.

**HORATIO**

And then it started like a guilty thing upon a fearful summons.*
*(*seems that the ghost had been frightened)*

**NARRATOR 1**

Enter Hamlet, the Prince of this castle. He mourns his father's death and his mother's, Queen Gertrude's, recent marriage to Claudius, his father's brother. Hamlet greets the guards.

**HAMLET**

The air bites shrewdly;* it is very cold. *(*cold cuts deep)*

**HORATIO**

It is a nipping and an eager* air. *(*nippy and cold)*

**HAMLET**

What hour now?

**HORATIO**

I think it lacks twelve.* *(*not yet midnight)*

**BERNARDO**

No, it is struck.

**NARRATOR 2**

Claudius, the new king, is celebrating his coronation. A flourish of trumpets interrupts their conversation.

**HORATIO**

What does this mean my lord?

**HAMLET**

The King doth wake and takes his draughts of wine.*
(*King is awake and drinking)
The kettledrum and the trumpet thus call out.

**HORATIO**

Is it a custom?

**HAMLET**

Ay, marry is it.
But to my mind, though I am native here
And to the manner born, it is a custom
More honored in the breach than the observance.*
(*even though Hamlet was born into nobility, this kind of festivity is seldom celebrated)

**HORATIO**

My lord, I came to see your father's funeral.

**HAMLET**

I pray thee, do not mock me; I think it was to see my mother's wedding.

**HORATIO**

Indeed, my lord, it followed hard upon.

**HAMLET**

Thrift, thrift, Horatio! The funeral baked meats
Did coldly furnish forth the marriage tables.
My father!—methinks I see my father!

**HORATIO**

Where, my lord?

**HAMLET**

In my mind's eye, Horatio.

**HORATIO**

My lord, I think I saw him.

**HAMLET**

Saw? Who?

**HORATIO**

My lord, the king your father. Here.

**HAMLET**

The king my father!

**HAMLET**

I will watch to-night; Perchance* 'twill walk again. (*maybe)

**HORATIO**

I warrant it will.

**HAMLET**

If it assume my noble father's person,
I'll speak to it, though hell itself should gape
And bid me hold my peace.

**NARRATOR 1**

The ghost enters.

**HORATIO**

Look my lord it comes.

**HAMLET**

Angels and ministers of grace* defend us! *(*guardian angels)*
It waves me forth, I'll follow it.

**BERNARDO**

Something is rotten* in the state of Denmark. *(*not right)*

**HAMLET**

Speak, I'll go no further.

**NARRATOR 2**

The ghost has the appearance of Hamlet's recently deceased father. It
speaks.

**GHOST**

I am thy father's spirit
Doomed for a certain time to walk the night.
If thou ever didst thy dear father love –
Revenge his foul* and most unnatural murder. *(*indecent)*

**HAMLET**

Murder?

**GHOST**

Murder most foul. Sleeping within my orchard
Thy uncle, in my ears did pour a poison.
If thou hast nature in thee, bear it not.*
*(*if you have natural feeling, do not accept this)*
The serpent that did sting thy father's life*
*(*the murderer that killed me)*
Now wears his crown.*
*(*is the current king)*

**HAMLET**

Yes, by heaven!*

*(\*Hamlet promises to avenge his father)*
O villain, villain, smiling damned villain!
Now to my word. I have sworn it.

**NARRATOR 1**

The Ghost leaves. Horatio and Bernardo catch up to Hamlet.

**HORATIO**

What news, my lord?

**HAMLET**

O, wonderful!

**HORATIO**

Good my lord, tell it.

**HAMLET**

No; you'll reveal it.

**BERNARDO**

Not I, my lord, by heaven.

**HAMLET**

You'll be secret?

**HORATIO**

Ay, by heaven, my lord.

**HAMLET**

Never make known what you have seen to-night.

**BERNARDO**

My lord, we will not.

**HAMLET**

Nay, but swear it.

**HORATIO**

In faith, My lord, not I.

**HAMLET**

Upon my sword.

**BERNARDO**

We have sworn, my lord, already.

**HAMLET**

Come hither, gentlemen, And lay your hands again upon my sword:
Never to speak of this that you have heard. Swear by my sword.

**NARRATOR 2**

The Ghost suddenly reappears and calls out from below…

**GHOST**

Swear.

**HAMLET**

Rest, rest perturbed* spirit.
(*worried)

**HORATIO**

O day and night, but this is wondrous strange.

**HAMLET**

There are more things in heaven and earth, Horatio,
Than are dreamt of in your philosophy.

**HORATIO**

So have I heard and do in part believe it.
But, look, the morn, in russet mantle clad,
Walks o'er the dew of yon high eastward hill.*
(*the sun is peeking over that eastern hill)

**HAMLET**

The time is out of joint.*
(* history has been tampered with. Hamlet's father should still be King. )
O cursed spite
That ever I was born to set it right!*
(* Hamlet protests that he has been chosen to revenge his father's murder)

**NARRATOR 2**

The next day within the castle, the new King of Denmark, Claudius,
enters with his new Queen, Gertrude, followed by her son Hamlet.

**CLAUDIUS**

Though my dear brother's death, the memory be green,* (* fresh)
But now, my dear Hamlet and my son —

**HAMLET**

A little more than kin and less than kind.
(* Hamlet and Claudius are closely related (kin) but
that they are not of the same sort or kind.)

**CLAUDIUS**

How is it Hamlet, my son, that the clouds still hang on you?

**HAMLET**

Not so, my lord: I am too much in the sun.

**GERTRUDE**

Good Hamlet. Cast thy knighted* colour off. (* *gloomy*)
And let thine eye look like a friend on Denmark.
Do not forever with thy veiled lids
Seek for thy noble father in the dust:
Good Hamlet. Thou know'st tis common. *

(* *It happens to everyone*)
All that live must die. Passing through nature to eternity.*
(* *everyone is born then lives and goes to heaven after death*)

**HAMLET**

Ay, madam, 'tis common.

**GERTRUDE**

If it be.

**CLAUDIUS**

Tis sweet and commendable in your nature, Hamlet,
To give these mourning duties to your father:
But, you must know, your father lost a father;
That father lost, lost his,
We pray you throw to earth,
This unprevailing* woe and think of me
(* *not usual*) As your father. Come away.

**NARRATOR 1**

King Claudius and Queen Gertrude leave Hamlet alone.

**HAMLET**

O that this too too solid flesh would melt.*
(* *I want my contaminated and unclean body to disappear so that I can be pure*)
Thaw and resolve itself into a dew!* (* *vapour*)
How weary, stale, flat and unprofitable,
Seem to me all the uses of this world!
But two months dead: nay, not so much, not two:
So excellent a king; that was, to this,
so loving to my mother
Must I remember? why, she would hang on him,
As if increase of appetite had grown
My mother married to my uncle, my father's brother
Within a month after she followed my poor father's body
Let me not think on it. Frailty thy name is woman.*

(* *all women are weak*)

**NARRATOR 2**

Change of scene to the chambers of Polonius, the Lord Chamberlain to the King. Polonius's son Laertes is about to board ship to sail south back to his school in France. Laertes sees his father again.

**LAERTES**

Here my father comes. A double blessing is a double grace,
Occasion smiles upon a second leave.

**POLONIUS**

There my blessing with thee!
And these few teachings in thy memory* (*remember this advice)
Give thy thoughts no tongue.* (* think and listen)
Be thou familiar, but by no means vulgar.
Beware of entrance to a quarrel, but being in,
Bear it that the opposed may beware of thee.*
(* If in a quarrel be serious so that you will be respected)
Give every man thine ear, but few thy voice* (* listen well but talk little)
Neither a borrower nor lender be* (* don't lend or borrow money)
For loan oft loses both itself and friend. (*you might lose your friends and the money)
And borrowing dulls the edge of husbandry.* (* thriftiness)
This above all, to thine own self be true
And it must follow as night the day
Thou canst not then be false to any man* (* be yourself)
Farewell. My blessing season* this in thee. (* ripen)

**LAERTES**

Most humbly do I take my leave my lord.

**NARRATOR 1**

Polonius turns to his daughter Ophelia. Ophelia carries a letter from Hamlet.

**POLONIUS**

How now, Ophelia! What is the matter?

**OPHELIA**

O, my lord, my lord, I have been so frightened!

**POLONIUS**

With what, in the name of God?

**OPHELIA**

My lord, as I was sewing in my closet,
Lord Hamlet, with his doublet all unbraced;* (* jacket unbuttoned)
No hat upon his head; Pale as his shirt;
His knees knocking each other;
And with a look so piteous comes before me.

**POLONIUS**

Ophelia, is Hamlet mad for thy love?

**OPHELIA**

He took me by the wrist and held me hard;
Then goes he to the length of all his arm;
And, with his other hand thus o'er his brow,
He falls to such perusal* of my face *(* study)*
As he would draw it. Long stay'd he so;
At last, a little shaking of mine arm
And thrice his head thus waving up and down,
He raised a sigh so piteous and profound
As it did seem to shatter all his bulk
And that done, he lets me go:
And, with his head over his shoulder turned,
He seemed to find his way without his eyes.

**POLONIUS**

Come, go with me: I will go seek the king.
This is the very ecstasy of love.

**OPHELIA**

My lord, I do not know; But truly, I do fear it.

**POLONIUS**

What is between you? Give me up the truth.

**OPHELIA**

My lord he hath importuned* me with love *(*pursued)*
In honourable fashion.

**NARRATOR 1**

Ophelia reads a letter given to her by Hamlet.

**OPHELIA**

To the celestial, and my soul's idol, the most beautified Ophelia
Doubt that the stars are fire; Doubt that the sun doth move;
Doubt truth be a liar;
But never doubt I love thee best. O dear Ophelia.

**POLONIUS**

Though this be madness, yet there is method in it.

**OPHELIA**

And hath given countenance* to his speech, *(*expression)*
My lord, with almost all the holy vows of heaven.

**POLONIUS**

Do not believe his vows.
I would not have you give words or talk with the Lord Hamlet.

**OPHELIA**

I shall obey my lord.

**NARRATOR 2**

Hamlet thinks constantly of his father's ghost and the promised revenge. He arranges for a troupe of actors to perform a play whose plot is parallel to that of Claudius's crime.

**HAMLET**

Oh what a rogue and peasant slave am I!* (* *I am ineffective*)
Is it not monstrous* that this actor here, (* *outrageous or wrong*)
Could drown the stage with tears
Yet I, a dull and muddy–mettled rascal* (*lacking in resolve*)
Can say nothing. Am I a coward?
I have heard that the guilty creatures sitting at a play
Have been struck so to the soul that presently
they have proclaimed their malefactions.*
(* *the criminals confessed their criminal acts*)
For murder, though it have no tongue, will speak
I'll have these players play something like the murder of my father
Before my uncle. I'll observe his looks and if he do blanche* (* *turn pale*)
I'll know my course.* The plays the thing (* *what I will do*)
Wherein I'll catch the conscience of the king.*
(* *Hamlet will know that Claudius killed Old King Hamlet*
*by Claudius's reaction to the play*)

**NARRATOR 1**

Hamlet's behaviour is considered mad. Polonius explains to the King and Queen that he considers Hamlet dangerous.

**POLONIUS**

Since brevity* is the soul of wit, (*being brief*)
I will be brief: your noble son is mad:
Mad call I it; for, to define true madness,
What is it but to be nothing else but mad?

**CLAUDIUS**

How may we try* this further? (* *examine*)

**POLONIUS**

You know, sometimes he walks for hours
Here in the lobby.

**GERTRUDE**

So he does indeed.

**POLONIUS**

At such a time I will loose my daughter to him.

**NARRATOR 2**

Claudius, Gertrude and Polonius exit. Hamlet is speaking to himself as he enters the lobby where Ophelia has been sent to read.

**HAMLET**

To be or not to be – that is the question:* *(* Should I live or die?)*
Whether 'tis nobler in the mind to suffer
the slings and arrows of outrageous fortune*
*(* is it better to accept those troubles that fate throws at us)*
Or to take arms against a sea of troubles*
*(* or should I fight against fate?)*
and by opposing end them. To die to sleep —
No more – and by a sleep to say we end
The heartache, and the thousand natural shocks
That flesh is heir to.*
*(* Hamlet longs for peace and he thinks peace can be found in death)*
To sleep; perchance* to dream; *(* maybe)*
ay there's the rub.* *(* difficulty)*
But that the dread of something after death,
The undiscovered country, from whose bourn* *(* borders)*
No traveler returns, puzzles the will
And makes us rather bear those ills we have.
Soft* now, the fair Ophelia. *(* quiet)*

**OPHELIA**

Good my lord,
How does your honor for this many as day?*
*(* haven't seen you, how are you?)*

**HAMLET**

I humbly thank you, well, well, well.

**OPHELIA**

My lord, I have letters of yours
That I have longed to re-deliver.
I pray you now receive them.

**HAMLET**

No not I,
I never gave you aught.* *(* anything)*

*Part Two: Hamlet*

**OPHELIA**

My honored lord, you know right well you did. Rich gifts wax poor
when givers prove unkind.*
*(\* nice presents convert to not-so-nice presents when the giver becomes mean)*

**HAMLET**

I did love you once.

**OPHELIA**

Indeed, my lord, you made me believe so.

**HAMLET**

You should not have believed me. I loved you not.

**OPHELIA**

I was the more deceived.

**HAMLET**

Go thy ways to a nunnery.* Where's your father?
*(\* Hamlet tells Ophelia to become a nun because  then she will not
have children. Having children would continue the cycle of life and death that
Hamlet thinks is bad)*

**OPHELIA**

At home my lord.

**HAMLET**

Denmark's a prison.

**OPHELIA**

Then is the world one.

**HAMLET**

A goodly one; in which there are many confines, wards and dungeons,
Denmark being one o' the worst.

**OPHELIA**

I think not so, my lord.

**HAMLET**

Why, then, 'tis none to you;
for there is nothing either good or bad,
but thinking makes it so: to me it is a prison.
Get thee to a nunnery.
Why wouldst thou be a breeder of sinners.*
*(\* have children)*

**OPHELIA**

O, help him, you sweet heavens!

**HAMLET**

What a piece of work is a man!
how noble in reason! how infinite in faculty!
in form and moving how express and admirable!
in action how like an angel! in apprehension how like a god!
the beauty of the world! the paragon* of animals! *(* best)*
And yet, to me, what is this quintessence* of dust? *(* essence)*
man delights not me: no, nor woman neither,
To a nunnery, go and quickly too. Farewell.

**OPHELIA**

O, what a noble mind is here overthrown.*

*(* Ophelia thinks Hamlet is becoming crazy)*
And I, of ladies most deject and wretched,
That sucked the honey of his music vows,
Now see that noble and most sovereign reason
Blasted. Oh woe is me.
To have seen what I have seen.

**NARRATOR 1**

Hamlet gives advice to the troupe of actors that will present the play whose plot is similar to Claudius's crime of killing the king and marrying the former king's widow.

**HAMLET**

Speak the speech, I pray you, as I pronounced it to you, trippingly* on the tongue. They are coming to the play. Be the players ready? *(* nimbly)*

**ACTOR KING**

I warrant your honor.

**HAMLET**

Go make you ready. How now? Will the king hear this piece of work?

**NARRATOR 2**

The King and Queen and their entourage enter to view the play. Hamlet speaks to Polonius.

**HAMLET**

My lord, you played once in the university, you say?

**POLONIUS**

That did I, my lord; and was accounted a good actor.

**HAMLET**

What did you enact?

**POLONIUS**

I did enact Julius Caesar: I was killed in the Capitol; Brutus killed me.

**HAMLET**

It was a brute part of him to kill so capital a calf.* *(* fool)*

**GERTRUDE**

Come hither,* my dear Hamlet, sit by me. *(* here)*

**NARRATOR 1**

The players perform. Enter a King and a Queen who embraces him and he her. He lies down and she, seeing him asleep, leaves.

**OPHELIA**

What means this, my lord?

**HAMLET**

Marry, it means mischief

**OPHELIA**

Tis brief, my lord.

**HAMLET**

As a woman's love. Mother, how like you the play?

**GERTRUDE**

The lady doth protest too much, methinks.*
*(* the actress complains too much, I think)*

**CLAUDIUS**

What do you call this play?

**HAMLET**

The Mouse-Trap.

**NARRATOR 2**

Anon comes in another man: takes off the crown, kisses it, pours poison into the sleeper's ear and leaves. The Queen returns, finds the King dead.

**HAMLET**

See? He poisons Gonzago in the garden for his estate.
You shall see anon how the murderer gets the love of Gonzago's wife.

**NARRATOR 1**

The poisoner returns, seems to condole with the Queen and sends the dead body away. He woos the Queen with gifts; she rejects them awhile, but in the end accepts love.

**OPHELIA**

See. The king rises.

**HAMLET**

What frightened with false fire?*(* *gun that shoots only blanks not real bullets*)

**GERTRUDE**

How fares my lord?

**POLONIUS**

Give over the play.

**CLAUDIUS**

Give me some light. Away.

**ALL**

Lights. Lights. Lights.

**NARRATOR 2**

The King rushes away and all follow. Hamlet trails his mother to her room. He thinks before approaching her.

**HAMLET**

Tis now the very witching time of night,
When churchyards yawn and hell itself breathes out.
Now could I drink hot blood,
And do such bitter business as the day
Would quake to look on. Soft! now to my mother.
O heart, lose not thy nature;
I will speak daggers to her, but use none;
My tongue and soul in this be hypocrites!* (* *not connected*)
Now mother, what is the matter?

**GERTRUDE**

Hamlet, thou hast thy father much offended.

**HAMLET**

Mother, you have my father much offended.

**NARRATOR 1**

Hamlet shows his mother a small musical instrument.

**HAMLET**

Will you play upon this pipe?

**GERTRUDE**

You know I cannot.

**HAMLET**

I pray you.

**GERTRUDE**

Believe me, I cannot.

**HAMLET**

'Tis as easy as lying: Govern* these holes with your fingers and thumb,
(* control)
Give it breath with your mouth, and It will discourse most eloquent music.
Look you, these are the stops.

**GERTRUDE**

But these cannot I command to any utterance of harmony;
I have not the skill.

**HAMLET**

Why, look you now, how unworthy a thing you make of me!
You would play upon me;
And there is much music, excellent voice, in this little pipe;
Yet cannot you make it speak.
Do you think I am easier to be played on than a pipe?
Call me what instrument you will, though you can fret* me,
(* both to fret a guitar and to alarm)
Yet you cannot play upon me.

**GERTRUDE**

Come, come, you answer with an idle tongue.* (* cruel statement)

**HAMLET**

Go, go, you question with a wicked tongue.

**GERTRUDE**

What wilt thou do? Thou wilt not murder me?
Help ho!

**NARRATOR 2**

Polonius has been eavesdropping on the mother-son conversation, hiding behind a curtain.

**POLONIUS**

What, ho! Help! Help!

**NARRATOR 1**

Hamlet draws his sword thinking that it is Claudius behind the curtain.

**HAMLET**

How now? A rat? Dead for a ducat, dead.*
(* I bet a ducat [money] that I've killed someone)

**POLONIUS**

O, I am slain.

**GERTRUDE**

O me, what hast thou done?

**HAMLET**

Nay, I know not. Is it the King?

**GERTRUDE**

O, what a rash* and bloody deed is this! (* impulsive)

**HAMLET**

A bloody deed — almost as bad, good mother
As kill a king, and marry with his brother.

**GERTRUDE**

As kill a king!

**HAMLET**

Ay, lady, 'twas my word.

**NARRATOR 2**

Hamlet lifts the curtain and sees that it is not Claudius but Polonius
whom he has killed.

**HAMLET**

Thou wretched, rash, intruding fool, farewell
I took thee for thy better.* Peace.
(* Hamlet thought that Polonius was Claudius)

**GERTRUDE**

What have I done, that thou darest wag thy tongue
In noise so rude against me?

**HAMLET**

Such an act that blurs the grace and blush of modesty.

**GERTRUDE**

O Hamlet, speak no more: Thou turn'st mine eyes into my very soul;
And there I see such black and grained spots.

**HAMLET**

Nay, but to live in the rank sweat of an enseamed* bed, (*defiled)

**GERTRUDE**

O, speak to me no more;
These words, like daggers, enter in mine ears;
No more, sweet Hamlet.

**HAMLET**

A murderer and a villain; A slave that is not twentieth part
Of your precedent lord.* *(\* previous husband)*

**GERTRUDE**

No more!

**NARRATOR 1**

The Ghost enters. Hamlet can see his father's ghostly form, but
Gertrude can not.

**HAMLET**

What would your gracious figure?

**GERTRUDE**

Alas he is mad.

**HAMLET**

Do you come your tardy son to chide?* *(\* slow son to scold)*

**GHOST**

Do not forget thy purpose.
But look amazement on thy mother sits: Speak to her, Hamlet.

**HAMLET**

How is it with you lady?

**GERTRUDE**

Alas, how is it with you,
That you do bend your eye on vacancy
And with the incorporal* air do hold discourse? *(\* bodiless)*
Whereon do you look?

**HAMLET**

On him, on him! Look you, how pale he glares!
Do you see nothing there?

**GERTRUDE**

No, nothing but ourselves.

**HAMLET**

Nor did you nothing hear?

SHAKESPEARE FOR READER'S THEATRE: *HAMLET, ROMEO AND JULIET, MIDSUMMER NIGHT'S DREAM*
BY JOHN POULSEN

**GERTRUDE**

No, nothing but ourselves.

**HAMLET**

Look where he goes, even now, out the portal.

**GERTRUDE**

O Hamlet, thou hast cleft my heart in twain.* *(* cracked my heart in two)*

**HAMLET**

I do repent Polonius's death: but heaven hath pleased it so,
To punish me with this and this with me,
That I must be their scourge and minister.*
*(* I must be the whip and the one who whips)*
I will bestow him, and will answer well
The death I gave him.
I must be cruel, only to be kind.

**NARRATOR 2**

Hamlet runs to Claudius's chamber to kill him.

**CLAUDIUS**

O, my offence is rank it smells to heaven;
It hath the primal eldest* curse upon it, *(* refers to Cain and Able)*
A brother's murder.
O wretched state! O bosom black as death.
Help, Angels!
Bow, stubborn knees; and, heart with strings of steel
Be soft as sinews of the newborn babe.
I pray all may be well.

**NARRATOR 1**

Hamlet sees Claudius on his knees, praying.

**HAMLET**

Now might I do it. Now he is praying.
And now I'll do it. And so he goes to heaven.
And so I am revenged.
A villain kills my father and for that
I, his sole son, do this same villain send to heaven.
Up sword. Later.
When he is drunk asleep, or in his rage.
That his soul may be as damned and black
As hell, whereto it goes.

**NARRATOR 2**

Hamlet leaves.

**CLAUDIUS**

My words fly up, my thoughts remain below.
Words without thoughts never to heaven go.

**NARRATOR 1**

Ophelia hearing of her father's death descends into madness. Claudius
and Gertrude watch her enter singing.

**OPHELIA**

He is dead and gone, He is dead and gone,
At his head a grass-green turf,
At his heels a stone.

**GERTRUDE**

Nay, but, Ophelia,—

**OPHELIA**

Pray you, mark.
White his shroud as the mountain snow,—

**CLAUDIUS**

How do you, pretty lady?

**OPHELIA**

God be at your table!

**CLAUDIUS**

Pretty Ophelia!

**OPHELIA**

Quoth she, you promised me to wed.
So would I have done, by yonder sun,
And thou hads't not come to my bed.

**CLAUDIUS**

How long hath she been thus?

**OPHELIA**

I cannot choose but weep, to think they should lay him
In the cold ground. Good night, ladies; good night, sweet ladies.

**CLAUDIUS**

O, this is the poison of deep grief; it springs
All from her father's death. O Gertrude, Gertrude,
When sorrows come, they come not single spies
But in battalions.* First, her father slain
(* *sorrows come in groups one after another*)
Now, your son is gone.

PART TWO: *HAMLET*

**NARRATOR 2**

Hamlet is sent by Claudius to England to be killed. Pirates take him off the ship and return him to Denmark. En route back to the castle Hamlet crosses through a graveyard and speaks to the gravedigger.

**HAMLET**

What man dost thou dig it for?

**GRAVEDIGGER**

For no man, sir.

**HAMLET**

For what woman then?

**GRAVEDIGGER**

For none neither.

**HAMLET**

Who is to be buried in it?

**GRAVEDIGGER**

Oh that was a woman, sir, but rest her soul, she's dead. Here's a skull now hath lain in the earth three and twenty years.

**HAMLET**

Whose was it?

**GRAVEDIGGER**

A pestilence on him for a mad rogue. He poured a flagon* of wine on
(* bottle)
my head once. This same skull, sir, was Yorick's skull, the King's jester.

**HAMLET**

Let me see. Alas poor Yorick! I knew him.
A fellow of infinite jest, of excellent fancy: he hath
borne me on his back a thousand times; and now,
How abhorred in my imagination it is! My gorge rises at it.
Here hung those lips that I have kissed
I know not how oft. Where be your jokes now?
Your gambols?* Your songs? Your flashes of merriment? (* games)
But soft, soft awhile! Here comes the King
The Queen, the courtiers. Who is this they follow?

**NARRATOR 1**

Hamlet hides and watches the ceremony. Laertes lowers his sister into the grave. Gertrude strews flowers onto Ophelia's body.

**LAERTES**

Lay her in the earth

And from her fair and unpolluted flesh
May violets spring.
A ministering angel shall my sister be.

**HAMLET**

What, the fair Ophelia?

**GERTRUDE**

Sweets to the sweet. Farewell.
I hoped thou should have been my Hamlet's wife.
I thought thy bride-bed to have decked, sweet maid,
And not have strewed thy grave.

**NARRATOR 2**

Laertes struck with grief jumps into the grave with his sister.

**LAERTES**

Hold off the earth awhile,
Till I have caught her in mine arms
Now pile you dust upon the quick and dead.
Till of this flat a mountain you have made.

**HAMLET**

What is he whose grief bears such an emphasis?
This is I Hamlet the Dane!

**NARRATOR 1**

Hamlet advances and leaps into the grave to grapple with Laertes.

**LAERTES**

The devil take thy soul.

**HAMLET**

I loved Ophelia. Forty thousand brothers
Could not with all their quantity of love
Make up my sum.

**CLAUDIUS**

O, he is mad, Laertes.

**GERTRUDE**

For love of God, forbear him.

**HAMLET**

Show me what thou will do.
Wouldst thou weep? Wouldst thou fight?
Wouldst thou tear thyself? Eat a crocodile?
I'll do it. Dost thou come here to whine?
To outface* me with leaping in her grave? (* *show more grief*)

Be buried quick with her, and so will I.
I'll rant as well as thou.

**GERTRUDE**

This is mere madness.

**HAMLET**

Here you, Laertes,
What is the reason you use me thus?
I loved you ever. But it is no matter.
Let Hercules himself do what he may.
The cat will mew, and dog will have his day.*
(* *whatever happens, even if Hercules arrives, the future cannot be stopped*)

**NARRATOR 2**

Later in private Laertes confronts the King about the death of Polonius.

**LAERTES**

How came he dead? I'll not be juggled with.* (* *tricked*)

**CLAUDIUS**

I am guiltless of your father's death.
Tis Hamlet. He which hath your noble father slain
Pursued my life.* What would you undertake
(* *Hamlet is trying to kill Claudius*)
To show yourself your father's son in deed
More than words?

**LAERTES**

To cut the murder's throat in the church.

**CLAUDIUS**

Revenge should have no bounds. But, good Laertes,
Will you do this, keep close within your chamber.* (* *room*)

**LAERTES**

But let Hamlet come;
It warms the very sickness in my heart,
That I shall live and tell him to his teeth, 'Thus dies thou.'

**CLAUDIUS**

If it be so, Laertes—As how should it be so? —
Will you be ruled by me?

**LAERTES**

Ay, my lord; So you will not over rule me to peace.

**CLAUDIUS**

You and Hamlet shall duel.

He will not peruse* the foils, so that with ease *(* inspect)*
Or with a little shuffling,* you may choose. *(* rearranging)*

**LAERTES**

I will do it.
And for that purpose I'll anoint* my sword *(* smear)*
With poison so that if I touch him lightly
It may be death.

**CLAUDIUS**

Let's further think of this. If this should fail.
Let us have a back or second. If he calls for drink
I'll have a chalice* for the occasion whereon but sipping *(* cup)*
Our purpose may hold there. It be poisoned as well.
We'll put the matter to the present plan.

**NARRATOR 1**

As the final scene opens the King is shaking Laertes's hand when
Hamlet enters. The King bides Hamlet and Laertes to shake hands.

**CLAUDIUS**

Come, Hamlet, come and take this hand from me.

**HAMLET**

Give me your pardon sir. I have done you wrong.
And hurt my brother.

**LAERTES**

I am satisfied in nature but in terms of my honour,
I stand aloof, and will no reconcilement.* *(* not forgive)*

**CLAUDIUS**

Give them the foils. Come on.

**LAERTES**

Come, one for me. This is too heavy; let me see another.

**HAMLET**

Come on sir.

**LAERTES**

Come my lord.

**NARRATOR 2**

Laertes has taken the sword with the poison on it. Laertes and Hamlet
fight.

**HAMLET**

One.

**LAERTES**

No.

**HAMLET**

Judgment?

**CLAUDIUS**

A hit, a very palpable* hit. *(\* obvious)*

**LAERTES**

Well again.

**NARRATOR 1**

Claudius poisons the wine and tries to get Hamlet to drink.

**CLAUDIUS**

Stay, give me drink. Hamlet, here's to thy health. Give him the cup.

**HAMLET**

I'll play this bout first; set it by awhile.
Come. Another hit; what say you?

**LAERTES**

A touch, a touch. I do confess it.

**NARRATOR 2**

Gertrude cheers for her son and picks up the poisoned cup.

**GERTRUDE**

Our son shall win. Here, Hamlet, take my napkin, rub thy brows.
The Queen carouses* to thy fortune, Hamlet. *(\* celebrates)*

**CLAUDIUS**

Gertrude, do not drink.

**GERTRUDE**

I will my lord; I pray you pardon me.

**NARRATOR 1**

Gertrude drinks.

**CLAUDIUS**

It is the poisoned cup; it is too late.

**HAMLET**

Come for the third Laertes, you do but dally.* *(\* delay)*

**LAERTES**

Say you so? Come on. Have at you now.

**NARRATOR 2**

Laertes wounds Hamlet; then in the scuffling they change rapiers and Hamlet wounds Laertes.

**LAERTES**

I am justly killed with mine own treachery.* *(* betrayal)*

**HAMLET**

How does the Queen?

**CLAUDIUS**

She swoons* to see them bleed. *(* faints)*

**GERTRUDE**

No, no, the drink, the drink! O my dear Hamlet!
The drink, the drink. I am poisoned.

**HAMLET**

O, villainy! Ho! Let the door be locked. Treachery! Seek it out.

**LAERTES**

It is here, Hamlet. Hamlet thou art slain;
No medicine in the world can do thee good.
In thee there is not half an hour's life;
The treacherous instrument is in thy hand.
Unbated and envenomed.* The foul practice *(* sharp and poisoned)*
Hath turned itself on me; lo, here I lie,
Never to rise again. Thy mother's poisoned.
I can no more. The King, the King's to blame.

**HAMLET**

The point envenomed too!
Then venom to thy work.

**NARRATOR 1**

Hamlet stabs Claudius.

**CLAUDIUS**

O, yet defend me friends; I am but hurt.

**HAMLET**

Here, thou incestuous, murderous, damned Dane,
Drink off this potion. Follow my mother.

**NARRATOR 2**

Hamlet forces Claudius to drink from the poisoned cup. The King dies.

**LAERTES**

He is justly served.
It is a poison tempered by himself.
Exchange forgiveness with me, noble Hamlet.

**HAMLET**

O, I die. Horatio!
The potent poison quite over crows* my spirit *(* triumphs over)*
The rest is silence.

**HORATIO**

Now cracks a noble heart. Good night sweet prince.
And flights of angels sing thee to thy rest.

**ALL**

The end.

## Chapter 6: Hamlet, 20-Minute Readers' Theatre Version

### CASTING SUGGESTIONS

<u>One reader per part</u>

<u>15 readers</u>
    Reader 1: Narrator 1
    Reader 2: Narrator 2
    Reader 3: Hamlet
    Reader 4: Claudius
    Reader 5: Gertrude
    Reader 6: Polonius
    Reader 7: Laertes
    Reader 8: Ophelia
    Reader 9: Horatio
    Reader 10: Guard
    Reader 11: Ghost
    Reader 12: Gravedigger
    Reader 13: Actor King (non-speaking)
    Reader 14: Actor Queen (non-speaking)
    Reader 15; Actor Poisoner (non-speaking)

<u>Using nine readers with some double casting</u>
    Reader 1: Narrator 1
    Reader 2: Narrator 2
    Reader 3 : Hamlet
    Reader 4: Claudius, Gravedigger
    Reader 5: Gertrude, Ghost
    Reader 6: Polonius, Actor Poisoner
    Reader 7: Laertes, Actor Queen
    Reader 8: Guard, Ophelia
    Reader 9: Horatio, Actor King

PART TWO: *HAMLET*

<u>Using seven readers with some double/triple casting</u>
>    Reader 1 : Hamlet
>    Reader 2: Guard, Ophelia, Actor Queen
>    Reader 3: Horatio, Polonius, Actor King
>    Reader 4: Ghost, Gertrude
>    Reader 5: Narrator 1, Narrator 2
>    Reader 6 : Laertes, Actor Poisoner
>    Reader 7 : Claudius, Gravedigger

# *HAMLET* 20-MINUTE READERS' THEATRE VERSION

**ALL**

Hamlet Prince of Denmark.

**GHOST**

By William Shakespeare.

**OPHELIA**

Adapted by John Poulsen.

**NARRATOR 1**

The story of Hamlet revolves around…

**HAMLET**

Prince Hamlet the Dane.

**NARRATOR 2**

His uncle…

**CLAUDIUS**

Claudius, the newly married King.

**NARRATOR 1**

Hamlet's mother…

**GERTRUDE**

Queen Gertrude. Recently widowed. Recently married.

**NARRATOR 2**

Hamlet's love…

**OPHELIA**

Ophelia. The whole castle has been expecting Hamlet and me to get married ever since we could walk.

**NARRATOR 1**

And Horatio…

**HORATIO**

Hamlet's good friend.

**NARRATOR 1**

Enter Hamlet, the Prince of this castle. He mourns his father's death and his mother's, Queen Gertrude's, recent marriage to Claudius, his father's brother. Hamlet greets the guards.

**HAMLET**

The air bites shrewdly;* it is very cold. (* *cold cuts deep*)

**HORATIO**

It is a nipping and an eager* air. (* *nippy and cold*)

**HAMLET**

What hour now?

**HORATIO**

I think it lacks twelve.* (* *not yet midnight*)

**GUARD**

No, it is struck.

**NARRATOR 2**

A ghost enters.

**HORATIO**

Look my lord it comes.

**HAMLET**

Angels and ministers of grace* defend us! (**guardian angels*)
It waves me forth, I'll follow it.

**GUARD**

Something is rotten* in the state of Denmark. (**not right*)

**HAMLET**

Speak, I'll go no further.

**NARRATOR 1**

The ghost has the appearance of Hamlet's recently deceased father. It
speaks.

**GHOST**

I am thy father's spirit
Doomed for a certain time to walk the night.
If thou ever didst thy dear father love –
Revenge his foul* and most unnatural murder. (* *indecent*)

**HAMLET**

Murder?

**GHOST**

Murder most foul. Sleeping within my orchard
Thy uncle, in my ears did pour a poison.
If thou hast nature in thee, bear it not.*
(**if you have natural feeling, do not accept this*)

SHAKESPEARE FOR READER'S THEATRE: HAMLET, ROMEO AND JULIET, MIDSUMMER NIGHT'S DREAM
BY JOHN POULSEN

The serpent that did sting* thy father's life ( * the murderer that killed me)
Now wears his crown.* ( *is the current king)

**HAMLET**

Yes, by heaven!* ( *Hamlet promises to avenge his father)
O villain, villain, smiling damned villain!
Now to my word. I have sworn it.
The time is out of joint.*
( * history has been tampered with. Hamlet's father should still be King. )
O cursed spite
That ever I was born to set it right!*
( * Hamlet protests that he has been chosen to revenge his father's murder)

**NARRATOR 2**

The next day within the castle, the new King of Denmark, Claudius, with his new Queen, Gertrude, are just leaving her son, Hamlet, to himself.

**CLAUDIUS**

How is it Hamlet, my son, that the clouds still hang on you?*
( * you are still depressed?)

**GERTRUDE**

Good Hamlet. Thou know'st tis common. * ( * It happens to everyone)
All that live must die. Passing through nature to eternity.*
( * Everyone is born then lives and goes to heaven after death)

**HAMLET**

O that this too too solid flesh would melt*.
( * I want my contaminated and unclean body to disappear so that I can be pure)
My mother married to my uncle, my father's brother
Within a month after she followed my poor father's body
Let me not think on it. Frailty thy name is woman.* ( * All women are weak)

**NARRATOR 1**

Change of scene to the chambers of Polonius, the Lord Chamberlain to the King, who enters with his son Laertes.

**POLONIUS**

There my blessing with thee.
And these few thoughts in thy memory* ( *remember this advice)
Give every man thine ear, but few thy voice * ( * listen well but talk little)
Neither a borrower nor lender be* ( * don't lend or borrow money)
For loan oft loses both itself and friend. ( *you might lose your friends and the money)
This above all, to thine own self be true
And it must follow as night the day
Thou canst not then be false to any man* ( * be yourself)
Farewell.

**LAERTES**

Most humbly do I take my leave my lord.

**NARRATOR 2**

Hamlet thinks constantly of his father's ghost and the promised revenge. He arranges for a troupe of actors to perform a play whose plot is similar to that of Claudius's crime.

**HAMLET**

Oh what a rogue and peasant slave am I!* *(* I am ineffective)*
Is it not monstrous* that this actor here, *(* outrageous or wrong)*
Could drown the stage with tears
Am I a coward?
I have heard that the guilty creatures sitting at a play
Have been struck so to the soul that presently
they have proclaimed* their malefactions.† *(* confessed †criminal acts)*
I'll have these players play something like the murder of my father
Before my uncle.
I'll observe his looks and if he do blanche* *(* turn pale)*
I'll know my course*. The plays the thing *(* what I will do)*
Wherein I'll catch the conscience of the king.* *(* Hamlet will know that Claudius killed Old King Hamlet by Claudius's reaction to the play)*

**NARRATOR 1**

Hamlet's behaviour is considered mad. He seems to be in constant confusion. He enters a room in which Ophelia is reading.

**HAMLET**

To be or not to be – that is the question:* *(* Should I live or die?)*
Whether 'tis nobler in the mind to suffer
the slings and arrows of outrageous fortune*
*(* is it better to accept those troubles that fate throws at us)*
Or to take arms against a sea of troubles* *(* or should I fight against fate?)*
and by opposing end them. To die to sleep –
No more – and by a sleep to say we end
The heartache, and the thousand natural shocks
That flesh is heir to.* *(* Hamlet longs for peace and he thinks peace can be found in death)*
Soft* now, the fair Ophelia. *(* quiet)*

**OPHELIA**

Good my lord,
How does your honor for this many as day?* *(* haven't seen you, how are you?)*

**HAMLET**

I humbly thank you, well, well, well.

**OPHELIA**

My lord, I have letters of yours

That I have longed to re-deliver.
I pray you now receive them.

**HAMLET**

No not I,
I never gave you aught.* *(\* anything)*

**OPHELIA**

My honoured lord, you know right well you did.
Rich gifts wax poor when givers prove unkind *
*(\* not present current or mini-size presents when the giver becomes mean)*

**HAMLET**

I did love you once.

**OPHELIA**

Indeed, my lord, you made me believe so.

**HAMLET**

You should not have believed me. I loved you not.

**OPHELIA**

I was the more deceived.

**HAMLET**

Get thee to a nunnery. Why wouldst thou be a breeder of sinners.
To a nunnery, go and quickly too.* Farewell.
*(\* Hamlet tells Ophelia to become a nun because then she will not
have children. Having children would continue the cycle of life and
death which Hamlet thinks is bad)*

**OPHELIA**

O, what a noble mind is here overthrown.* *(\*Ophelia thinks Hamlet is becoming crazy)*
Oh woe is me.
To have seen what I have seen.

**NARRATOR 2**

Hamlet gives advice to the troupe of actors that will present the play.
The plot that is similar to Claudius's crime of killing the king and
marrying the former king's widow.

**HAMLET**

Speak the speech, I pray you, as I pronounced it to you,
trippingly* on the tongue. *(\* nimbly)*
They* are coming to the play. Be the players ready?
*(\* the King & Queen)*

**NARRATOR 1**

The King and Queen and their entourage enter to view the play.

**GERTRUDE**

Come hither,* my dear Hamlet, sit by me. *(* here)*

**NARRATOR 2**

The players perform. A King and a Queen enter. She embraces him. He lies down and she, seeing him asleep, leaves.

**NARRATOR 1**

In comes another man: takes off the crown and kisses it. He pours poison into the sleeper's ear and leaves. The Queen returns, finds the King dead.

**NARRATOR 2**

The poisoner returns and woos the Queen with gifts. She embraces the poisoner.

**OPHELIA**

What means this, my lord?

**HAMLET**

Marry, it means mischief.

**OPHELIA**

Tis brief, my lord.

**HAMLET**

As a woman's love. Mother, how like you the play?

**GERTRUDE**

The lady doth protest too much, methinks.*
*(* the actress complains too much, I think)*
See. The king rises.

**CLAUDIUS**

Give me some light. Away.

**NARRATOR 1**

The King rushes away and all except Gertrude and Hamlet follow.

**HAMLET**

Now mother, what is the matter?

**GERTRUDE**

Hamlet, thou hast thy father much offended.

**HAMLET**

Mother, you have my father much offended.

**GERTRUDE**

Come, come, you answer with an idle tongue.* *(* cruel statement)*

**HAMLET**

Go, go, you question with a wicked tongue.

**GERTRUDE**

What wilt thou do? Thou wilt not murder me?
Help ho!

**NARRATOR 2**

Polonius has been hiding behind a curtain, eavesdropping on the mother-son conversation.

**POLONIUS**

What, ho! Help!

**NARRATOR 1**

Hamlet draws his sword thinking that it is Claudius behind the curtain and stabs through the curtain.

**HAMLET**

How now? A rat? Dead for a ducat, dead.*
(* I bet a ducat [money] that I've killed someone)

**POLONIUS**

O, I am slain.

**GERTRUDE**

O me, what hast thou done?

**HAMLET**

Nay, I know not. Is it the King?

**GERTRUDE**

O, what a rash* and bloody deed is this! (* impulsive)

**HAMLET**

A bloody deed – almost as bad, good mother,
As kill a king, and marry with his brother.

**NARRATOR 2**

Hamlet lifts the curtain and sees that it is not Claudius but Polonius who he has killed.

**HAMLET**

Thou wretched, rash, intruding fool, farewell
I took thee for thy better.* Peace. (* Hamlet thought that Polonius was Claudius)

**NARRATOR 1**

Later Hamlet crosses through a graveyard and speaks to a gravedigger.

PART TWO: *HAMLET*

**HAMLET**

What man dost thou dig it for?

**DIGGER**

A pestilence on him for a mad rogue.
He poured a flagon* of wine on my head once. *(\* bottle)*
This same skull, sir, was Yorick's skull, the King's jester.

**HAMLET**

Alas poor Yorick! I knew him.
A fellow of infinite jest, of excellent fancy.
Where be your jokes now?
But soft, soft awhile! Here comes the King
The Queen, the courtiers. Who is this they follow?

**NARRATOR 2**

Hamlet hides and watches the ceremony. He realizes that it is Ophelia's funeral. She has died from grief at death of her father Polonius. Laertes lowers his sister into the grave. Gertrude strews flowers onto Ophelia's body.

**GERTRUDE**

Sweets to the sweet. Farewell.
I hoped thou should have been my Hamlet's wife.

**NARRATOR 1**

Laertes struck with grief jumps into the grave with his sister.

**LAERTES**

Hold off the earth awhile,
Till I have caught her in mine arms
Now pile you dust upon the quick* and dead. *(\* living)*

**NARRATOR 2**

Hamlet advances and leaps into the grave to grapple with Laertes.

**HAMLET**

What is he whose grief bears such an emphasis?
This is I Hamlet the Dane!

**LAERTES**

The devil take thy soul.

**HAMLET**

I loved Ophelia. Forty thousand brothers
Could not with all their quantity of love
Make up my sum.

**CLAUDIUS**

O, he is mad, Laertes.

**HAMLET**

Show me what thou will do.
I'll do it. Dost thou come here to whine?
To outface* me with leaping in her grave? *(* show more grief)*
Be buried quick with her, and so will I.
I'll rant as well as thou.

**GERTRUDE**

This is mere madness.

**HAMLET**

Here you, Laertes,
What is the reason you use me thus?
I loved you ever. But it is no matter.
Let Hercules himself do what he may.
The cat will mew, and dog will have his day.*
*(* whatever happens, even if Hercules arrives, the future cannot be stopped)*

**NARRATOR 1**

Later in private Laertes schemes with the King.

**CLAUDIUS**

I am guiltless of your father's death.
'Tis Hamlet. What would you undertake
To show yourself your father's son in deed
More than words.

**LAERTES**

To cut the murder's throat in the church.

**CLAUDIUS**

You and Hamlet shall duel.
He will not peruse* the foils, so that with ease *(* inspect)*
Or with a little shuffling*, you may choose. *(* rearranging)*

**LAERTES**

I will do it.
And for that purpose I'll anoint* my sword *(* smear)*
With poison so that if I touch him lightly
It may be death.

**CLAUDIUS**

Let's further think of this. If this should fail,
Let us have a back or second. If he calls for drink
I'll have a chalice* for the occasion. *(* cup)*

It be poisoned as well.

**NARRATOR 2**

The final scene contains the duel. Laertes looks for the foil with the poison tip.

**CLAUDIUS**

Give them the foils. Come on.

**LAERTES**

Come, one for me. This is too heavy; let me see another.

**HAMLET**

Come on sir.

**LAERTES**

Come my lord.

**NARRATOR 1**

Laertes has taken the sword with the poison on it. Laertes and Hamlet fence. Hamlet scores a point.

**HAMLET**

One.

**LAERTES**

No.

**HAMLET**

Judgment?

**CLAUDIUS**

A hit, a very palpable* hit. (*obvious)

**LAERTES**

Well again.

**NARRATOR 2**

Claudius poisons the wine and tries to get Hamlet to drink.

**CLAUDIUS**

Stay, give me drink. Hamlet, here's to thy health. Give him the cup.

**HAMLET**

I'll play this bout first; set it by awhile. Come. Another hit; what say you?

**LAERTES**

A touch, a touch. I do confess it.

**NARRATOR 1**

Gertrude cheers for her son and takes the poisoned cup.

**GERTRUDE**

Our son shall win. Here, Hamlet, take my napkin, rub thy brows.
The Queen carouses* to thy fortune, Hamlet. (* *celebrates*)

**CLAUDIUS**

Gertrude, do not drink.

**GERTRUDE**

I will my lord; I pray you pardon me.

**NARRATOR 2**

Gertrude drinks.

**CLAUDIUS**

It is the poisoned cup; it is too late.

**HAMLET**

Come for the third Laertes, you do but dally.* (* *delay*)

**LAERTES**

Say you so? Come on. Have at you now.

**NARRATOR 1**

Laertes wounds Hamlet; then in the scuffling they change rapiers and
Hamlet wounds Laertes.

**LAERTES**

I am justly killed with mine own treachery.* (* *betrayal*)

**HAMLET**

How does the Queen?

**CLAUDIUS**

She swoons* to see them bleed. (* *faints*)

**GERTRUDE**

No, no, the drink, the drink! O my dear Hamlet! The drink, the drink.
I am poisoned.

**HAMLET**

O, villainy! Ho! Let the door be locked. Treachery! Seek it out.

**LAERTES**

It is here, Hamlet. Hamlet thou art slain;
No medicine in the world can do thee good.
Lo, here I lie, Never to rise again.

Thy mother's poisoned. I can no more.
The King, the King's to blame.

**HAMLET**

The point envenomed* too! (* *made poisonous*)
Then venom to thy work.

**NARRATOR 2**

Hamlet stabs Claudius.

**CLAUDIUS**

O, yet defend me friends; I am but hurt.

**HAMLET**

Here, thou incestuous, murderous, damned Dane,
Drink off this potion. Follow my mother.

**NARRATOR 1**

Hamlet forces Claudius to drink from the poisoned cup. The King
dies.

**LAERTES**

He is justly served.
It is a poison tempered by himself.
Exchange forgiveness with me, noble Hamlet.

**HAMLET**

O, I die. Horatio!
The potent poison quite over crows* my spirit (* *triumphs over*)
The rest is silence.

**HORATIO**

Now cracks a noble heart. Good night sweet prince.
And flights of angels sing thee to thy rest.

**ALL**

The end.

PART TWO: HAMLET

## Chapter 7: *Hamlet*: Readers' Theatre Director's Script

This *Director's Script* has suggestions for directing an abridged Readers' Theatre production of Hamlet. The suggestions correspond with the *Hamlet: 20-Minute Readers' Theatre Version* found in this book. This version of *Hamlet* has a running time of about 20 minutes—from the time the actors start their entrance to when they walk off stage.

## INTRODUCTION

Bold indicates suggested direction. If there is no bold directorial suggestion connected to the line, the actors should briefly freeze while other lines are being said and then interpret their line as they see fit. They should use off stage focus, by delivering the line straight ahead.

Text after the character's name without bold or italics are the words to be spoken. Print a copy of the script (*Hamlet*: 20-Minute Readers' Theatre Version) for each reader. The first rehearsal should be a read-through where actors read their assigned parts. After the read-through, performers should highlight or underline their lines. If an actor has more than one character, lines for each should be highlighted in different colours. Have readers write in pencil directorial notes (such as when to stand, sit, and move forward), as well as clarification of line meaning or line intention.

Italics in smaller font indicate meaning. Sometimes a specific word is defined, other times the phrase is clarified. The format begins with an asterisk behind a word or phrase. The clarification follows in italics.

The casting suggestions below require as few as seven and as many as 15 actors. If you have 15 performers there are parts for all. Using triple casting as few as seven performers can be accommodated. The Actor King, Queen, and Poisoner have no spoken lines, they only mime their parts. This may be suitable for some students.

## DIRECTORIAL PARAMETERS

Actors use off-stage focus for this presentation. They assume that all action takes place toward the audience. If they are speaking to someone, they pretend the person is standing in front of them.

The performing area is pre-set. Before the audience arrives the performers' chairs and stools are arranged in a straight line mid-stage with about one meter between each seat. The characters enter to sit on chairs that have been pre-set sideways with the backs towards stage left. Narrators sit at the ends of the line, farthest stage right and stage left, on stools that place them slightly higher than the performers sitting on chairs.

If the audience is sitting on the floor, stretch a rope or lay some tape to indicate where the audience is to sit. If using chairs, all audience seats will be set out.

The actors' seating is pre-arranged. The primary consideration in seating is to have Hamlet in the middle chair with Ophelia on one side and Gertrude on the other. Claudius sits next to Gertrude. Next to Ophelia sits her brother Laertes and then her father Polonius.

Narrators do not use Back to Audience (BTA) for entrances, or Front to Audience (FTA) for exits. They use the Freeze convention, so that when they finish saying a line they stop moving until their next line. Checking their scripts unobtrusively is acceptable.

As much as possible, actors should say their lines directly to the audience. Reading is acceptable, but speaking directly forward using offstage focus can improve the production by making actors easier to see and hear.

Front to Audience (FTA) direction requires that actors spin to face the audience before saying their line. Generally, actors should be spinning and breathing in as the previous speaker is saying the last three words of their line. For example, the Guard is the first actor to spin FTA She should spin as Horatio says "it lacks." She should also be taking in air so she can start her line loudly and slowly as Horatio finishes saying "twelve."

Drop Head (DH) and Raise Head (RH) direction is used when the performer will be needed shortly. Actors drop their heads at the end of their line and bring their heads up as the final words in the previous lines are being said. The raising of the head should be accompanied with an intake of breath so the next line can be said immediately and loudly. For example, Hamlet is the first to use this convention. He would breathe in and raise his head as the Narrator says "…Horatio and the guard." Hamlet then says his line deliberately allowing the audience to focus on him.

## CASTING SUGGESTIONS

Casting can be fluid up until performance. At performance, should you have fewer than the actors originally cast, consider using some or all of the following double casting suggestions. For example, if the Actor Poisoner and Narrator 1 are missing on the day of performance, have the actor playing Polonius take on the Actor Poisoner role and Narrator 2 read the lines of Narrator 1. With the exception of combining the Narrator roles, it is important that the actors taking on extra parts highlight their new lines in a different and distinctive manner.

One reader per part

15 readers
    Reader 1: Narrator 1
    Reader 2: Narrator 2
    Reader 3: Hamlet
    Reader 4: Claudius
    Reader 5: Gertrude
    Reader 6: Polonius
    Reader 7: Laertes
    Reader 8: Ophelia
    Reader 9: Horatio
    Reader 10: Guard
    Reader 11: Ghost
    Reader 12: Gravedigger
    Reader 13: Actor King
    Reader 14: Actor Queen
    Reader 15: Actor Poisoner


Using nine readers with some double casting.
    Reader 1: Narrator 1
    Reader 2: Narrator 2
    Reader 3: Hamlet
    Reader 4: Claudius, Gravedigger
    Reader 5: Gertrude, Ghost
    Reader 6: Polonius, Actor Poisoner
    Reader 7: Laertes, Actor Queen
    Reader 8: Guard, Ophelia
    Reader 9: Horatio, Actor King

<u>Using seven readers with some double/triple casting.</u>
    Reader 1: Hamlet
    Reader 2: Guard, Ophelia, Actor Queen
    Reader 3: Horatio, Polonius, Actor King
    Reader 4: Ghost, Gertrude
    Reader 5: Narrator 1, Narrator 2
    Reader 6 : Laertes, Actor Poisoner
    Reader 7: Claudius, Gravedigger,

## ENTRANCE

Actors enter in pairs or trios speaking to one another as though they are nobility. They enter from as many different upstage and downstage areas as possible. Some characters enter from behind the audience.

Narrators enter first. Hamlet enters slowly. He should reach his chair last. All actors freeze facing upstage in front of their designated chair or stool. Gertrude checks that all actors are in place, then she raises her script toward upstage and all actors turn to sit facing the audience. When all actors are settled, Gertrude again raises her script toward the audience and all actors say in unison the title.

**Bold = suggested direction**
Regular = text to be spoken by the actor.
*Italics = \*definition or clarification of line meaning.*

# *HAMLET* READERS' THEATRE DIRECTOR'S SCRIPT

**ALL**

Hamlet Prince of Denmark.
**(All but Ghost, Ophelia, Narrators, Hamlet, Claudius, Gertrude, Ophelia, Guard, and Horatio turn to face upstage and then sit still – BTA)**

**GHOST**

By William Shakespeare.
**(BTA)**

**OPHELIA**

Adapted by John Poulsen

**NARRATOR 1**

The story of Hamlet revolves around…
**(Freeze. Narrators freeze after each line unless instructed otherwise.)**

**HAMLET**

Prince Hamlet the Dane.
**(DH)**

**NARRATOR 2**

His uncle
**(Freeze. Narrators freeze after each line unless instructed otherwise.)**

**CLAUDIUS**

Claudius, the newly married King.
**(BTA)**

**NARRATOR 1**

Hamlet's mother.

**GERTRUDE**

Queen Gertrude. Recently widowed. Recently married.
**(BTA)**

**NARRATOR 2**

Hamlet's love.

**OPHELIA**

Ophelia. The whole castle has been expecting Hamlet and me to get married ever since we could walk.
**(BTA)**

**NARRATOR 1**

And Horatio.

**HORATIO:**

Hamlet's good friend.

**NARRATOR 1**

Enter Hamlet, the Prince of this castle. He mourns his father's death and his mother's, Queen Gertrude's, recent marriage to Claudius, his father's brother. Hamlet greets Horatio and the guard.

**HAMLET**

**(RH -Looks at audience as though he is cold.)**
The air bites shrewdly;* it is very cold. (* *cold cuts deep*)

**HORATIO**

It is a nipping and an eager* air. (* *nippy and cold*)

**HAMLET**

What hour now?

**HORATIO**

**(Looks up at the moon.)**
I think it lacks twelve.* (* *not yet midnight*)

**GUARD**

**(FTA)**
No, it is struck.

**NARRATOR 2**

A ghost enters.

**HORATIO**

**(Points directly above audience.)**
Look my lord it comes.

**HAMLET**

(Looks where Horatio is pointing.)
Angels and ministers of grace* defend us! (*guardian angels)
It waves me forth, I'll follow it.

**GUARD**

Something is rotten* in the state of Denmark. (*not right)
(Guard and Horatio turn BTA)

**HAMLET**

Speak, I'll go no further.
(Freeze, looks above the audience as though Ghost is in front
and above him.)

**NARRATOR 1**

The ghost has the appearance of Hamlet's recently deceased father. It
speaks.

**GHOST**

(FTA, stares at first row audience as though Hamlet is in front
and below him.)
I am thy father's spirit
Doomed for a certain time to walk the night.
If thou ever didst thy dear father love –
Revenge his foul* and most unnatural murder. (*indecent)

**HAMLET**

Murder?

**GHOST**

Murder most foul. Sleeping within my orchard
Thy uncle, in my ears did pour a poison.
If thou hast nature in thee, bear it not.*
(*if you have natural feeling do not accept this)
The serpent that did sting thy father's life* (*the murderer that killed me)
Now wears his crown.* (*is the current king)
(BTA)

**HAMLET**

Yes, by heaven!* (*Hamlet promises to avenge his father)
O villain, villain, smiling damned villain!
Now to my word. I have sworn it.
The time is out of joint.*
(History has been tampered with. Hamlet's father should still be King.)
O cursed spite
That ever I was born to set it right!*

*(\* Hamlet protests that he has been chosen to revenge his father's murder)*

**NARRATOR 2**

The next day within the castle, the new King of Denmark, Claudius with his new Queen, Gertrude are just leaving her son Hamlet to himself.

**CLAUDIUS**

**(FTA, looks straight ahead as though he owns the castle.)**
How is it Hamlet, my son, that the clouds still hang on you?* *(\* you are still depressed?)*
**(Holds out hand expecting Gertrude will place her hand on his, freeze.)**

**GERTRUDE**

Good Hamlet. Thou know'st tis common.* *(\* It happens to everyone)*
All that live must die. Passing through nature to eternity.* *(\* Everyone is born then lives and goes to heaven after death)*
**(Gertrude places her hand in front of herself as though placing it on Claudius's hand. With a flourish, Claudius and Gertrude BTA)**

**HAMLET**

O that this too too solid flesh would melt*

*(\* I want my contaminated and unclean body to disappear so that I can be pure)*
My mother married to my uncle, my father's brother
Within a month after she followed my poor father's body
Let me not think on it. Frailty thy name is woman*

*(\* All women are weak)*
**(DH)**

**NARRATOR 1**

Change of scene to the chambers of Polonius, the Lord Chamberlain to the King, who enters with his son Laertes.

**POLONIUS**

**(Polonius and Laertes FTA)**
There my blessing with thee.
And these few thoughts in thy memory* *(\*remember this advice)*
Give every man thine ear, but few thy voice * *(\* listen well but talk little)*
Neither a borrower nor lender be* *(\* don't lend or borrow money)*
For loan oft loses both itself and friend.* *(\*you might lose your friends and the money)*
This above all, to thine own self be true
And it must follow as night the day
Thou canst not then be false to any man* *(\* be yourself)*
Farewell.

**LAERTES**

Most humbly do I take my leave my lord.
**(Laertes and Polonius BTA)**

**NARRATOR 2**

Hamlet thinks constantly of his father's ghost and the promised revenge. He arranges for a troupe of actors to perform a play whose plot is similar to that of Claudius's crime.

**HAMLET**

**(RH)**
Oh what a rogue and peasant slave am I!* *(* I am ineffective)*
Is it not monstrous* that this actor here, *(* outrageous or wrong)*
Could drown the stage with tears
Am I a coward?
I have heard that the guilty creatures sitting at a play
Have been struck so to the soul that presently
they have proclaimed* their malefactions. † *(* confessed †criminal acts)*
I'll have these players play something like the murder of my father
Before my uncle.
I'll observe his looks and if he do blanche* *(* turn pale)*
I'll know my course.* The plays the thing *(* what I will do)*
Wherein I'll catch the conscience of the king,*
*(* Hamlet will know that Claudius killed Old King Hamlet*
*by Claudius's reaction to the play)*

**NARRATOR 1**

Hamlet's behaviour is considered mad. He seems to be in constant confusion. He enters a room in which Ophelia is reading.

**HAMLET**

To be or not to be – that is the question* *(* Should I live or die?)*
Whether 'tis nobler in the mind to suffer
the slings and arrows of outrageous fortune*
*(* is it better to accept those troubles that fate throws at us)*
Or to take arms against a sea of troubles* *(* or should I fight against fate?)*
and by opposing end them. To die to sleep –
No more – and by a sleep to say we end
The heartache, and the thousand natural shocks
That flesh is heir to.*
*(* Hamlet longs for peace and he thinks peace can be found in death)*
Soft* now, the fair Ophelia. *(* quiet)*

**OPHELIA**

**(FTA)**
Good my lord,
How does your honor for this many as day?*

SHAKESPEARE FOR READER'S THEATRE: *HAMLET, ROMEO AND JULIET, MIDSUMMER NIGHT'S DREAM*
BY JOHN POULSEN

*(\* haven't seen you, how are you?)*
**(Stand and curtsey)**

HAMLET

I humbly thank you, well, well, well.
**(Stand and bow)**

OPHELIA

My lord, I have letters of yours
That I have longed to re-deliver.
I pray you now receive them.
**(Holds out script to audience)**

HAMLET

No not I,
I never gave you aught\*. *(\* anything)*

OPHELIA

**(Ophelia draws back hand. Looks straight ahead as though Hamlet is in front of her.)**
My honored lord, you know right well you did.
Rich gifts wax poor when givers prove unkind.\*

*(\* nice presents convert to not-so-nice presents when the giver becomes mean)*

HAMLET

**(Steps toward audience as though Ophelia is in front of him.)**
I did love you once.

OPHELIA

Indeed, my lord, you made me believe so.

HAMLET

**(Steps back)**
You should not have believed me. I loved you not.

OPHELIA

I was the more deceived.

HAMLET

Get thee to a nunnery. Why wouldst thou be a breeder of sinners. To a nunnery, go and quickly too.\* Farewell.
*(\* Hamlet tells Ophelia to become a nun because then she will not have children.*
*Having children would continue the cycle of life and death which Hamlet thinks is bad)*
**(Sits)**

OPHELIA

O, what a noble mind is here overthrown\*
*(\* Ophelia thinks Hamlet is becoming crazy)*
Oh woe is me.

To have seen what I have seen.
**(Sits BTA)**

**NARRATOR 2**

Hamlet gives advice to the troupe of actors that will present the play. The plot that is similar to Claudius's crime of killing the king and marrying the former king's widow.

**HAMLET**

Speak the speech, I pray you, as I pronounced it to you,
trippingly* on the tongue. *(* nimbly)*
They* are coming to the play. Be the players ready? *(* the King & Queen)*

**NARRATOR 1**

The King and Queen and their entourage enter to view the play.
**(Claudius and Gertrude spin looking forward, FTA)**

**GERTRUDE**

Come hither,* my dear Hamlet, sit by me. *(* here)*
**(DH Claudius DH)**

**NARRATOR 2**

**(As the Narrators relate the story, leaving spaces for the Actors to mime, the Actor King, Actor Queen and Actor Poisoner mime the story. Actor Queen and Actor King stand and step forward as they are announced. Actor Queen, King, and Poisoner may mime without scripts.)**
The players perform. A King and a Queen enter. She embraces him.
**(The Actor King steps forward, opening his arms facing the audience. The Queen steps forward and mime embraces the Actor King. The Actor King embraces only air as he also mime embraces the Actor Queen.)**
He lies down and she seeing him asleep leaves.
**(Actor King steps backward, sits down and tilts head to the side and sleeps. Actor Queen turns, walks to chair, sits and freezes.)**

**NARRATOR 1**

In comes another man: takes off the crown, kisses it,
**(Actor Poisoner stands and reaches for a mimed crown, picks it up, kisses it and places it on his head.)**
pours poison into the sleeper's ear and leaves.
**(Reaches into a mimed breast pocket, picks out a mimed vial, takes the stopper out, and tips the vial into a mimed ear directly in front of him. Turns, faces up stage, and freezes.)**
The Queen returns, finds the King dead.

(The Actor Queen stands, steps forward, and reaches her hand out as though gently shaking the Actor King's shoulder. Actor King turns BTA Actor Queen freezes.)

NARRATOR 2

The poisoner returns and woos the Queen with gifts.
(Actor Poisoner turns FTA and kneels lifting a mimed present to the Actor Queen. Actor Queen accepts the mimed present opens the box and carefully sets down the mimed box on a mimed table. She removes a crown and places the crown on her head.)
She embraces the poisoner.
(Actor Poisoner and Actor Queen embrace using offstage focus, miming a hug facing forward. They return to their chairs and sit and both BTA)

OPHELIA

(FTA)
What means this, my lord?

HAMLET

Marry, it means mischief.

OPHELIA

Tis brief, my lord.
(BTA)

HAMLET

As a woman's love. Mother, how like you the play?

GERTRUDE

(RH)
The lady doth protest* too much, methinks.[†] (*the actress complains; †I think)
See. The king rises.
(Freeze)

CLAUDIUS

(RH)
Give me some light. Away.
(BTA)

NARRATOR 1

The King rushes away and all except Gertrude and Hamlet follow.

HAMLET

Now mother, what is the matter?

**GERTRUDE**

Hamlet, thou hast thy father much offended.

**HAMLET**

Mother, you have my father much offended.

**GERTRUDE**

Come, come, you answer with an idle tongue*. *(* cruel statement)*

**HAMLET**

Go, go, you question with a wicked tongue.

**GERTRUDE**

What wilt thou do? Thou wilt not murder me?
Help ho!
**(Leans back in chair, one arm up to defend self, freeze.)**

**NARRATOR 2**

Polonius has been hiding behind a curtain, eavesdropping on the mother-son conversation.

**POLONIUS**

**(Spins FTA)**
What, ho!
**(Stands)**
Help!

**NARRATOR 1**

Hamlet draws his sword thinking that it is Claudius behind the curtain and stabs through the curtain.

**HAMLET**

**(Rolls his script into a tight cylinder. Stands.)**
How now?
**(Uses script as a sword and stabs forward.)**
A rat? Dead for a ducat, dead.* *(* I bet a ducat [money] that I've killed someone)*
**(Freeze in a lunge.)**

**POLONIUS**

O, I am slain (dies).
**(Steps backwards, sits, dies, and BTA)**

**GERTRUDE**

**(Comes out of freeze.)**
O me, what hast thou done?

**HAMLET**

**(Stand straight)**

Nay, I know not. Is it the King?

**GERTRUDE**

O, what a rash* and bloody deed is this! *(\* impulsive)*

**HAMLET**

A bloody deed – almost as bad, good mother
As kill a king, and marry with his brother.
**(Gertrude spins BTA)**

**NARRATOR 2**

Hamlet lifts the curtain and sees that it is not Claudius but Polonius
who he has killed.

**HAMLET**

**(Mimes lifting a curtain to see who he killed.)**
Thou wretched, rash, intruding fool, farewell
I took thee for thy better*. Peace. *(\* Hamlet thought that Polonius was Claudius)*
**(Sits. Freeze.)**

**NARRATOR 1**

Later Hamlet crosses through a graveyard and speaks to a gravedigger.

**HAMLET**

**(Gravedigger spins FTA and mimes digging with his rolled
script as shovel.)**
What man dost thou dig it for?

**GRAVEDIGGER**

A pestilence on him for a mad rogue.
He poured a flagon* of wine on my head once. *(\* bottle)*
This same skull, sir, was Yorick's skull, the King's jester.
**(BTA)**

**HAMLET**

**(Stands. Holds up script to stage right as though it is a skull.)**
Alas poor Yorick! I knew him.
A fellow of infinite jest, of excellent fancy.
Where be your jokes now?
**(Returns script and crouches.)**
But soft, soft awhile! Here comes the King
The Queen, the courtiers. Who is this they follow?
**(Sits and DH)**

**NARRATOR 2**

Hamlet hides and watches the ceremony. He realizes that it is Ophelia's
funeral. She has died from grief at the death of her father Polonius.

**(Laertes spins FTA, stands, raises his script to shoulder height and lowers his script slowly.)**

Laertes lowers his sister into the grave.

**(Gertrude FTA, stands and mimes throwing flowers as though they are coming from the script.)**

Gertrude strews flowers onto Ophelia's body.

**(Laertes freezes.)**

**GERTRUDE**

Sweets to the sweet. Farewell.
I hoped thou should have been my Hamlet's wife.

**NARRATOR 1**

Laertes struck with grief jumps into the grave with his sister.

**LAERTES**

**(Laertes jumps forward and kneels facing audience.)**
Hold off the earth awhile,
Till I have caught her in mine arms
**(Mimes cradling his sister in his arms.)**
Now pile you dust upon the quick* and dead. *(* living)*
**(Freeze)**

**NARRATOR 2**

Hamlet advances and leaps into the grave to grapple with Laertes.

**HAMLET**

**(RH)**
What is he whose grief bears such an emphasis?
This is I Hamlet the Dane!

**LAERTES**

**(Stands up speaks straight ahead.)**
The devil take thy soul.

**HAMLET**

**(Stands speaks straight ahead.)**
I loved Ophelia. Forty thousand brothers
Could not with all their quantity of love
Make up my sum.

**CLAUDIUS**

**(FTA, stands.)**
O, he is mad, Laertes.

**HAMLET**

**(Steps forward.)**
Show me what thou will do.

I'll do it. Dost thou come here to whine?
To outface* me with leaping in her grave? *(* show more grief)*
Be buried quick with her, and so will I.
I'll rant as well as thou.

**GERTRUDE**

This is mere madness.

**HAMLET**

**(Laertes steps forward in challenge.)**
Here you, Laertes,
What is the reason you use me thus?
I loved you ever. But it is no matter.
Let Hercules himself do what he may.
The cat will mew, and dog will have his day.*
*(* whatever happens, even if Hercules arrives, things cannot be stopped)*
**(Hamlet and Gertrude sit and DH Claudius and Laertes sit, freeze.)**

**NARRATOR 1**

Later in private Laertes schemes with the King.

**CLAUDIUS**

**(Sits slightly forward.)**
I am guiltless of your father's death.
Tis Hamlet. What would you undertake
To show yourself your father's son in deed
More than words.

**LAERTES**

**(Sits slightly forward.)**
To cut the murder's throat in the church.

**CLAUDIUS**

**(Sits farther forward.)**
You and Hamlet shall duel.
He will not peruse* the foils, so that with ease *(* inspect)*
Or with a little shuffling,* you may choose. *(* rearranging)*

**LAERTES**

**(Sits farther forward.)**
I will do it.
And for that purpose I'll anoint* my sword *(* smear)*
With poison so that if I touch him lightly
It may be death.

**CLAUDIUS**

**(Both sit slowly up. First Claudius then Laertes.)**
Let's further think of this. If this should fail,
Let us have a back or second. If he calls for drink
I'll have a chalice* for the occasion. *(* cup)*
It be poisoned as well.
**(Both sit neutral. Freeze.)**

**NARRATOR 2**

The final act in contains the duel. Laertes looks for the foil with the poison tip.

**CLAUDIUS**

Give them the foils. Come on.

**LAERTES**

**(Stand)**
Come, one for me. This is too heavy; let me see another.

**HAMLET**

**(Stand)**
Come on sir.

**LAERTES**

**(Rolls up script, stabs forward with a flourish.)**
Come my lord.

**NARRATOR 1**

Laertes has taken the sword with the poison on it.
**(Hamlet rolls up script and moves into 'en garde' position - back hand up, front foot pointed ahead, back foot sideways, and sword straight forward.)**
Laertes and Hamlet fence.
**(Tightly choreograph the fencing. It is all directed to the audience using offstage focus. The following is repeated later in this scene. Laertes stabs forward, Hamlet rocks back and then stabs forward. Laertes knocks Hamlet's sword to the side and then stabs forward. Hamlet's sword is knocked sideways, but he recovers and spins the tip of his sword in a small circle then flicks. Laertes's sword is spun in a circle and then knocked aside. Hamlet stabs forward.)**
Hamlet scores a point.

**HAMLET**

One.

**LAERTES**

No.

**HAMLET**

Judgment?

**CLAUDIUS**

A hit, a very palpable* hit. *(\* obvious)*

**LAERTES**

Well again.
**(Both fencers go into 'en garde' position.)**

**NARRATOR 2**

Claudius poisons the wine and tries to get Hamlet to drink.
**(Claudius steps forward and mimes plucking a small pill from his breast pocket, picking up a large wine glass, and dropping the pill into the glass.)**

**CLAUDIUS**

Stay, give me drink. Hamlet, here's to thy health. Give him the cup.

**HAMLET**

I'll play this bout first; set it by awhile.
**(Both fighters step forward closer to the audience. Fight begins with the same choreography as above. Laertes stabs forward, Hamlet rocks back and then stabs forward. Laertes knocks Hamlet's sword to the side and then stabs forward. Hamlet's sword is knocked sideways but he recovers and spins the tip of his sword in a small circle then flicks. Laertes's sword is spun in a circle and then is knocked aside. Hamlet stabs forward. Then Laertes makes a desperate contraction, moving his stomach back while sweeping Hamlet's sword up and away. Then Laertes tries to slice down on Hamlet's head. Hamlet raises his sword, knocks Laertes's sword aside and quickly thrusts his front foot forward while stretching forward with his sword.)**
Come. Another hit; what say you?
**(Both stand and step back.)**

**LAERTES**

A touch, a touch. I do confess it.

**NARRATOR 1**

Gertrude cheers for her son and takes the poisoned cup.

**GERTRUDE**

(RH Gertrude stands and steps forward slightly. Offers script as though it is a napkin.)

Our son shall win. Here, Hamlet, take my napkin, rub thy brows.

(She mimes picking up a large wine glass.)

The Queen carouses* to thy fortune, Hamlet. (* celebrates)

**CLAUDIUS**

(Gertrude raises the wine glass. Claudius stands as though he will grab the glass.)

Gertrude, do not drink.

**GERTRUDE**

(Gertrude swings the glass as though she is keeping it away from Claudius.)

I will my lord; I pray you pardon me.

**NARRATOR 2**

Gertrude drinks.

(Gertrude flourishes the mimed glass in the air as though congratulating Hamlet and drinks.)

**CLAUDIUS**

(Shrinks sideways.)

It is the poisoned cup; it is too late.

(Freeze)

**HAMLET**

Come for the third Laertes, you do but dally.* (* delay)

(Small flourish to the right then turns slightly left keeping his sword raised.)

**LAERTES**

Say you so? Come on. Have at you now.

(Laertes stabs forward desperately. Hamlet feels his back where he was stabbed and turns front bringing his sword down fast. Laertes drops his sword, as though Hamlet knocked it out of his hand. This action may be more of a throw, as Laertes's sword should land in front of Hamlet. Hamlet picks up Laertes's sword and throws his sword down in front of Laertes still looking straight ahead. Laertes picks up the sword.)

**NARRATOR 1**

Laertes wounds Hamlet; then in the scuffling they change rapiers and Hamlet wounds Laertes.

(Both fighters step forward closer to the audience. Fight is the same choreography as above. Laertes stabs forward, Hamlet rocks back and then stabs forward. Laertes knocks Hamlet's sword to the side and then stabs forward. Hamlet's sword is knocked sideways but he recovers and spins the tip of his sword in a small circle then flicks. Laertes's sword is spun in a circle and then is knocked aside. Hamlet stabs forward. Then Laertes makes a desperate contraction, moving his stomach back while sweeping Hamlet's sword up and away. Then Laertes tries to slice down on Hamlet's head. Hamlet raises his sword, knocks Laertes's sword aside and quickly thrusts his front foot forward while stretching forward with his sword.)

**LAERTES**

I am justly killed with mine own treachery.* *(* betrayal)*
(Laertes touches his chest where he was stabbed and falls slowly to his knees.)

**HAMLET**

(Stands erect.)
How does the Queen?

**CLAUDIUS**

(Steps forward. Gertrude steps forward and falters.)
She swoons* to see them bleed. *(* faints)*

**GERTRUDE**

No, no, the drink, the drink! O my dear Hamlet! The drink, the drink.
I am poisoned.
(Slowly sinks to the floor.)

**HAMLET**

O, villainy! Ho! Let the door be locked. Treachery! Seek it out.

**LAERTES**

(On his knees facing front.)
It is here, Hamlet. Hamlet thou art slain;
No medicine in the world can do thee good.
Lo, here I lie, Never to rise again.
Thy mother's poisoned. I can no more.
The King, the King's to blame.
(Freeze)

**HAMLET**

The point envenomed* too! *(* made poisonous)*
Then venom to thy work.
(Hamlet quickly stabs forward.)

**NARRATOR 2**

Hamlet stabs Claudius.

**CLAUDIUS**

**(Claudius touches the place he was stabbed and kneels facing forward.)**

O, yet defend me friends; I am but hurt.

**HAMLET**

Here, thou incestuous, murderous, damned Dane,
Drink off this potion. Follow my mother.
**(Hamlet drops his script, reaches for a mimed wine glass with his right hand and mimes grabbing Claudius hair. Claudius responds by dropping his head back. In mime, Hamlet now has Claudius's head pulled back. He brings the glass to Claudius's mimed mouth and pours.)**

**NARRATOR 1**

Hamlet forces Claudius to drink from the poisoned cup. The King dies.
**(Claudius mimes swallowing, then slowly falls to the floor.)**

**LAERTES**

He is justly served.
It is a poison tempered by himself.
Exchange forgiveness with me, noble Hamlet.
**(Slowly falls to the floor.)**

**HAMLET**

O, I die. Horatio!
**(Horatio FTA)**
The potent poison quite over crows* my spirit (* *triumphs over*)
The rest is silence.
**(Hamlet reaches the floor and lies still. Also lying on the floor are Gertrude, Claudius, Laertes, and Hamlet. It is preferable if they lay slightly on top of one another.)**

**HORATIO**

**(Stands and walks forward to just behind the pile of bodies.)**
Now cracks a noble heart. Good night sweet prince.
And flights of angels sing thee to thy rest.

**ALL**

**(All stand downstage in a single line facing the audience. Actors who were sitting stand and move downstage. Actors who were dead stand up. All actors grasp hands with the people on either**

side of them. Gertrude leads the bow by raising her hands, all others raise hands at the same time. Led by Gertrude, in unison they say…)

The end.

(Then bow still holding hands. After the bow, actors drop hands and exit from where they entered. They reconnect with the person they entered with and exit chatting as though they are nobility. Hamlet leaves last, sighing.)

# Part Three: Romeo and Juliet

## Chapter 8: *Romeo and Juliet* Background

### NUTSHELL

*Romeo and Juliet* is a story about star-crossed lovers, meaning they are predetermined by fate to ill fortune. The story may be based on a real Verona incident from the 3rd century. The play's popularity rests on its action-oriented plot, important themes, comedy-to-tragedy structure, beautiful poetry, and fiery characters.

### SYNOPSIS

The play begins with a prologue that sets out the plot and some of the themes including: star-crossed lovers, hate versus love, and passions. The play is set in Verona, Italy, where the people are passionate in both love and hatred. The play's action starts with a riot that peaks with the entrance of the elderly heads of the Montague and Capulet families, eager to join in the fight. The Prince stops the battle and threatens death to anyone who disturbs the peace again.

Romeo, in love with love, is a romantic searching for meaning in his life and finds it like a thunderbolt from above in the person of Juliet. Even after Romeo and Juliet find that their passions are centered on someone from their enemies' camp, they resolve to marry, hoping their love will solve the rancor between the two houses.

Then Tybalt, Juliet's cousin, kills Romeo's good friend Mercutio. In a moment of passion Romeo kills Tybalt and is subsequently banished from Verona. The Friar who married the star-crossed lovers devises a plan whereby Juliet appears to be dead for 42 hours allowing Romeo to sneak back to Verona and carry his love away when she awakes. The plan backfires and Romeo finds Juliet apparently dead. He takes poison and dies. Juliet awakes and kills herself. The Capulets and the Montagues reconcile at the gravesite.

## SOURCES

The basic Romeo and Juliet story can be found in Latin stories from as early as the 3rd century. In 1530, Luigi da Porto published a story in Italian that he said was based on an actual incident in Verona that had as the two lovers, Romeus Montague and Giulietta Capulet. The theme of young impetuous love can be found in many stories that abounded in Shakespeare's time but the 1562 poem by Arthur Brooke *The Tragical Historye of Romeus and Juliet* is very closely aligned with the plot structure in the Shakespearean play. The poem, at 3,020 lines long, probably gave William the plot as well as most major characters, including Friar Laurence, the Nurse, and Tybalt. One important difference was that Brooke's work had as a theme the righteous deaths of the young lovers because of their disobedience.

The other important document Shakespeare was probably familiar with was William Painter's, *Palace of Pleasure,* which could be found in London before 1580. *Palace of Pleasure* contained over 100 stories, including the basic plot of *Romeo and Juliet.* In Painter's story Juliet hopes "that our soules passing from this light, may eternally liue together in the place of euerlasting ioy." Shakespeare, however, rejects the idea that a double suicide can count as a happy ending and appears to hold the parents' pointless feud responsible for the tragedy.

## PUBLISHING HISTORY

Shakespeare's company changed its name in 1597. Before March 17, 1597, they were The Lord Hunsdon's Men, referring to the nobleman George Carey Hunsdon. After March 17, they were the Lord Chamberlain's Men, reflecting George's promotion to Lord Chamberlain. *Romeo and Juliet* was first published in 1597 in what is called the First Quarto (Q1). Q1 states on the title page that *Romeo and Juliet* had been "…(with great applause) played publicly, by the Right Honourable Lord Hunsdon his servants." This points to a performance date before March 17, 1597.

However, the company had been known as The Chamberlain's Men before 1597. George Carey's father, Baron Henry Carey Hunsdon, died on July 22, 1596. He was the Lord Chamberlain until his death and the patron of The Lord Chamberlain's Men. So Shakespeare's company was The Lord Hunsdon's Men between the death of Henry on July 22, 1596, and the ascension of his son, George to Lord Chamberlain on March 17, 1597.

This kind of research is very interesting to Shakespearean scholars. It is a form of detective work that points to answers, but can never give a concrete fact. In this case what is known indicates that *Romeo and Juliet* played before March 17, 1597, and after July 22, 1596.

Other issues with regard to *Romeo and Juliet* include 'who published the First Quarto' and 'was it approved by Shakespeare'? The first printed appearance of *Romeo and Juliet* is the Quarto of 1597, now referred to as Q1. The title page states that Q1 was printed by John Danter. About the time Danter printed *Romeo and Juliet* his shop was raided by the authorities and his presses were destroyed because he was printing material he did not have the legal right to print. This suggests that *Romeo and Juliet* was also illegally printed.

Q1 was previously referred to as the Bad Quarto because the text is of poor quality. The tradition is that Q1 is a pirated version based on the acting scripts of the first actors who played Paris or Romeo. Recently, this 'Bad Quarto' has gained respectability. There are now suggestions that this should be considered the original script as Shakespeare intended it, because Q1 is a fast-moving, action-packed version of the play, which would have had great appeal for Elizabethan audiences. Q1 is also unique in that it provides insight into performing Shakespeare's work, because some of the stage directions indicate how the play may have originally been staged. It may be that Shakespeare printed Q1 from his initial notes just after the production went up. Then he had the longer version (Q2) printed two years later, in 1599, after the play had matured via performance.

The Second Quarto or Q2 has as its title, *The Most Excellent and Lamentable Tragedy of Romeo and Juliet*. It states that it is "newly corrected, augmented, and amended." Q2 at about 25,850 lines is one and a half times the length of Q1. Most of the extra 800 lines are in the form of introspection, lyricism, and characterization. Q2 was probably created from Shakespeare's rough notes and have odd stage directions such as, "Enter Will Kemp," which referred to the comedic actor who played the part, not the character. Most modern versions of *Romeo and Juliet* are based on Q2. A Q3 was printed in 1609 that was based on Q2. All other versions, including the *First Folio* that was printed in 1623, seven years after Shakespeare's death, are essentially the same as *Q2*.

The differences between *Q1* and *Q2* can be examined in a piece of text just after the "Romeo Romeo wherefore art thy Romeo?" speech.

Q1 states:

> Tis but thy name that is mine enemie.
> Whats Mountague? It is nor hand nor foote,
> Nor arme, nor face, nor any other part.
> Whats in a name? That which we call a Rose,

Q2 states:

> Tis but thy name that is mine enemie
> Thou art thy selfe, though not a Mountague,
> Whats Montague? It is nor hand nor foote,
> Nor arme, nor face, o be some other name
> Belonging to a man.
> Whats in a name that which we call a rose.

The spelling is the original from the Q1 and Q2 documents. There are four lines in Q1 versus six in Q2. This reflects the difference in length between the documents, with Q2 being about one and a half times longer than Q1.

Is Q2 clearer? Perhaps, depending on the actor. Some actors prefer the punctuation in Q1, especially after "Whats in a name?" The question mark makes delivery of the line easier compared to no punctuation in Q2. However, the line from Q2, "o be some other name..." has a certain power. Examination of these sections of text illustrate that Q1 is not so bad and it often simply comes down to individual preference when considering which Quarto is best.

## WHY *ROMEO AND JULIET* IS EXTRAORDINARY

Romeo falls in love with Juliet before he knows her name. Sudden and dramatic love is very exciting. Add young forbidden love and there is excitement galore just within the plot.

And there is more. *Romeo and Juliet* starts like a romantic comedy. Everything is light, boys fight but nobody is injured. It feels a bit like a playground where even the oldest can act very badly because the monitor, the Prince, makes sure nobody gets hurt. The Prince breaks up the scuffle, sending most boys home, then takes one to his office.

The first half features love sonnets. Romeo meeting Juliet is a wonderful sonnet that runs: ABAB CBCB DEDE FF. Romeo says the first 4 lines, then Juliet has 4, Romeo says 1, Juliet says 1, Romeo 2, Juliet 1, and

Romeo finishes with the last line. The poem builds to love's first kiss – a classic romantic comedy moment.

Then suddenly Mercutio dies and the play becomes a tragedy. Tybalt dies and now there are bodies and consequences. Romeo is to be killed on sight or banished. Juliet takes a potion to feign death. Romeo buys a poison that kills within seconds. Even though *Romeo and Juliet* starts like a comedy the prologue makes clear that this is a tragedy.

The prologue makes the audience omnipresent. They know more than any one character and hold that advantage till the discovery of the dead lovers. This is the only Shakespeare play where audiences know the outcome of the play from the beginning and know more than any character, minor or major. Fate drives the story and the audience has the role of fate's recorder.

The main characters shine. Romeo and Juliet are lovely in their naïve world of love spiced with the heat of young passion. Tybalt and Mercutio are also passionate and hot-blooded. Even the old characters are hot-blooded, bent on revenge. Within seconds, Old Capulet goes from a harmless old man to threatening death when his daughter disobeys him.

Last but not least are Shakespeare's world-famous lines, which have permeated our language. When someone wants to be romantic they might say, "Good Night, Good night! Parting is such sweet sorrow" or "Romeo, Romeo wherefore art thou Romeo?" When examining the concept of objects and their connected names, "A rose by any other name would smell as sweet" is a fast and understood encapsulation of the concept.

## IMPORTANT PRODUCTIONS OF ROMEO AND JULIET

### 1596

Though versions of *Romeo and Juliet* could have played before 1596, they are best considered prototypes of Q1. Shakespeare probably began writing Romeo and Juliet in the early 1590s finishing it in 1595. In between it is likely that Shakespeare's company worked with him to develop the script. During the plague years (1592-1594) the Chamberlain's Men toured outside London, possibly playing an early version of *Romeo and Juliet* as part of their repertoire.

### 1662

William Davenant adapted the play, but it was not well received. Thomas Betterton, the most popular actor of the Restoration, played Mercutio.

**1670**

A popular adaptation ran that had alternate endings. One night the lovers lived, the next they died.

**1750**

David Garrick and Spranger Barry fanned their rivalry and lined their pockets with the *Romeo and Juliet* war. Audiences in London were encouraged to see both productions, running at the same time. Garrick and Barry had such box-office success with this they played *King John* and *Richard III* as rivals as well. Garrick's adaptation also included a final duologue for the lovers as well as a dirge for Juliet.

**1830**

Shakespeare's play inspired Vincenzo Bellini's opera *I Capuleti e I Montecchi*.

**1845**

Charlotte Cushman was one of the first women to play Romeo. Her sister Susan often played opposite as Juliet.

**1869-1880**

Pyotor Ilyich Tchaikovsky composed numerous versions of a symphony titled *Romeo and Juliet*. He called it an Overature-Fantasia and in 1937 it was choreographed as a ballet.

**1882**

Henry Irving, at age 44, starred in a production that was better received when a younger actor replaced him.

**1900**

Clémént Maurice's *Roméo et Juliette* was the first adaptation of a Shakespeare play to film.

**1935**

John Gielgud directed Laurence Olivier and Peggy Ashcroft at the New Theatre, London. Gielgud and Olivier played Romeo and Mercutio. They switched roles regularly, with Olivier eventually settling into the Mercutio role.

**1936**

Prokofiev's famous ballet was first presented to the Bolshoi, who pronounced it undanceable. Luckily, the Kirov Ballet significantly reworked and revised it, presenting it in 1940 in Leningrad.

**1936**

George Cukor's film starred a 43-year-old Leslie Howard and 34-year-old Norma Shearer. Most comments indicate the stars were too old for the parts.

PART THREE: *ROMEO & JULIET*

**1961**

The Jerome Robbins and Robert Wise's *West Side Story* movie was preceded by the Broadway Musical in 1957. This production was advertised as freely adapted from Shakespeare's work.

**1968**

Franco Zeffirelli directed the relatively young and unknown actors Leonard Whiting and Olivia Hussey. An early scene where they meet during the song, "What is a Youth" is a classic. This version was a manifestation of the 1960s. It focused on innocence of youth versus the inflexibility of the establishment.

**1978**

The BBC produced a version that was very close to Q1, which was lackluster in part because it focused on the importance of the older generation. Brooke's original poem made the same mistake.

**1996**

Baz Luhrmann's version starring Leonardo DiCaprio and Claire Dace is a modern adaptation where the Montagues and Capulets are warring mafia-like organizations. The script was heavily cut and augmented with a contemporary sound track that sometimes overshadowed the poetry. It made record profits, probably because it focused on an almost reckless pace and infectious energy that typified music videos of the 1990s.

**2006**

A modernized, deeply cut French-Canadian *Roméo and Juliette* film is directed by Yves Desgagnés. It has nudity.

## WRAP-UP

*Romeo and Juliet* is one of the most produced plays on the planet. Its staying power over the centuries is a tribute to Shakespeare's skill. He created a plot that starts light and effortlessly turns dark. The characters are all strong, interesting, believable, and still relevant today, 400 years after it was created. Ben Jonson, one of Shakespeare's peers, thought *Romeo and Juliet* was one of Shakespeare's best plays. It is also one of Shakespeare's earliest plays, which shows Shakespeare was a talented writer from the beginning.

# Chapter 9: *Romeo and Juliet,* 45-Minute Readers' Theatre Version

## CASTING SUGGESTIONS

<u>One reader per part</u>

<u>17 readers</u>
Reader 1: Romeo
Reader 2: Benvolio
Reader 3: Juliet
Reader 4: Nurse
Reader 5: Narrator
Reader 6 : Tybalt
Reader 7: Sampson
Reader 8: Gregory
Reader 9: Abram
Reader 10: Capulet
Reader 11: Montague
Reader 12: Prince
Reader 13: Lady Capulet
Reader 14: Mercutio
Reader 15: Narrator 2
Reader 16: Paris
Reader 17: Friar Laurence

<u>Using nine readers with some double/triple casting</u>
Reader 1: Romeo,
Reader 2: Benvolio, Montague
Reader 3: Juliet
Reader 4: Nurse, Abram,
Reader 5: Narrator 1, Narrator 2
Reader 6 : Tybalt, Prince, Paris
Reader 7: Sampson, Capulet
Reader 8: Gregory, Lady Capulet
Reader 9: Friar Laurence

### *Romeo and Juliet*: 45-minute Readers' Theatre Version

**ALL**

Romeo and Juliet.

**BENVOLIO**

By William Shakespeare.

**LADY CAPULET**

Adapted by John Poulsen.

**NARRATOR 1**

The story of Romeo and Juliet revolves around...

**ROMEO**

Romeo Montague who is in love with love.

**NARRATOR 2**

Romeo's kinsman...

**BENVOLIO**

The thoughtful and brave Benvolio.

**NARRATOR 1**

On the other side is the beautiful...

**JULIET**

Juliet Capulet who is only weeks away from her 14th birthday.

**NARRATOR 2**

And Juliet's...

**NURSE**

Old and faithful Nurse.

**NARRATOR 1**

Also Juliet's cousin...

**TYBALT**

The fiery and dangerous Tybalt.

**NARRATOR 2**

The story starts by describing the tense situation in the city of Verona where two families have been fighting one another for generations.

**ALL**

Two households,* both alike in dignity *(* families)*

**LADY CAPULET**

In fair Verona where we lay our scene

**MONTAGUE & CAPULET**

From ancient grudge break to new mutiny* *(* eruptions of violence)*

**PRINCE**

When civil* blood makes civil* hands unclean *(* citizens')*

**MONTAGUE & CAPULET**

From forth the fatal loins of these two foes*

*(* children born to these two enemies are destined to be enemies)*

**ROMEO & JULIET**

A pair of star-crossed* lovers take their life. *(* going against destiny)*

**NARRATOR 1**

The play begins with two Capulets, Sampson and Gregory, seeing some Montagues approaching.

**SAMPSON**

My naked* weapon is out. Quarrel, I will back thee. *(* unsheathed, ready)*

**GREGORY**

I will frown as they pass by, and let them take it as they list*. *(* please)*

**SAMPSON**

Nay as they dare, I will bite my thumb at them, which is a disgrace to them if they bear it (bites thumb).

**ABRAM**

Do you bite your thumb at me, sir?

**SAMPSON**

I do bite my thumb, sir.

**GREGORY**

Do you quarrel sir?

**ABRAM**

Quarrel sir? No, sir.

**SAMPSON**

But if you do, sir, I am for you.* I serve as good a man as you.
*(* I will fight you)*

**ABRAM**

No better?

**GREGORY**

Say 'better.' Here comes one of our kinsmen.

**SAMPSON**

Yes, better sir.

**ABRAM**

You lie.

**NARRATOR 2**

They fight. Benvolio, one of Romeo's kinsmen, arrives. Benvolio draws his sword to stop the quarrel. Benvolio is followed closely by Tybalt, Juliet's cousin.

**BENVOLIO**

Put up your swords. You know not what you do.

**TYBALT**

What, art thou drawn among these heartless hinds?* (* *good-for-nothings*)
Turn thee Benvolio! Look upon thy death.

**BENVOLIO**

I do but keep the peace.

**TYBALT**

What, drawn,* and talk of peace. I hate the word (* *sword out and ready*)
As I hate hell, all Montagues and thee.
Have at thee coward.

**NARRATOR 1**

Benvolio and Tybalt sword fight. The father of Capulets enters.

**CAPULET**

What noise is this. Give me my sword, ho!

**NARRATOR 2**

The father of the Montagues enters.

**MONTAGUE**

Thou villain Capulet! Hold me not, let me go!

**NARRATOR 1**

The Prince of Verona enters and stops the fighting.

**PRINCE**

Rebellious subjects, enemies to peace

Will they not hear? What, ho! You men. You beasts.
Three civil brawls, bred of an airy* word *(* imagined insult)*
By thee old Capulet and Montague
Have thrice disturbed the quiet of our streets.
If ever you disturb our streets again,
Your lives shall pay the forfeit of the peace.
Away, on pain of death, all men depart.

**NARRATOR 2**

Later Benvolio talks to Romeo.

**BENVOLIO**

Good morning, cousin.

**ROMEO**

Is the day so young?

**BENVOLIO**

But new struck nine.

**ROMEO**

Ay me! Sad hours seem long.

**BENVOLIO**

What sadness lengthens Romeo's hours?

**ROMEO**

Not having that which having makes them short.

**BENVOLIO**

Love?

**ROMEO**

Aye, love
She hath forsworn to love, and in that vow
Do I live dead that live to tell it now?* *(* I am dead without love)*

**BENVOLIO**

Be ruled by me; forget to think of her.

**ROMEO**

O teach me how I should forget to think!

**BENVOLIO**

By giving liberty unto thine eyes.* *(* let your eyes see other women)*
Examine other beauties.
At the feast of ancient Capulet
Sups the fair Rosaline whom thou so loves;
With all the admired beauties of Verona.

Go thither, and with untainted eye.* (* *fresh, unbiased*)
Compare her face with some that I shall show
And I will make thee think thy swan a crow.

**ROMEO**

One fairer than my love? The all-seeing sun
Ne'er saw her match since first the world begun.

**NARRATOR 1**

The Capulet household is preparing for the masked ball they will host later that evening. Lady Capulet and the nurse speak to Juliet about marrying Paris.

**LADY CAPULET**

Tell me, daughter Juliet
How stands your disposition* to be married? (* *how do you feel about*)

**JULIET**

It is an honor that I dream not of.

**LADY CAPULET**

Well, think of marriage now. Younger than you,
Here in Verona, ladies of esteem
Are made already mothers. By my count
I was your mother much upon these years* (* *same age as you*)
That you are now a maid. Thus then in brief:
The valiant Paris seeks you for his love.

**NURSE**

A man, young lady! Lady, such a man
as all the world.

**LADY CAPULET**

Verona's summer hath not such a flower.

**NURSE**

He's a flower, in faith – a very flower.

**LADY CAPULET**

What say you? Can you love the gentleman?
This night you shall behold him at our feast.
So shall you share all that he doth possess,
By having* him, making yourself no less. (* *marrying*)

**NURSE**

No less? Nay, bigger! Women grow bigger* by men. (* *become pregnant*)

**LADY CAPULET**

Speak briefly, can you like of Paris's love?

**JULIET**

I'll look to like, if looking liking move.

**NARRATOR 2**

The festivities begin and Capulet greets the guests to his masked ball.

**CAPULET**

Welcome Gentlemen and Ladies!
Come musicians play.
A hall, a hall! Give room! And foot it* girls. *(* dance)*
Quench* the fire, the room is grown too hot. *(* put out)*

**NARRATOR 1**

Capulet sits beside a kinsman and reminisces.

**CAPULET**

For you and I are past our dancing days.
Twas five and twenty years since we were masked.

**NARRATOR 2**

Romeo enters masked. He sees Juliet and immediately falls in love.

**ROMEO**

O, she doth teach the torches to burn bright.
It seems she hangs upon the cheek of night.
As a rich jewel in a disagreeable ear
Beauty too rich for use, for earth too dear!
So shows a snowy dove trooping with crows
As yonder lady over her fellows shows
Did my heart love till now? Forswear it, sight!* *(* I deny that I loved till now)*
For I never saw true beauty till this night.

**NARRATOR 1**

Tybalt hears Romeo and becomes angry.

**TYBALT**

This, by his voice, should be a Montague
Fetch me my rapier.* What, dares the slave *(* sword)*
Come hither, covered with a mask,
To sneer and scorn at our solemnity?* *(* festivities)*
Now, by stock and honor of my kin.
To strike him dead I hold it not a sin.

**NARRATOR 2**

Capulet admonishes Tybalt to leave Romeo alone.

PART THREE: *ROMEO & JULIET*

**CAPULET**

> Let him alone. Verona brags of Romeo
> To be a virtuous and well governed youth.

**NARRATOR 1**

> Romeo approaches Juliet and takes her hand. They fall quickly and deeply in love.

**ROMEO**

> If I profane* with my unworthy hand (* *blemish or disrespect*)
> Thy holy hand, the gentle sin is this
> My lips, two blushing pilgrims, ready stand
> To smooth that rough touch with a tender kiss.

**JULIET**

> Good pilgrim, you do wrong your hand too much
> Which mannerly devotion shows in this;
> For saints have hands the pilgrims' hands do touch
> And palm to palm is holy pilgrims' kiss.*
> (* *your touch is not too rough, to heal it with a kiss is not necessary,*
> *clasping hands is acceptable*)

**ROMEO**

> Have saints not lips? and holy pilgrims too?

**JULIET**

> Ay, pilgrim, lips that they must use in prayer.

**ROMEO**

> O then dear saint, let the lips do what hands do!* (**they kiss*)
> They pray: Grant thou, lest faith turn to despair.

**JULIET**

> Saints do not move, though grant for prayers' sake.*
> (* *even though statues of Saints do not move, the real Saints grant prayers*)

**ROMEO**

> Then move not while my prayer's effect I take.* (* *they kiss*)

**NARRATOR 2**

> Romeo kisses Juliet.

**JULIET**

> Then have my lips the sin that they have took?* (* *now my lips have sin?*)

**ROMEO**

> Sin from my lips? O trespass sweetly urged!
> Give me my sin again.

**NARRATOR 1**

    The nurse interrupts Romeo and Juliet kissing.

**NURSE**

    Madam, your mother craves a word with you.

**ROMEO**

    Who is her mother?

**NURSE**

    Her mother is the lady of the house, Lady Capulet.

**ROMEO**

    Is she a Capulet?
    O dear account! My life is my foe's debt.* *(* I owe my enemy my life)*

**NARRATOR 2**

    Romeo leaves the party quickly. Exit all but Juliet and her Nurse.

**JULIET**

    Come hither Nurse. What is yond gentleman?
    Go ask his name. If he be married
    My grave is like to be my wedding bed.* *(* I will kill myself if he is married)*

**NURSE**

    His name is Romeo, and a Montague
    The only son of your great enemy.

**JULIET**

    My only love sprung from my only hate!
    Too early seen unknown, and known too late!
    Prodigious* birth of love it is to me. *(* extraordinary)*
    That I must love a loathed enemy.

**NARRATOR 1**

    Later, Romeo climbs an orchard wall to return to Capulet's house and
    Juliet.

**ROMEO**

    But soft!* What light through yonder window breaks? *(* wait)*
    It is the East, and Juliet is the sun.
    Arise, fair* sun, and kill the envious moon, *(* beautiful)*
    Who is already sick and pale with grief
    That thou her maid art far more fair than she.
    It is my lady; O, it is my love.
    O that she knew she were!
    See how she leans her cheek upon her hand!
    O that I were a glove upon that hand,

PART THREE: ROMEO & JULIET

SHAKESPEARE FOR READER'S THEATRE: *HAMLET, ROMEO AND JULIET, MIDSUMMER NIGHT'S DREAM*
BY JOHN POULSEN

That I might touch that cheek.

**JULIET**

Ay me!

**ROMEO**

She speaks. Oh speak again bright angel.

**JULIET**

O Romeo, Romeo! Wherefore art thou Romeo?*
(* *Why are you a Montague*)
Deny thy father and refuse thy name;
Or, if thou wilt not, be but sworn my love
And I'll no long be a Capulet.

**ROMEO**

Shall I hear more, or shall I speak at this?

**JULIET**

'Tis but thy name that is my enemy.
Thou art thyself, not a Montague.
What's a Montague? It is nor hand, nor foot,
Nor arm, nor face, nor any other part.
Belonging to a man. O be some other name!
What's in a name? That which we call a rose
By any other name would smell as sweet.
So Romeo would, were he not Romeo called.
Retain that dear perfection which he owes
Without that title. Romeo doff* thy name (* *discard*)
And for thy name, which was no part of thee,
Take all myself.

**ROMEO**

Call me but love, and I'll be new baptized.*(* *take a new name*)
Henceforth I never will be Romeo.

**JULIET**

What man art thou that, thus bescreened* in night (* *concealed*)
So stumblest on my counsel?*(* *snooping on my thoughts*)

**ROMEO**

By a name
I know not how to tell thee who I am
My name, dear saint, is hateful to myself
Because it is an enemy to thee.
Had I it written, I would tear the word.

**JULIET**

Art thou not Romeo and a Montague?

**ROMEO**

Neither fair saint, if either thee dislike.

**JULIET**

How camest thou hither, tell me, and wherefore?
The orchard walls are high and hard to climb.
And the place death, considering who thou art,
If any of my kinsmen find thee here.

**ROMEO**

With loves light wings did I over perch* these walls. (* *fly over*)
For stony limits cannot hold love out.
And what love can do, that dares love attempt*
(*"one will risk anything for love")
Therefore thy kinsmen are no stop to me.

**JULIET**

If they see thee, they will murder thee.

**ROMEO**

Alack, there lies more peril in thine eye* (* *danger in your look*)
Than twenty of their swords. Look but thou sweet
And I am proof against their hate.* (* *invulnerable against their anger*)

**JULIET**

I would not for all the world they saw thee here.

**ROMEO**

I have nights cloak to hide me from their eyes;
And but thou love me, let them find me here.
My life were better ended by their hate
Than death prorogued, wanting of thy love.* (*"*die slowly of a broken heart*")

**JULIET**

Do you love me? O gentle Romeo
If thou dost love pronounce it faithfully.

**ROMEO**

Lady, by yonder blessed moon I swear…

**JULIET**

O, swear not by the moon, the inconsistent moon
That monthly changes in her circled orb
Lest that thy love prove likewise variable.*
(* *Don't make promises by the moon that changes every night or your love might also change*)

PART THREE: *ROMEO & JULIET*

**ROMEO**

What shall I swear by? My dearest…

**JULIET**

I have no joy of this contract tonight.
It is too rash, too unadvised, too sudden.

**ROMEO**

Wilt thou leave me so unsatisfied?

**JULIET**

What satisfaction canst thou have tonight?

**ROMEO**

The exchange of thy love's faithful vow for mine.

**JULIET**

My love is deep; the more I give to thee
The more I have, for both are infinite
I hear some noise within. Dear love adieu.

**NARRATOR 2**

Romeo turns to leave.

**JULIET**

Romeo!

**ROMEO**

My sweet?

**NARRATOR 1**

Juliet hears the nurse call from within the house.

**NURSE**

Juliet!

**JULIET**

I hear some noise within; dear love, adieu!
Anon,* good nurse! Sweet Montague, be true. (* just a moment)
Stay but a little, I will come again.

**ROMEO**

O blessed, blessed night! I am afeard.
Being in night, all this is but a dream.

**JULIET**

Three words, dear Romeo, and good night indeed.
If that thy bent* of love be honourable, (* your intentions)
Thy purpose marriage, send me word to-morrow,

**NURSE**

Madam!

**JULIET**

I come, anon.—But if thou mean'st not well,*
(* *if you don't want to marry me*)
I do beseech thee—

**NURSE**

Madam!

**JULIET**

By and by, I come:—
 To cease thy suit, and leave me to my grief:*
(* *leave me alone and let me suffer*)
Tomorrow will I send.

**ROMEO**

So thrive my soul—

**JULIET**

A thousand times good night!

**ROMEO**

A thousand times the worse, to want* thy light. (* *to be without*)

**JULIET**

Hist! Romeo, hist!* (* *psst*)

**ROMEO**

It is my soul that calls upon my name.

**JULIET**

Romeo!

**ROMEO**

My dear?

**JULIET**

At what o'clock to-morrow
Shall I send to thee?

**ROMEO**

At the hour of nine.

**JULIET**

I will not fail. 'Tis twenty years till then.
I have forgot why I did call thee back.

SHAKESPEARE FOR READER'S THEATRE: *HAMLET, ROMEO AND JULIET, MIDSUMMER NIGHT'S DREAM*
BY JOHN POULSEN

**ROMEO**

Let me stand here till thou remember it.

**JULIET**

I shall forget, to have thee still stand there,
Remembering how I love thy company.

**ROMEO**

And I'll stay, to have thee still forget
Forgetting any other home but this.

**JULIET**

Sweet, so would I
Good night, good night! Parting is such sweet sorrow,
that I shall say good night till it be morrow.* (* morning)

**NARRATOR 2**

Romeo leaves Juliet and asks Friar Laurence to marry him and Juliet
later that day. Friar Laurence agrees.

**FRIAR**

For this alliance may so happy prove
To turn your households' rancor* to pure love. (* mutual hate)

**ROMEO**

O, let us hence! I stand on sudden haste.* (* I need to hurry)

**FRIAR**

Wisely and slow. They stumble that run fast.

**NARRATOR 1**

Romeo meets his friends and they tease him.

**BENVOLIO**

Here comes Romeo, here comes Romeo.

**MERCUTIO**

Signior, Romeo, bon jour! You gave us the counterfeit* (* the slip)
fairly last night.

**ROMEO**

Good morrow to you both. What counterfeit did I give you?

**MERCUTIO**

The slip, sir, the slip; can you not conceive?

**ROMEO**

Pardon, good Mercutio, my business was great; and in
such a case as mine, a man may strain courtesy.

**MERCUTIO**

Thy wits run the wild-goose chase. I have done.
For thou hast more of the wild-goose in one of
thy wits than I have in my whole five.

**NARRATOR 2**

Romeo meets Juliet's nurse and they conspire how the two star-crossed
lovers will be married after 'shrift', that is, after confession

**ROMEO**

Bid her devise
Some means to come to shrift this afternoon*
(* ask Juliet to find a way to go to confession this afternoon)
And there she shall at Friar Laurence's cell
Be shrived* and married. (* forgiven)

**NURSE**

Pray you sir, that you not lead her into a fool's paradise.
Nor double deal* with her. For the gentlewoman is young. (* cheat)

**NARRATOR 1**

Juliet waits anxiously for her Nurse, who is three hours late, to return.

**JULIET**

The clock struck nine when I did send the nurse;
In half an hour she promised to return.
Old folks, many feign* as they were dead (* pretend)
Unwieldy, slow, heavy and pale as lead.

**NARRATOR 2**

The nurse enters tired and worn.

**NURSE**

I am a weary.* (* tired)

**JULIET**

O Lord, why lookest thou so sad?
Through news be sad, yet tell them merrily;
If good, thou shamest the music of sweet news
By playing it to me with so sour a face.*
(* you are ruining the good news with your bad mood)

**NURSE**

Give me leave awhile.
Fie how my bones ache!

**JULIET**

I would thou had my bones and I thy news.

140

**NURSE**

Do you not see that I am out of breath?

**JULIET**

How art thou out of breath when thou hast breath
To say to me that thou art out of breath?
Sweet, sweet, sweet Nurse, tell me, what says my love?

**NURSE**

Your love says like an honest gentleman, and a courteous, and a
kind and a handsome, and I warrant* a virtuous–where is your *(\* agree)*
mother?

**JULIET**

Where is my mother? How oddly thou repliest.
Your love says, like an honest gentleman,
"Where is your mother?"

**NURSE**

Have you leave to go to shrift* to-day? *(\* confession)*

**JULIET**

I have.

**NURSE**

Then hie* you hence to Friar Laurence's cell; *(\* get)*
There stays a husband to make you a wife.
Now comes the wanton* blood up in your cheeks. *(\*aroused, lustful)*
I must fetch a ladder by which your
love must climb a bird's nest* soon when it is dark. *(\* your balcony)*
I am the drudge, and toil* in your delight; *(\* your servant and work for you)*
But you shall bear the burden soon at night
Go: I'll to dinner; hie you to the cell.

**NARRATOR 1**

Romeo arrives at Friar Laurence's room. They wait for Juliet.

**ROMEO**

Do thou but close our hands with holy words.
Then love-devouring death do what he dare –
It is enough I may but call her mine.

**FRIAR**

These violent delights have violent ends.
Therefore love moderately: long love doth so
Too swift arrives as tardy as too slow.

**NARRATOR 2**

Juliet arrives.

**JULIET**

My true love is grown to such an excess
I cannot sum up half my wealth.

**FRIAR**

Come, come with me, and we will make short work;
For by your leaves, you shall not stay alone
Till Holy Church incorporate two in one.*
(* you will not be allowed to be alone until you are married)

**NARRATOR 1**

After the secret wedding Romeo's friends are accosted by Tybalt, Juliet's
cousin.

**BENVOLIO**

I pray thee, good Mercutio, let's retire
The day is hot, the Capulets abroad
And if we meet, we shall not escape a brawl.
For now, these hot days, is the mad blood stirring.*
(* let's leave. We are going to meet some Capulets and there will be a fight)

**MERCUTIO**

Thou wilt quarrel with a man eating nuts, having no other reason
But because thou hast hazel eyes.

**BENVOLIO**

By my head, here come the Capulets.

**MERCUTIO**

By my heel, I care not.

**NARRATOR 2**

Tybalt enters.

**TYBALT**

Mercutio, thou consortest* with Romeo. (* hang out)

**MERCUTIO**

Consortest? What, dost thou make us minstrels?

**BENVOLIO**

Either withdraw unto some private place,
Reason coldly of your grievances* (* speak reasonably about your differences)
Or else depart. Here all eyes gaze on us.

**NARRATOR 1**

Romeo enters.

**TYBALT**

Romeo, thou art a villain, therefore turn and draw.

**ROMEO**

I see thou knowest me not. Farewell.

**TYBALT**

Boy, this shall not excuse the injuries
That thou hast done me: therefore turn and draw.

**ROMEO**

I do protest I never injured thee
But love thee better than thou canst devise.* (* imagine)
Good Capulet, which name I tender
as dearly as my own, be satisfied.

**NARRATOR 2**

Romeo and Tybalt agree to walk away in peace. Mercutio, Romeo's
friend takes offense at Tybalt's insults and challenges Tybalt. They fight.

**MERCUTIO**

Tybalt, you ratcatcher*, will you walk? (* sneaky cat)

**TYBALT**

I am for you.

**ROMEO**

Gentlemen for shame! Forbear this outrage!* (* end this violence)
Tybalt, Mercutio, the Prince hath forbid this.

**NARRATOR 1**

Romeo comes between the two fighters. Tybalt, under Romeo's arm,
stabs Mercutio.

**MERCUTIO**

A plague* on both your houses. (* curse)

**BENVOLIO**

What, art thou hurt?

**ROMEO**

The hurt cannot be much.

**MERCUTIO**

No, tis not so deep as a well, nor so wide as a church door, but 'tis enough. Twill serve. Ask for me tomorrow and you will find me a grave man. Why the devil came you between us? I was hurt under your arm.

**ROMEO**

I thought all for the best.

**MERCUTIO**

A plague on both your houses. They have made worms meat of me.

**NARRATOR 2**

Romeo, seeing his friend die, threatens Tybalt.

**ROMEO**

Mercutio's soul is but a little way above our heads.
Staying for thine to keep him company.
Either thou or I, or both, must go with him.

**TYBALT**

Thou, wretched boy, shalt with him hence.

**NARRATOR 1**

They fight and Tybalt falls. Benvolio urges Romeo to flee.

**BENVOLIO**

Romeo, away, be gone!
The Prince will doom thee death.
If thou art taken. Hence, be gone, away.

**ROMEO**

O, I am fortune's fool!* *(* fate's dupe)*

**BENVOLIO**

Why dost thou stay?

**NARRATOR 2**

Romeo flees to Friar Laurence's cell and bemoans his fate.

**ROMEO**

I am banished. Heaven is here
Where Juliet lives; and every cat and dog
Live here in heaven and may look upon her.
But Romeo may not.

**FRIAR**

Go, get thee to Juliet's love as was decreed
Then be gone before the watch be set,*(* before morning)
Sojourn* in Mantua, till I can call thee back. *(* hide)*

144

**NARRATOR 1**

After their wedding night, Romeo and Juliet bid one another a tearful farewell for Romeo must flee to Mantua.

**JULIET**

Wilt thou be gone?

**ROMEO**

I must be gone and live, or stay and die.

**JULIET**

Then, window, let day in, and let life out.

**ROMEO**

Farewell, farewell! One kiss, and I'll descend.

**JULIET**

O Fortune, fortune! All men call thee fickle.

**NARRATOR 2**

Juliet's mother, Lady Capulet, enters to tell her daughter of the upcoming marriage with Paris in three days.

**LADY CAPULET**

Ho, daughter! Are you up?
Evermore weeping for your cousin's death?
Some grief shows much of love;
But much of grief shows still want of wit.* (* too much weeping is foolish)
Weep thou for the villain lives which slaughtered him.
That same villain Romeo.

**JULIET**

Ay, madam, from the reach of these my hands
Would none but I might revenge my cousin's death.

**LADY CAPULET**

But now I'll tell thee joyful tidings, girl.
Next Thursday morn, Paris
Shall happily make thee a joyful bride.

**JULIET**

He shall not make me a joyful bride.
I wonder at this haste, that I must wed
Ere he that should be husband comes to woo.

**NARRATOR 1**

Juliet's father enters.

SHAKESPEARE FOR READER'S THEATRE: *HAMLET, ROMEO AND JULIET, MIDSUMMER NIGHT'S DREAM*
BY JOHN POULSEN

PART THREE: ROMEO & JULIET

**CAPULET**

Things have fallen out so unluckily
That we have had no time to move our daughter
Juliet you loved your kinsman Tybalt dearly
And so did I. Well we were born to die.
How now, wife? Have your delivered to her our decree?*

*(\* told Juliet our decision)*

**LADY CAPULET**

Ay sir, but she will none

**NARRATOR 2**

Capulet becomes angry at hearing that Juliet will not wed Paris.

**CAPULET**

Hang thee young baggage!* Disobedient wretch. *(\* rogue)*
I tell thee what — get thee to church a Thursday
Or never after look me in the face.

**JULIET**

Good father, I beseech you on my knees.

**CAPULET**

Speak not, reply not, do not answer me!
Wife we scarce thought us blest
That God had lent us but this only child;
But now I see this one is one too much
And that we have a curse in having her.

**LADY CAPULET**

You are too hot.* *(\* angry)*

**CAPULET**

I'll give you to my friend.
And you be not,* hang, beg, starve, die in the streets. *(\* and if you won't)*
For, by my soul, I'll never acknowledge thee.

**NARRATOR 1**

Juliet runs to Friar Laurence's cell where she cries for help.

**JULIET**

Come weep with me – past hope, past cure, past help!

**FRIAR**

Ah, Juliet, I already know thy grief: I hear thou must, on Thursday next
be married to Paris.

**JULIET**

If in thy wisdom thou canst give no help
I long to die if what thou speakest speak not of remedy.

**FRIAR**

Hold, daughter. I do spy a kind of hope.
Wilt thou undertake a thing like death
If, rather than to marry Paris
Thou hast the strength of will to slay thyself…

**JULIET**

Oh bid me leap, rather than marry Paris,
From off the battlements* of any tower. *(* walls)*

**FRIAR**

Then it is likely thou wilt undertake
A thing like death
That cop'st with death himself to escape from it.
And, if thou darest, I'll give thee remedy.

**JULIET**

O bid me hide nightly in a charnel house * *(* grave)*
Overcovered quiet with dead men's rattling bones.* *(* covered with bones)*

**FRIAR**

Hold, then. Go home, be merry, give consent* *(* agree to)*
To marry Paris. Then to-morrow night lie alone
Take thou this vial, being then in bed
And this distilling liquid drink thou off;* *(* drink all of the liquid)*
When presently through all thy veins shall run
A cold and drowsy humour.
In this borrowed likeness of shrunk death* *(* you will appear to be dead)*
Thou shalt continue for two-and-forty hours,
And then awake as from a pleasant sleep.

**JULIET**

Give me, give me! O, tell not me of fear!

**FRIAR**

Romeo and I will watch thy waking.
And that very night shall Romeo bear thee hence to Mantua.

**JULIET**

Love, give me strength. Farewell dear father.

**NARRATOR 2**

Juliet returns home and reports that she is better.

PART THREE: ROMEO & JULIET

**CAPULET**

How now, my headstrong!* Where have you been? *(\* stubborn)*

**JULIET**

Where I have learned me to repent the sin of disobedient opposition
And beg your pardon: pardon, I beseech you!
Henceforward I am ever ruled by you.

**CAPULET**

Send for Paris; go tell him of this:
I'll have this knot knit up to morrow morning.

**JULIET**

I met the youthful lord at Laurence's cell;
And gave him what love I might,
Not over stepping the bounds of modesty.

**NARRATOR 1**

Lady Capulet sees Juliet to bed.

**JULIET**

I pray thee leave me to myself tonight.

**LADY CAPULET**

Need you my help?

**JULIET**

No madam. Please you, let me now be left alone.

**LADY CAPULET**

Good night. Get thee to bed, and rest; for thou has need.

**NARRATOR 2**

Juliet alone in her room takes the poison and falls into a death like sleep.

**JULIET**

Farewell! God knows when we shall meet again.
I have a faint cold fear thrills through my veins.
Come vial.
What if this mixture do not work at all?
Shall I be married then to-morrow morning?
How if, when I am laid into the tomb,
I wake before the time that Romeo
Come to redeem me?
Romeo, I come! This do I drink to thee.

**NARRATOR 1**

In the morning the Nurse comes to waken Juliet.

**NURSE**

Mistress! What mistress! Juliet! Sweetheart! Bride?
What dressed, and in your clothes?
I needs must wake you. Lady. Lady! Lady!

**NARRATOR 2**

Capulet and Lady Capulet enter.

**LADY CAPULET**

What noise is here?

**NURSE**

Oh lamentable day. Look.

**LADY CAPULET**

O me. My child, my only life.
Revive, look up, or I will die with thee.
Help. Help.

**CAPULET**

Bring Juliet forth. Her lord is come.

**NURSE**

She is dead, deceased.

**CAPULET**

Death, that hath taken her hence, make me wail.
Ties up my tongue and will not let me speak.

**NARRATOR 1**

The next day Juliet's parents take her seemingly lifeless body to Capulet's family tomb and lay her on top of their family grave.

**NARRATOR 2**

Later Romeo enters the grave. The letter telling him that Juliet is only feigning death did not arrive.

**NARRATOR 1**

Romeo has only heard that Juliet is dead.

**ROMEO**

Thou detestable maw,* thou womb of death *(* jaws)*
Gorged with the dearest morsel of the earth,
Thus I enforce thy rotten jaws to open,
And in spite I'll cram thee with more food.*
*(* Even though you might not want more bodies I am going to force you to take me)*

**NARRATOR 2**

Paris who has been hiding threatens Romeo and Romeo begs him to leave.

**PARIS**

Stop thy unhallowed toil,* vile Montague. (* *sinful work*)
Obey and go with me: for thou must die.

**ROMEO**

I must indeed: and therefore came I hither.
Good gentle youth, tempt not a desperate man.
Fly thee hence and leave me. Be gone.
Live and hereafter say
A madman's mercy bade thee run away.

**PARIS**

I do defy thee.
And apprehend thee for a felon.

**ROMEO**

Wilt thou provoke me? Then have at thee.

**NARRATOR 1**

They fight and Romeo slays Paris.

**PARIS**

I am slain! If thou be merciful
Open the tomb and lay me with Juliet.

**ROMEO**

In faith I will.

**NARRATOR 2**

Romeo then kneels at Juliet's body.

**ROMEO**

O my love! My wife!
Death, that hath sucked the honey of the breath
Hath had no power yet upon thy beauty.
Here, will I remain
With worms that are thy chambermaids. O here
Will I set up my everlasting rest.

**NARRATOR 1**

Romeo drinks some fast acting poison he brought with him and dies.

**ROMEO**

From this world-wearied flesh. Eyes, look your last!

Arms, take your last embrace! and, lips, O you
The doors of breath, seal with a righteous kiss
A dateless bargain to engrossing* death! *(* all encompassing)*
Come, bitter conduct, come, unsavory* guide! *(* distasteful)*
Here's to my love!
O true apothecary!* *(* pharmacist)*
Thy drugs are quick. Thus with a kiss I die.

**NARRATOR 2**

Friar Lawrence enters and Juliet awakens.

**FRIAR**

Alack. What blood is this which stains
The stony entrance of this sepulcher?* *(* grave)*
Romeo! O, pale!! Who else? What Paris too?
The lady stirs.

**JULIET**

O comfortable friar! Where is my lord?
I do remember well where I should be,
And here I am. Where is my Romeo?

**FRIAR**

I hear some noise. Lady come from that nest
Of death, contagion,* and unnatural sleep. *(* infection)*
Come, come away
Thy husband in thy bosom there lies dead.
And Paris too. Come I'll dispose of thee
Among a sisterhood of holy nuns.
I dare no longer stay.

**JULIET**

Go, get thee hence, for I will not away.

**NARRATOR 1**

The Friar leaves.

**JULIET**

What's here? A cup, closed in my true love's hand?
Poison, I see, hath been his timeless end.
Drunk all, and left no friendly drop
To help me after? I will kiss thy lips.
Haply some poison yet doth hang on them
To make me die with a restorative.* *(* healing medicine)*
Thy lips are warm.
O happy dagger! This is thy sheath; there rust and let me die.

**NARRATOR 2**

Romeo and Juliet lay dead in one another's arms on the tomb. Enter the Prince, Friar Lawrence, Capulet and Montague.

**MONTAGUE**

My wife is dead tonight!
Grief of my son's exile hath stopped her breath.
What further woe conspires against mine age?

**PRINCE**

Look and thou shalt see.
Bring forth the parties of suspicion.

**FRIAR**

Here I stand, both to impeach and purge
Myself condemned and myself excused.*
(* will explain both to justify and to criticize)

**PRINCE**

Say at once what thou dost know in this.

**FRIAR**

Romeo, there dead, was husband to that Juliet.
And she, there dead, Romeo's faithful wife.
I married them; and their stolen marriage day
Was Tybalt's doomsday.* (* day of death)
To remove grief from her, you
Would have married her to Paris.
Then she comes to me with wild looks.
She would kill herself, so I gave her
A sleeping potion.
Miscarried by my fault, let my old life
Be sacrificed.

**PRINCE**

We still have known thee for a holy man.

**CAPULET**

O brother Montague, give me thy hand
This is for my daughter. For no more
Can I demand.

**MONTAGUE**

But I can give thee more;
For I will raise her statue in pure gold

**PRINCE**

A gloomy peace this morning with it brings.

PART THREE: ROMEO & JULIET

Go hence, to have more talk of these sad things.
For never was a story of more woe
Than this of Juliet and her Romeo.

**ALL**

The end.

SHAKESPEARE FOR READER'S THEATRE: *HAMLET, ROMEO AND JULIET, MIDSUMMER NIGHT'S DREAM*
BY JOHN POULSEN

# Chapter 10: *Romeo and Juliet,* 20-Minute Readers' Theatre Version

## CASTING SUGGESTIONS

<u>One reader per part</u>

<u>15 readers</u>
    Reader 1: Romeo
    Reader 2: Benvolio
    Reader 3: Juliet
    Reader 4: Nurse
    Reader 5: Mercutio
    Reader 6 : Tybalt
    Reader 7: Sampson
    Reader 8: Gregory
    Reader 9: Abram
    Reader 10: Capulet
    Reader 11: Friar Laurence
    Reader 12: Prince
    Reader 13: Lady Capulet
    Reader 14: Narrator 1
    Reader 15 : Narrator 2

<u>Using nine readers with some double casting</u>
    Reader 1 : Romeo,
    Reader 2: Benvolio
    Reader 3: Juliet
    Reader 4: Nurse, Abram,
    Reader 5: Narrator 1, Narrator 2
    Reader 6 : Tybalt, Prince
    Reader 7: Sampson, Capulet
    Reader 8: Gregory, Lady Capulet
    Reader 9 : Friar Laurence, Mercutio

<u>Using seven readers with some double/triple casting</u>
Reader 1 : Romeo,
Reader 2: Benvolio, Friar Laurence
Reader 3: Juliet, Abrams
Reader 4: Nurse, Gregory
Reader 5: Narrator 1, Narrator 2
Reader 6 : Tybalt, Prince, Lady Capulet
Reader 7: Sampson, Capulet, Mercutio

SHAKESPEARE FOR READER'S THEATRE: HAMLET, ROMEO AND JULIET, MIDSUMMER NIGHT'S DREAM
BY JOHN POULSEN

## Romeo and Juliet: 20-Minute Readers' Theatre Version

**ALL**

Romeo and Juliet

**BENVOLIO**

By William Shakespeare

**LADY CAPULET**

Adapted by John Poulsen

**NARRATOR 1**

The story of Romeo and Juliet revolves around…

**ROMEO**

Romeo Montague who is in love with love.

**NARRATOR 2**

Romeo's cousin...

**BENVOLIO**

The thoughtful and brave Benvolio.

**NARRATOR 1**

On the other side is the beautiful...

**JULIET**

Juliet Capulet who is only days away from her 14th birthday.

**NARRATOR 2**

And Juliet's...

**NURSE**

Old and faithful Nurse.

**NARRATOR 1**

Also Juliet's cousin...

**TYBALT**

The fiery and dangerous Tybalt.

**NARRATOR 2**

The story starts by describing the tense situation in the city of Verona where two families have been fighting one another for generations.

**ALL**

Two households,* both alike in dignity *(* families)*

**LADY CAPULET**

In fair Verona where we lay our scene

**CAPULET**

From ancient grudge break to new mutiny* (* *eruptions of violence*)

**PRINCE**

Where civil* blood makes civil* hands unclean (* *citizens'*)

**CAPULET**

From forth the fatal loins of these two foes*
(* *children born to these two enemies are destined to be enemies*)

**ROMEO & JULIET**

A pair of star-crossed* lovers take their life. (* *going against destiny*)

**NARRATOR 1**

The play begins with two Capulets, Sampson and Gregory, seeing some Montagues approaching.

**SAMPSON**

My naked* weapon is out. Quarrel, I will back thee. (* *unsheathed, ready*)

**GREGORY**

I will frown as they pass by, and let them take it as they list.* (* *please*)

**SAMPSON**

Nay as they dare, I will bite my thumb at them, which is a disgrace to them if they bear it (bites thumb).

**ABRAM**

Do you bite your thumb at me, sir?

**SAMPSON**

I do bite my thumb, sir.

**GREGORY**

Do you quarrel sir?

**ABRAM**

Quarrel sir? No, sir.

**SAMPSON**

But if you do, sir, I am for you.* I serve as good a man as you.
(* *I will fight you*)

**ABRAM**

No better?

**GREGORY**

Say 'better.' Here comes one of our kinsmen.

**SAMPSON**

Yes, better sir.

**ABRAM**

You lie.

**NARRATOR 2**

They fight, Benvolio, one of Romeo's kinsmen, arrives. Benvolio draws his sword to stop the quarrel. Benvolio is closely followed by Tybalt, Juliet's cousin.

**BENVOLIO**

Put up your swords. You know not what you do

**TYBALT**

What, art thou drawn among these heartless hinds?* (* *good-for-nothings*)
Turn thee Benvolio! Look upon thy death.

**BENVOLIO**

I do but keep the peace.

**TYBALT**

What, drawn,* and talk of peace. I hate the word (* *sword out and ready*)
As I hate hell, all Montagues and thee.
Have at thee coward.

**NARRATOR 1**

Benvolio and Tybalt sword fight. The father of Capulets enters and threatens all the Montagues.

**CAPULET**

What noise is this. Give me my sword, ho!

**NARRATOR 2**

The Prince of Verona enters and stops the fighting.

**PRINCE**

What ho, you men you beasts.
Old Capulet and Montague
If ever you disturb our streets again,
Your lives shall pay the forfeit of the peace.
Away, on pain of death, all men depart.

**NARRATOR 1**

The enemies depart. Later old Capulet, Juliet's father, greets the guests arriving at his masked ball.

**CAPULET**

Welcome Gentlemen and Ladies!
Come musicians play.
A hall, a hall! Give room! And foot it* girls. *(* dance)*
Quench* the fire, the room is grown too hot. *(* put out)*

**NARRATOR 2**

Romeo enters masked. He sees Juliet.

**ROMEO**

O, she doth teach the torches to burn bright.
It seems she hangs upon the cheek of night.
Did my heart love till now? Forswear it, sight!*
*(* I deny that I loved till now)*
For I never saw true beauty till this night.

**NARRATOR 1**

Romeo approaches Juliet and shakes her hand. They fall quickly and
deeply in love.

**ROMEO**

If I profane* with my unworthy hand *(* blemish or disrespect)*
Thy holy hand, the gentle sin is this
My lips, two blushing pilgrims, ready stand
To smooth that rough touch with a tender kiss

**JULIET**

Good pilgrim, you do wrong your hand too much
Which mannerly devotion shows in this;
For saints have hands the pilgrims' hands do touch
And palm to palm is holy pilgrims' kiss.*
*(* your touch is not too rough, to heal it with a kiss is not necessary,
clasping hands is acceptable)*

**ROMEO**

Have saints not lips? and holy pilgrims too?

**JULIET**

Ay, pilgrim, lips that they must use in prayer.

**ROMEO**

O then dear saint, let the lips do what hands do!
They pray: Grant thou, lest faith turn to despair.

**JULIET**

Saints do not move, though grant for prayers' sake.*
*(* even though statues of Saints do not move, the real Saints grant prayers)*

**ROMEO**

Then move not while my prayer's effect I take.* *(* they kiss)*

**NARRATOR 2**

Romeo kisses Juliet.

**JULIET**

Then have my lips the sin that they have took?* *(* now my lips have sin?)*

**ROMEO**

Sin from my lips? O trespass sweetly urged!
Give me my sin again.

**NARRATOR 1**

The nurse interrupts Romeo and Juliet kissing.

**NURSE**

Madam, your mother craves a word with you.

**ROMEO**

Who is her mother?

**NURSE**

Her mother is the lady of the house, Lady Capulet.

**ROMEO**

Is she a Capulet?
O dear account! My life is my foe's debt.* *(* I owe my enemy my life)*

**NARRATOR 1**

Romeo leaves the party quickly. Exit all but Juliet and her Nurse.

**JULIET**

Come hither Nurse. What is yond gentleman?
Go ask his name. If he be married
My grave is like to be my wedding bed.* *(* I will kill myself if he is married)*

**NURSE**

His name is Romeo, and a Montague
The only son of your great enemy.

**JULIET**

My only love sprung from my only hate!
Too early seen unknown, and known too late!
Prodigious* birth of love it is to me. *(* extraordinary)*
That I must love a loathed enemy.

PART THREE: *ROMEO & JULIET*

**NARRATOR 2**

Later, Romeo climbs an orchard wall to return to Capulet's house. He hides under Juliet's balcony.

**ROMEO**

But soft!* What light through yonder window breaks? *(* wait)*
It is the East, and Juliet is the sun.
Arise, fair* sun, and kill the envious moon, *(* beautiful)*
Who is already sick and pale with grief
That thou her maid art far more fair than she.
See how she leans her cheek upon her hand!
O that I were a glove upon that hand,
That I might touch that cheek.

**JULIET**

Ay me!

**ROMEO**

She speaks. Oh speak again bright angel.

**JULIET**

O Romeo, Romeo! Wherefore art thou Romeo?*
*(* Why are you a Montague)*
Deny thy father and refuse thy name;
Or, if thou wilt not, be but sworn my love
And I'll no longer be a Capulet.

**ROMEO**

Shall I hear more, or shall I speak at this?

**JULIET**

Tis but thy name that is my enemy.
Thou art thyself, not a Montague.
What's a Montague? It is nor hand, nor foot,
Nor arm, nor face, nor any other part
Belonging to a man. O be some other name!
What's in a name? That which we call a rose
By any other name would smell as sweet.
So Romeo would, were he not Romeo called.
Retain that dear perfection which he owes
Without that title. Romeo doff* thy name *(* discard)*
And for thy name, which was no part of thee,
Take all myself.

**ROMEO**

Call me but love, and I'll be new baptized;
Henceforth I never will be Romeo.

**JULIET**

What man art thou that, thus bescreened* in night *(* concealed)*
So stumblest on my counsel?* *(* snooping on my thoughts)*

**ROMEO**

By a name
I know not how to tell thee who I am
My name, dear saint, is hateful to myself
Because it is an enemy to thee.
Had I it written, I would tear the word.

**JULIET**

How camest thou hither, tell me, and wherefore?
The orchard walls are high and hard to climb.
And the place death, considering who thou art,
If any of my kinsmen find thee here.

**ROMEO**

With loves light wings did I over perch* these walls. *(* fly over)*
For stony limits cannot hold love out.
And what love can do, that dares love attempt*
*(*one will risk anything for love)*
Therefore thy kinsmen are no stop to me.

**JULIET**

If they see thee, they will murder thee.

**ROMEO**

Alack, there lies more peril in thine eye* *(* danger in your look)*
Than twenty of their swords. Look but thou sweet
And I am proof against their hate.* *(* invulnerable against their anger)*

**JULIET**

My ears have not drunk a hundred words
Of thy tongues uttering, yet I know the sound
Art thou not Romeo, and a Montague?

**ROMEO**

Neither fair maid, if either thee dislike.

**JULIET**

Do you love me? O gentle Romeo
If you dost love, pronounce it faithfully.

**ROMEO**

Lady, by yonder blessed moon, I vow.

**NARRATOR 1**

Romeo turns to leave.

**JULIET**

Romeo!

**ROMEO**

My sweet?

**NARRATOR 2**

Juliet hears the nurse call from within the house.

**NURSE**

Juliet!

**JULIET**

I hear some noise within; dear love, adieu!
Anon,* good nurse! Sweet Montague, be true. *(* just a moment)*
Stay but a little, I will come again.

**ROMEO**

O blessed, blessed night! I am afraid.
 Being in night, all this is but a dream,

**JULIET**

Dear Romeo, good night indeed.
If that thy bent* of love be honourable, *(* your intentions)*
Thy purpose marriage, send me word to-morrow,
Romeo!

**ROMEO**

My dear?

**JULIET**

At what o'clock to-morrow
Shall I send to thee?

**ROMEO**

At the hour of nine.

**JULIET**

I will not fail.
Good night, good night! Parting is such sweet sorrow,
that I shall say good night till it be morrow.* *(* morning)*

**NARRATOR 1**

The next day Romeo meets Juliet's nurse and they conspire how the two
star-crossed lovers will be married after 'shrift', that is, after confession

**ROMEO**

Bid Juliet devise
Some means to come to shrift this afternoon*
(* ask Juliet to find a way to go to confession this afternoon)
And there she shall at Friar Laurence's cell
Be shrived* and married. (* forgiven)

**NURSE**

Pray you sir, that you not lead her into a fool's paradise.
Nor should deal* with her. For the gentlewoman is young. (* cheat)

**NARRATOR 2**

After the secret wedding, Romeo's friends are accosted by Tybalt,
Juliet's cousin.

**BENVOLIO**

I pray thee, good Mercutio, let's retire
The day is hot, the Capulets abroad
And if we meet, we shall not escape a brawl.
For now, these hot days, is the mad blood stirring.*
(* let's leave. We are going to meet some Capulets and there will be a fight)

**NARRATOR 1**

Tybalt enters

**TYBALT**

Mercutio, thou consortest* with Romeo. (* hang out)

**MERCUTIO**

Consortest? What, dost thou make us minstrels?

**BENVOLIO**

Either withdraw unto some private place,
Reason coldly of your grievances* (* speak reasonably about your differences)
Or else depart. Here all eyes gaze on us.

**NARRATOR 2**

Romeo enters.

**TYBALT**

Romeo, thou art a villain, therefore turn and draw.

**ROMEO**

I see thou knowest me not. Farewell.

**TYBALT**

Boy, this shall not excuse the injuries
That thou hast done me: therefore turn and draw.

**ROMEO**

I do protest I never injured thee
But love thee better than thou canst devise* (* *imagine*)
Good Capulet, which name I tender
as dearly as my own, be satisfied.

**NARRATOR 1**

Romeo and Tybalt agree to walk away in peace. Mercutio, Romeo's
friend takes offense at Tybalt's insults and challenges Tybalt.

**MERCUTIO**

Tybalt, you ratcatcher,* will you walk? (* *sneaky cat*)

**TYBALT**

I am for you.

**ROMEO**

Gentlemen for shame! Forbear this outrage!* (* *end this violence*)
Tybalt, Mercutio, the Prince hath forbid this.

**NARRATOR 2**

Romeo comes between the two fighters. Tybalt, under Romeo's arm,
stabs Mercutio.

**MERCUTIO**

A plague* on both your houses. (* *curse*)

**BENVOLIO**

What, art thou hurt?

**ROMEO**

The hurt cannot be much.

**MERCUTIO**

No, tis not so deep as a well, nor so wide as a church door, but 'tis
enough. Twill serve. Ask for me tomorrow and you will find me a grave
man. Why the devil came you between us? I was hurt under your arm.

**ROMEO**

I thought all for the best.

**MERCUTIO**

A plague on both your houses. They have made worms meat of me.

**NARRATOR 1**

Romeo, seeing his friend die, threatens Tybalt.

SHAKESPEARE FOR READER'S THEATRE: HAMLET, ROMEO AND JULIET, MIDSUMMER NIGHT'S DREAM
BY JOHN POULSEN

**ROMEO**

Mercutio's soul is but a little way above our heads.
Staying for thine to keep him company.
Either thou or I, or both, must go with him.

**TYBALT**

Thou, wretched boy, shalt with him hence.

**NARRATOR 2**

They fight and Romeo kills Tybalt. Benvolio urges Romeo to flee.

**BENVOLIO**

Romeo, away, be gone!
The Prince will doom thee death.
If thou art taken. Hence, be gone, away.

**ROMEO**

O, I am fortune's fool!* (* *fate's dupe*)

**BENVOLIO**

Why dost thou stay?

**NARRATOR 1**

Romeo flees to Friar Laurence's cell and bemoans his fate.

**ROMEO**

I am banished. Heaven is here
Where Juliet lives; and every cat and dog
Live here in heaven and may look upon her.
But Romeo may not.

**FRIAR**

Go, get thee to Juliet's love as was decreed
Then be gone before the watch be set,* (* *before morning*)
Sojourn* in Mantua, till I can call thee back. (* *hide*)

**NARRATOR 2**

After their wedding night bid one another a tearful farewell, for Romeo
must flee to Mantua.

**JULIET**

Wilt thou be gone?

**ROMEO**

I must be gone and live, or stay and die.

**JULIET**

Then, window, let day in, and let life out.

**ROMEO**

Farewell, farewell! One kiss, and I'll descend.

**JULIET**

O Fortune, fortune! All men call thee fickle.

**NARRATOR 1**

Romeo leaves and Juliet's mother, Lady Capulet, enters to tell her daughter of the upcoming marriage with Paris in three days.

**LADY CAPULET**

Ho, daughter! Are you up?
Evermore weeping for your cousin's death?
Weep thou for the villain lives which slaughtered him.
That same villain Romeo.

**JULIET**

Ay, madam, from the reach of these my hands
Would none but I might revenge my cousin's death.

**LADY CAPULET**

But now I'll tell thee joyful tidings, girl.
Next Thursday morn, Paris
Shall happily make thee a joyful bride.

**JULIET**

He shall not make me a joyful bride.
I wonder at this haste, that I must wed
Ere he that should be husband comes to woo.

**NARRATOR 2**

Juliet runs to Friar Laurence's cell where she cries for help.

**JULIET**

Come weep with me – past hope, past cure, past help!

**FRIAR**

Ah, Juliet, I already know thy grief: I hear thou must, on Thursday next be married to Paris.

**JULIET**

If in thy wisdom thou canst give no help
I long to die if what thou speakest speak not of remedy.

**FRIAR**

Hold, daughter. I do spy a kind of hope.
Wilt thou undertake a thing like death
If, rather than to marry Paris

Thou hast the strength of will to slay thyself…

**JULIET**

Oh bid me leap, rather than marry Paris
From off the battlements* of any tower. *(* walls)*

**FRIAR**

Then it is likely thou wilt undertake
A thing like death
That cop'st with death himself to escape from it,*
*(* you will have to cope with death to free yourself from death)*
*And, if thou darest, I'll give thee remedy.*

**JULIET**

O bid me hide nightly in a charnel house * *(* grave)*
Overcovered quiet with dead men's rattling bones* *(* covered with bones)*

**FRIAR**

Hold, then. Go home, be merry, give consent* *(* agree)*
To marry Paris. Then to-morrow night lie alone
Take thou this vial, being then in bed
And this distilling liquid drink thou off;* *(* drink all of the liquid)*
When presently through all thy veins shall run
A cold and drowsy humour.
In this borrowed likeness of shrunk death* *(* you will appear to be dead)*
Thou shalt continue for two-and-forty hours,
And then awake as from a pleasant sleep.

**JULIET**

Give me, give me! O, tell not me of fear!

**FRIAR**

Romeo and I will watch thy waking.
And that very night shall Romeo bear thee hence to Mantua.

**JULIET**

Love, give me strength. Farewell dear father.

**NARRATOR 1**

Juliet returns home. Then alone in her room she takes the poison and
falls into a death-like sleep.

**JULIET**

Farewell! God knows when we shall meet again.
I have a faint cold fear thrills through my veins.
Romeo, I come! This do I drink to thee.

PART THREE: ROMEO & JULIET

**NARRATOR 2**

The next day Juliet's parents take her seemingly lifeless body to Capulet's family tomb and lay her on top of their family grave.

**NARRATOR 1**

Later Romeo enters the grave. The letter telling him that Juliet is only feigning death did not arrive.

**NARRATOR 2**

Romeo has only heard that Juliet is dead.

**ROMEO**

Thou detestable maw,* thou womb of death *(*jaws)*
Gorged with the dearest morsel of the earth,
Thus I enforce thy rotten jaws to open,
And in spite I'll cram thee with more food.*
*(* Even though you might not want more bodies I am going to force you to take me)*
O my love! My wife!
Death, that hath sucked the honey of the breath
Hath had no power yet upon thy beauty.
Here, will I remain
With worms that are thy chambermaids. O here
Will I set up my everlasting rest.

**NARRATOR 1**

Romeo drinks some fast acting poison he brought with him and dies.

**ROMEO**

From this world-wearied flesh. Eyes, look your last!
Arms, take your last embrace! and, lips, O you
The doors of breath, seal with a righteous kiss
A dateless bargain to engrossing* death! *(* all encompassing)*
Come, bitter conduct, come, unsavory guide! *(* distasteful)*
Here's to my love!
O true apothecary!* *(* pharmacist)*
Thy drugs are quick. Thus with a kiss I die.

**NARRATOR 2**

Juliet awakens.

**JULIET**

What's here? A cup, closed in my true love's hand?
Poison, I see, hath been his timeless end.
Drunk all, and left no friendly drop
To help me after? I will kiss thy lips.
Haply some poison yet doth hang on them
To make me die with a restorative.* *(* healing medicine)*

Thy lips are warm.
O happy dagger! This is thy sheath; there rust and let me die.

**NARRATOR 1**

Romeo and Juliet lay dead in one another's arms on the tomb. The story ends with the Capulet's and Montague's seeing the errors of their ways and offering mutual friendship.

**PRINCE**

For never was a story of more woe

**ROMEO & JULIET**

Than this of Juliet and her Romeo.

**ALL**

The end.

## Chapter 11: *Romeo and Juliet* Readers' Theatre Director's Script

This *Director's Script* has suggestions for directing an abridged Readers' Theatre production of *Romeo and Juliet*. The suggestions correspond with the *Romeo and Juliet Readers' Theatre: 20-Minute Version* found in this book. The 20-Minute version of *Romeo and Juliet* has a running time of about 20 minutes—from the time the actors start their entrance to when they walk off stage.

### INTRODUCTION

Bold indicates suggested direction. If there is no bold directorial suggestion connected to the line, the actors should briefly freeze while other lines are being said and then interpret their line as they see fit. They should use off stage focus, by delivering the line straight ahead.

Text after the character's name without bold or italics are the words to be spoken. Print a copy of the script *(Romeo and Juliet Readers' Theatre: 20-Minute Version)* for each reader. The first rehearsal should be a read-through where actors read their assigned parts. After the read-through, performers should highlight or underline their lines. If an actor has more than one character, lines for each should be highlighted in different colours. Have readers write in pencil directorial notes (such as when to stand, sit, and move forward), as well as clarification of line meaning or line intention.

Italics in smaller font indicate meaning. Sometimes a specific word is defined, other times the phrase is clarified. The asterisk follows the word or phrase. Left justified on the next line is the clarification.

The casting suggestions below require as few as seven and as many as 15 actors. If you have 15 performers, there are parts for all. Using triple casting, as few as seven performers can be accommodated.

### DIRECTORIAL PARAMETERS

Actors use off-stage focus for this presentation. They assume that all action takes place toward the audience. If they are speaking to someone, they pretend the person is standing in front of them.

The performing area is pre-set. Before the audience arrives the performers' chairs and stools are arranged in a gentle semi-circle with the centre of the semi-circle farthest from the audience and the ends closest to the audience. Put about one meter between each seat. The actors enter and sit on chairs set sideways with the chair backs towards stage left. Narrators sit at the ends of the line, farthest stage right and left, on stools that place them closer to the audience and slightly higher than the performers sitting on chairs. If double casting, the minimal costume pieces needed to clarify a character change are pre-arranged under the appropriate chairs.

If the audience is sitting on the floor, stretch a rope or lay some tape to indicate where the audience is to sit. If using chairs, all audience seats will be set out.

The actors' seating is pre-arranged with the primary consideration having Romeo and Juliet sitting at the centre. Lady Capulet and Capulet sit next to Juliet. Benvolio and Mercutio sit next to Romeo.

Narrators do not use Back to Audience (BTA) for exits or Front to Audience (FTA) for entrances. They usually use the Freeze convention, so that when they finish saying a line they stop moving until their next line. The direction to freeze means movement is kept to a minimum. Should actors need to check their scripts, they should do so with minimal disruption.

As much as possible the actors should say their lines directly to the audience. Reading is acceptable, but speaking directly forward using offstage focus can improve the production by making actors easier to see and hear.

Front to Audience (FTA) direction requires that actors spin to face the audience before saying their line. Generally actors should be spinning and breathing in as the previous speaker is saying the last words of their line. For example, Abrams is the first to spin FTA He should spin as the Sampson is saying "… if they…". He should also be taking in air so he can start his line loudly and slowly as Sampson finishes saying "…bear it."

Drop Head (DH) and Raise Head (RH) direction is used when the performer will be needed shortly. The actors drop their heads at the end of their line and bring their heads up as the final words in the previous line are being said. The raising of the head should be accompanied with an intake of breath so the next line can be said immediately and loudly. For example, the Nurse is the first to use this convention. She would breathe in and raise her head as the Narrator says, "And Juliet's." The Nurse then says "Old and faithful Nurse," deliberately allowing the audience to focus on her.

## CASTING SUGGESTIONS

Casting can be fluid up until performance. At performance, should you have fewer actors than originally cast, consider using some or all of the following double casting suggestions. It is important that actors taking on extra parts highlight their new lines in a different and distinctive manner.

<u>One reader per part</u>

<u>15 readers</u>
    Reader 1 : Romeo
    Reader 2: Benvolio
    Reader 3: Juliet
    Reader 4: Nurse
    Reader 5: Mercutio
    Reader 6 : Tybalt
    Reader 7: Sampson
    Reader 8: Gregory
    Reader 9: Abram
    Reader 10: Capulet
    Reader 11: Friar Laurence
    Reader 12: Prince
    Reader 13: Lady Capulet
    Reader 14: Narrator 1
    Reader 15 : Narrator 2

<u>Using nine readers with some double casting</u>
    Reader 1 : Romeo,
    Reader 2: Benvolio
    Reader 3: Juliet
    Reader 4: Nurse, Abram,
    Reader 5: Narrator 1, Narrator 2
    Reader 6 : Tybalt, Prince
    Reader 7: Sampson, Capulet
    Reader 8: Gregory, Lady Capulet
    Reader 9 : Friar Laurence, Mercutio

Using seven readers with some double/triple casting
Reader 1: Romeo,
Reader 2: Benvolio, Friar Laurence
Reader 3: Juliet, Abrams
Reader 4: Nurse, Gregory
Reader 5: Narrator 1, Narrator 2
Reader 6 : Tybalt, Prince, Lady Capulet
Reader 7: Sampson, Capulet, Mercutio

## ENTRANCE

Half the cast, led by Juliet, enter stage right and the other half, led by Romeo, enter stage left. Romeo and Juliet start the entrance. They make eye contact, give a small signal and then take three small steps on stage, lock eyes and stop. They soften, give a small sigh and move slowly to their seats. Others swarm on, step past the lovers, and lock eyes with an opposite enemy in angry manner and mutter under their breath one of these insults: rascally knave *(wicked cheat)* or coxcomb *(conceited)*.

Abram and Gregory lock eyes. Gregory mutters, "thin faced gull." Abrams, hearing the insult, says, "thin faced gull?" and returns, "vain bibble babble." Gregory hears the insult and mutters, "vain bibble babble?" Both move to their seats locking eyes on the other as much as possible.

All actors stand facing upstage in front of their seats. As soon as Gregory and Abrams arrive Lady Capulet gives a signal and all sit facing the audience. At another signal by Lady Capulet, all in unison say the title.

**Bold = suggested direction**
Regular = text to be spoken by the actor.
*Italics = \*definition or clarification of line meaning.*

## *ROMEO AND JULIET* READER'S THEATRE DIRECTOR'S SCRIPT

**ALL**

Romeo and Juliet
**(All but Narrators, Benvolio, Romeo, and Lady Capulet, DH and freeze. Narrators use the freeze form of entrance and exit.)**

**BENVOLIO**

By William Shakespeare
**(Freeze)**

**LADY CAPULET**

Adapted by John Poulsen
**(DH)**

**NARRATOR 1**

The story of Romeo and Juliet revolves around…
**(Freeze. Narrators freeze after each line unless instructed otherwise.)**

**ROMEO**

Romeo Montague who is in love with love.

**NARRATOR 2**

Romeo's cousin…

**BENVOLIO**

The thoughtful and loyal Benvolio.
**(DH)**

**NARRATOR 1**

On the other side is the beautiful…

**JULIET**

**(RH)**
Juliet Capulet who is only days away from her 14ᵗʰ birthday.
**(DH)**

**NARRATOR 2**

And Juliet's…

**NURSE**

**(RH)**
Old and faithful Nurse.
**(DH)**

**NARRATOR 1**

Also Juliet's cousin...

**TYBALT**

**(RH)**
The fiery and dangerous Tybalt.
**(Freeze)**

**NARRATOR 2**

The story starts with a chorus describing the tense situation in the city of Verona where the two families have been fighting one another for generations.

**ALL**

**(RH—Following the lead of Lady Capulet all say in unison…)**
Two households,* both alike in dignity *(\* families)*
**(Romeo, Juliet, Prince, Lady Capulet and Capulet—Freeze. Sampson & Gregory—DH All others turn to face upstage and then sit still – BTA)**

**LADY CAPULET**

In fair Verona where we lay our scene
**(BTA)**

**CAPULET**

From ancient grudge break to new mutiny* *(\* eruptions of violence)*

**PRINCE**

Where civil* blood makes civil* hands unclean *(\* citizens')*
**(BTA)**

**CAPULET**

From forth the fatal loins of these two foes*
*(\* children born to these two enemies are destined to be enemies)*
**(BTA)**

**ROMEO & JULIET**

A pair of star-crossed* lovers take their life. *(\* going against destiny)*
**(BTA)**

**NARRATOR 1**

The play begins with two Capulets, Sampson and Gregory, seeing some Montagues approaching.

**SAMPSON**

**(RH)**

My naked* weapon is out. Quarrel I will back thee. *(* unsheathed, ready)*
**(Roll script into a sword and show it.)**

**GREGORY**

**(RH)**
I will frown as they pass by, and let them take it as they list.* *(* please)*
**(Frown using off stage focus.)**

**SAMPSON**

Nay as they dare, I will bite my thumb at them, which is a disgrace to them if they bear it.
**(Bite thumb in an insulting manner, directing action straight ahead.)**

**ABRAM**

**(FTA — deliver the first words clearly)**
Do you bite your thumb at me, sir?

**SAMPSON**

I do bite my thumb, sir.
**(Bite thumb in an insulting manner)**

**GREGORY**

Do you quarrel sir?

**ABRAM**

Quarrel sir? No, sir.

**SAMPSON**

But if you do, sir, I am for you.* I serve as good a man as you.
*(* I will fight you)*

**ABRAM**

No better?
**(Stand)**

**GREGORY**

Say 'better.' Here comes one of our kinsmen.
**(Stand)**

**SAMPSON**

Yes, better sir.
**(Stand)**

**ABRAM**

You lie.
**(Rolls script into a sword and slashes in a large figure eight, left then right. Gregory, using offstage focus, defends against the first slash and Sampson defends against the second. Repeat**

the figure eight and defense. Use peripheral vision to make movements match. Freeze in the middle of action.)

**NARRATOR 2**

They fight. Benvolio one of Romeo's kinsmen arrives. Benvolio draws his sword to stop the quarrel. Benvolio is closely followed by Tybalt, Juliet's cousin.

**BENVOLIO**

(FTA Rolls the script into a sword, stands
and urcs the sword forward and up. Abram's, Sampson's, and Gregory's swords flick up. Freeze.)
Put up your swords. You know not what you do.

**TYBALT**

(FTA Rolls script into a sword stands and stabs forward.)
What, art thou drawn among these heartless hinds?* (* good-for-nothings)
Turn thee Benvolio! Look upon thy death.

**BENVOLIO**

I do but keep the peace.
(Backing up as though the point of Tybalt's sword is at his throat.)

**TYBALT**

What, drawn,* and talk of peace. I hate the word (* sword out and ready)
As I hate hell, all Montagues and thee.
Have at thee coward.
(Tybalt thrusts forward. Benvolio moves head to one side and parries upward and sideways with his sword. Benvolio's brings his sword parallel to the floor in front and above his head. Tybalt strikes down and their swords clash in mime. Struggle as Tybalt forces his sword down and Benvolio's sword is forced closer to himself. This is all done using offstage focus so the movements must be coordinated using peripheral vision. Sampson, Abrams, and Gregory engage in the previous figure eight choreography. All freeze when the narrator speaks.)

**NARRATOR 1**

Benvolio and Tybalt sword fight. The father of Capulets enters and threatens all the Montagues.

**CAPULET**

(FTA Waveing his rolled script, he stands slowly.)
What noise is this? Give me my sword, ho!
(On "ho!" the fights start. Benvolio knocks Tybalt's sword away and thrusts forward making Tybalt back up. Sampson, Abrams,

**and Gregory engage in the figure eight choreography. All freeze when the Narrator speaks.)**

**NARRATOR 2**

The Prince of Verona enters and stops the fighting.

**PRINCE**

**(FTA)**
What ho, you men you beasts.
Old Capulet and Montague
If ever you disturb our streets again,
Your lives shall pay the forfeit of the peace.
Away, on pain of death, all men depart.
**(All sit. All but Capulet BTA)**

**NARRATOR 1**

The enemies depart. Later that evening old Capulet, Juliet's father, greets the guests arriving at his masked ball.

**CAPULET**

Welcome Gentlemen and Ladies!
Come musicians play.
A hall, a hall! Give room! And foot it* girls. *(* dance)*
Quench* the fire, the room is grown too hot. *(* put out)*
**(BTA)**

**NARRATOR 2**

Romeo enters masked. He sees Juliet.

**ROMEO**

**(FTA)**
O, she doth teach the torches to burn bright.
It seems she hangs upon the cheek of night.
Did my heart love till now? Forswear it, sight!*
*(* I deny that I loved till now)*
For I never saw true beauty till this night.

**NARRATOR 1**

**(Romeo reaches his right hand for Juliet's hand. Juliet spins FTA and reaches her right hand forward as though taking Romeo's hand. They freeze looking forward as though their eyes are locked in love.)**
Romeo approaches Juliet and shakes her hand. They fall quickly and deeply in love.

**ROMEO**

If I profane* with my unworthy hand *(* blemish or disrespect)*

PART THREE: ROMEO & JULIET

Thy holy hand, the gentle sin is this
**(Stands slowly while saying the following lines. Juliet's hand must react to the change in level.)**
My lips, two blushing pilgrims, ready stand
To smooth that rough touch with a tender kiss* *(\* they kiss)*

**JULIET**

Good pilgrim, you do wrong your hand too much
**(Standing. Romeo's hand must react to the difference in level.)**
Which mannerly devotion shows in this;
For saints have hands the pilgrims' hands do touch
**(The right hands must pivot so that the palms face the audience, fingers pointing up.)**
And palm to palm is holy pilgrims' kiss.*
*(\* your touch is not too rough, to heal it with a kiss is not*

*necessary, clasping hands is acceptable)*

**ROMEO**

**(Steps forward bringing hand closer to self, keeping palm forward.)**
Have saints not lips? and holy pilgrims too?

**JULIET**

**(Steps forward bringing hand closer to self, palm forward.)**
Ay, pilgrim, lips that they must use in prayer.

**ROMEO**

O then dear saint, let the lips do what hands do!
**(Romeo and Juliet reach faces forward and mime kiss.)**
They pray: Grant thou, lest faith turn to despair.

**JULIET**

Saints do not move, though grant for prayers' sake.*

*(\* even though statues of Saints do not move, the real Saints grant prayers)*

**ROMEO**

Then move not while my prayer's effect I take. *(\* they kiss)*
**(Romeo and Juliet reach faces forward and mime kiss. Longer this time.)**

**NARRATOR 2**

Romeo kisses Juliet.

**JULIET**

**(Both retreat slightly.)**
Then have my lips the sin that they have took?* *(\* now my lips have sin?)*

PART THREE: *ROMEO & JULIET*

**ROMEO**

Sin from my lips? O trespass sweetly urged!
Give me my sin again.
**(Romeo and Juliet arc faces forward and mime kiss. Freeze.)**

**NARRATOR 2**

The nurse interrupts Romeo and Juliet kissing.

**NURSE**

**(Break freeze. Romeo and Juliet sit. At the same time Nurse FTA)**
Madam, your mother craves a word with you.

**ROMEO**

Who is her mother?

**NURSE**

Her mother is the lady of the house, Lady Capulet.
**(Freeze)**

**ROMEO**

Is she a Capulet?
O dear account! My life is my foe's debt.* (* I owe my enemy my life)
**(DH)**

**NARRATOR 1**

Romeo leaves the party quickly. Exit all but Juliet and her Nurse.

**JULIET**

Come hither Nurse. What is yond gentleman?
Go ask his name. If he be married
My grave is like to be my wedding bed.* (* I will kill myself if he is married)

**NURSE**

His name is Romeo, and a Montague
The only son of your great enemy.
**(BTA)**

**JULIET**

My only love sprung from my only hate!
Too early seen unknown, and known too late!
Prodigious* birth of love it is to me. (* extraordinary)
That I must love a loathed enemy.
**(Freeze)**

**NARRATOR 2**

Later, Romeo climbs an orchard wall to return to Capulet's house. He hides under Juliet's balcony.

**ROMEO**

**(RH)**
But soft!* What light through yonder window breaks? (* *wait*)
It is the East, and Juliet is the sun.
Arise, fair* sun, and kill the envious moon, (* *beautiful*)
Who is already sick and pale with grief
That thou her maid art far more fair than she.
See how she leans her cheek upon her hand!
O that I were a glove upon that hand,
That I might touch that cheek.

**JULIET**

Ay me!

**ROMEO**

**(Kneels on one knee)**
She speaks. Oh speak again bright angel.

**JULIET**

**(Stands)**
O Romeo, Romeo! Wherefore art thou Romeo?*
(* *Why are you a Montague?*)
Deny thy father and refuse thy name;
Or, if thou wilt not, be but sworn my love
And I'll no longer be a Capulet.

**ROMEO**

**(Sits)**
Shall I hear more, or shall I speak at this?

**JULIET**

'Tis but thy name that is my enemy.
Thou art thyself, not a Montague.
What's a Montague? It is nor hand, nor foot,
Nor arm, nor face, nor any other part
Belonging to a man. O be some other name!
What's in a name? That which we call a rose
By any other name would smell as sweet.
So Romeo would, were he not Romeo called.
Retain that dear perfection which he owes
Without that title. Romeo doff* thy name (* *discard*)
And for thy name, which was no part of thee,
Take all myself.

**ROMEO**

**(Stands slowly)**
Call me but love, and I'll be new baptized;

Henceforth I never will be Romeo.

**JULIET**

What man art thou that, thus bescreened* in night *(* concealed)*
So stumblest on my counsel?* *(* snooping on my thoughts)*

**ROMEO**

By a name
I know not how to tell thee who I am
My name, dear saint, is hateful to myself
Because it is an enemy to thee.
Had I it written, I would tear the word.

**JULIET**

**(Using off stage focus, stands on chair looking down at Romeo.
Romeo looks up at Juliet.)**
How camest thou hither, tell me, and wherefore?
The orchard walls are high and hard to climb.
And the place death, considering who thou art,
If any of my kinsmen find thee here.

**ROMEO**

With loves light wings did I over perch* these walls. *(* fly over)*
For stony limits cannot hold love out.
And what love can do, that dares love attempt* *(*one will risk anything for love)*
Therefore thy kinsmen are no stop to me.

**JULIET**

If they see thee, they will murder thee.

**ROMEO**

Alack, there lies more peril in thine eye* *(* danger in your look)*
Than twenty of their swords. Look but thou sweet
And I am proof against their hate.* *(* invulnerable against their anger)*

**JULIET**

My ears have not drunk a hundred words
Of thy tongues uttering, yet I know the sound
Art thou not Romeo, and a Montague?

**ROMEO**

Neither fair maid, if either thee dislike.

**JULIET**

Do you love me? O gentle Romeo
If you dost love, pronounce it faithfully.

**ROMEO**

Lady by yonder blessed moon, I vow.

**NARRATOR 1**

Romeo turns to leave.

**JULIET**

Romeo!

**ROMEO**

My dear?

**NARRATOR 2**

Juliet hears the nurse call from within the house.

**NURSE**

**(FTA)**
Juliet!
**(DH)**

**JULIET**

I hear some noise within; dear love, adieu!
Anon, good nurse! Sweet Montague, be true.
Stay but a little, I will come again.

**ROMEO**

O blessed, blessed night! I am afraid.
Being in night, all this is but a dream,

**JULIET**

Dear Romeo, good night indeed.
If that thy bent* of love be honourable, *(* your intentions)*
Thy purpose marriage, send me word to-morrow,
Romeo!

**ROMEO**

My dear?

**JULIET**

At what o'clock to-morrow
Shall I send to thee?

**ROMEO**

At the hour of nine.
**(Sits and freeze)**

**JULIET**

**(Stepping down from the chair.)**
I will not fail.

Good night, good night! Parting is such sweet sorrow,
**(Sitting down)**
that I shall say good night till it be morrow.* *(* morning)*
**(BTA)**

### NARRATOR 1

The next day Romeo meets Juliet's nurse and they conspire how the two star-crossed lovers will be married after 'shrift', that is, after confession.
**(Nurse RH)**

### ROMEO

Bid Juliet devise
 Some means to come to shrift this afternoon*
*(* ask Juliet to find a way to go to confession this afternoon)*
And there she shall at Friar Laurence's cell
Be shrived* and married. *(* forgiven)*
**(Freeze)**

### NURSE

Pray you sir, that you not lead her into a fool's paradise.
Nor double deal* with her. For the gentlewoman is young. *(* cheat)*
**(BTA, Romeo DH)**

### NARRATOR 2

After Romeo and Juliet's secret wedding, Romeo's friends are confronted by Tybalt, Juliet's cousin.

### BENVOLIO

**(FTA)**
I pray thee, good Mercutio, let's retire
**(Mercutio FTA)**
The day is hot, the Capulets abroad
And if we meet, we shall not escape a brawl.
For now, these hot days, is the mad blood stirring.*

*(* let's leave. We are going to meet some Capulets and there will be a fight)*

### NARRATOR 1

Tybalt enters.

### TYBALT

**(FTA)**
Mercutio, thou consortest* with Romeo. *(* hang out)*

### MERCUTIO

Consortest? What, dost thou make us minstrels?

### BENVOLIO

Either withdraw unto some private place,

Reason coldly of your grievances* *(* speak reasonably about your differences)*
Or else depart. Here all eyes gaze on us.

**NARRATOR 2**

Romeo enters.
**(Romeo RH)**

**TYBALT**

Romeo, thou art a villain, therefore turn and draw.
**(Slowly stands, rolling script into sword.)**

**ROMEO**

I see thou knowest me not. Farewell.

**TYBALT**

Boy, this shall not excuse the injuries
That thou hast done me: therefore turn and draw.
**(Freeze)**

**ROMEO**

I do protest I never injured thee
But love thee better than thou canst devise* *(* imagine)*
Good Capulet, which name I tender
as dearly as my own, be satisfied.

**NARRATOR 1**

Romeo and Tybalt agree to walk away in peace. Mercutio, Romeo's friend takes offense at Tybalt's insults and challenges Tybalt.

**MERCUTIO**

**(Stands rolling script rolled into a sword. Points sword forward.)**
Tybalt, you ratcatcher,* will you walk? *(* sneaky cat)*

**TYBALT**

I am for you.
**(Tybalt attacks in a swooping arc from high to low intending to cut Mercutio's left leg. Mercutio protects by holding his sword perpendicular to the floor, point down, and sweeping Tybalt's sword away from his left leg. Mercutio's sword stays pointed to the ground and sweeps to protect his right leg. Tybalt attacks with the swooping arc from high to low intending to cut Mercutio's right leg. Tybalt raises his sword to cut straight down and Mercutio raises his sword to protect his head. Freeze.)**

**ROMEO**

**(Stands. Romeo extends his arm.)**
Gentlemen for shame! Forbear this outrage!* *(* end this violence)*

Tybalt, Mercutio, the Prince hath forbid this.
**(Tyblat moves slowly while the Narrator 2 speaks. Tybalt rocks back on his heel bringing his sword hilt to his belly, but point to the audience. He lunges forward stabbing straight ahead and freezes.)**

NARRATOR 2

Romeo comes between the two fighters. Tybalt, under Romeo's arm, stabs Mercutio.
**(Romeo drops arm.)**

MERCUTIO

**(Slowly comes out of his freeze and touches where he was stabbed near his heart.)**
A plague* on both your houses. *(* curse)*

BENVOLIO

What, art thou hurt?

ROMEO

The hurt cannot be much.

MERCUTIO

**(Mercutio slowly sinks to his knees during the following.)**
No, tis not so deep as a well, nor so wide as a church door, but 'tis enough. Twill serve. Ask for me tomorrow and you will find me a grave man. Why the devil came you between us? I was hurt under your arm.

ROMEO

I thought all for the best.

MERCUTIO

**(Sits)**
A plague on both your houses. They have made worms meat of me.
**(BTA)**

NARRATOR 1

Romeo, seeing his friend die, threatens Tybalt.

ROMEO

**(Rolling his script into a sword.)**
Mercutio's soul is but a little way above our heads.
Staying for thine to keep him company.
Either thou or I, or both, must go with him.

TYBALT

**(Tybalt and Romeo extend their swords front, ready to fight.)**
Thou, wretched boy, shalt with him hence.

SHAKESPEARE FOR READER'S THEATRE: HAMLET, ROMEO AND JULIET, MIDSUMMER NIGHT'S DREAM
BY JOHN POULSEN

**NARRATOR 2**

They fight
**(This fight begins the same way as the last. Tybalt attacks with the swooping arc from high to low intending to cut Romeo's right leg. Tybalt raises his sword to cut straight down. Romeo thrusts quickly forward and freezes. Tybalt contracts as though stabbed and backs up to sitting. BTA)** and Romeo kills Tybalt. Benvolio urges Romeo to flee.

**BENVOLIO**

**(Steps forward)**
Romeo, away, be gone!
The Prince will doom thee death.
If thou art taken. Hence, be gone, away.

**ROMEO**

O, I am fortune's fool!* *(* fate's dupe)*
**(Sit and freeze)**

**BENVOLIO**

Why dost thou stay?
**(Sit and BTA)**

**NARRATOR 1**

Romeo flees to Friar Laurence's cell and bemoans his fate.

**ROMEO**

I am banished. Heaven is here
Where Juliet lives; and every cat and dog
Live here in heaven and may look upon her.
But Romeo may not.

**FRIAR**

**(FTA)**
Go, get thee to Juliet's love as was decreed
Then be gone before the watch be set,* *(* before morning)*
Sojourn* in Mantua, till I can call thee back. *(* hide)*
**(DH)**

**NARRATOR 2**

After their wedding night Romeo and Juliet bid one another a tearful farewell for Romeo must flee to Mantua.

**JULIET**

**(FTA)**
Wilt thou be gone?

**ROMEO**

(Lean forward)
I must be gone and live, or stay and die.

**JULIET**

(Lean forward)
Then, window, let day in, and let life out.

**ROMEO**

Farewell, farewell! One kiss, and I'll descend.
**(Romeo and Juliet close eyes and kiss at the same time. Romeo opens his eyes and BTA)**

**JULIET**

(Opens eyes)
O Fortune, fortune! All men call thee fickle.
**(Freeze)**

**NARRATOR 1**

Romeo leaves and Juliet's mother, Lady Capulet, enters to tell her daughter of the upcoming marriage with Paris in three days.

**LADY CAPULET**

(FTA)
Ho, daughter! Are you up?
Evermore weeping for your cousin's death?
Weep thou for the villain lives which slaughtered him.
That same villain Romeo.

**JULIET**

Ay, madam, from the reach of these my hands
Would none but I might revenge my cousin's death.

**LADY CAPULET**

But now I'll tell thee joyful tidings, girl.
Next Thursday morn, Paris
Shall happily make thee a joyful bride.
**(Freeze)**

**JULIET**

He shall not make me a joyful bride.
I wonder at this haste, that I must wed
Ere he that should be husband comes to woo.
**(Lady Capulet BTA)**

**NARRATOR 2**

Juliet runs to Friar Laurence's cell where she cries for help.

**JULIET**

Come weep with me – past hope, past cure, past help!

**FRIAR**

**(FTA)**
Ah, Juliet, I already know thy grief: I hear thou must, on Thursday next
be married to Paris.

**JULIET**

If in thy wisdom thou canst give no help
I long to die if what thou speakest speak not of remedy.

**FRIAR**

Hold, daughter. I do spy a kind of hope.
Wilt thou undertake a thing like death
If, rather than to marry Paris
Thou hast the strength of will to slay thyself…

**JULIET**

Oh bid me leap, rather than marry Paris
From off the battlements* of any tower. (* walls)

**FRIAR**

Then it is likely thou wilt undertake
A thing like death
That cop'st with death himself to escape from it.
And, if thou darest, I'll give thee remedy.

**JULIET**

O bid me hide nightly in a charnel house * (* grave)
Overcovered quiet with dead men's rattling bones* (* covered with bones)

**FRIAR**

Hold, then. Go home, be merry, give consent* (* agree)
To marry Paris. Then to-morrow night lie alone
Take thou this vial, being then in bed
**(While saying the next lines, roll script into tube. Hold script
half way making the it look shorter, as though it is a tube. Mime
taking a cork off the top of the tube and replacing it.)**
And this distilling liquid drink thou off;* (* drink all of the liquid)
When presently through all thy veins shall run
A cold and drowsy humour.
In this borrowed likeness of shrunk death* (* you will appear to be dead)
Thou shalt continue for two-and-forty hours,
And then awake as from a pleasant sleep.

PART THREE: ROMEO & JULIET

**JULIET**

(**Reaching forward as though for the tube.**)
Give me, give me! O, tell not me of fear!

**FRIAR**

Romeo and I will watch thy waking.
And that very night shall Romeo bear thee hence to Mantua.
(**BTA**)

**JULIET**

Love, give me strength. Farewell dear father.

**NARRATOR 1**

Juliet returns home. Then alone in her room she takes the poison and
falls into a death like sleep.

**JULIET**

(**While saying the next lines, Juliet uses the same motions as
Friar Laurence previously. She rolls the script into a tube, holds
the script half way making the script look shorter, as though it is
a tube. Mimes taking a cork off the top of the tube, then drinks.**)
Farewell! God knows when we shall meet again.
I have a faint cold fear thrills through my veins.
Romeo, I come! This do I drink to thee.
(**DH**)

**NARRATOR 2**

The next day Juliet's parents take her seemingly lifeless body to Capulet's
family tomb and lay her on top of their family grave.

**NARRATOR 1**

Later Romeo enters the grave. The letter telling him that Juliet is only
feigning death did not arrive.

**NARRATOR 2**

Romeo has only heard that Juliet is dead.

**ROMEO**

(**FTA**)
Thou detestable maw,* thou womb of death (*jaws)
Gorged with the dearest morsel of the earth,
Thus I enforce thy rotten jaws to open,
And in spite I'll cram thee with more food.*
(* Even though you might not want more bodies I am going to force you to take me)
(**Stands slowly**)
O my love! My wife!
Death, that hath sucked the honey of the breath

Hath had no power yet upon thy beauty.
Here, will I remain
With worms that are thy chambermaids. O here
Will I set up my everlasting rest.

**NARRATOR 1**

Romeo drinks some fast acting poison he brought with him and dies.

**ROMEO**

From this world-wearied flesh. Eyes, look your last!
Arms, take your last embrace! and, lips, O you
**(Close eyes briefly)**
The doors of breath, seal with a righteous kiss
**(While saying the next lines, Romeo uses the same motions as Friar Laurence and Juliet. He rolls the script into a tube, holds the script half way making the script look shorter, as though it is a tube. Mimes taking a cork from the top of the tube and drinks.)**
A dateless bargain to engrossing* death! (* *all encompassing*)
Come, bitter conduct, come, unsavory guide! (* *distasteful*)
Here's to my love!
O true apothecary! (**pharmacist*)
Thy drugs are quick. Thus with a kiss I die.
**(Romeo closes his eyes briefly. Opens them and slowly falls to the floor.)**

**NARRATOR 2**

Juliet awakens.

**JULIET**

**(RH and stands. Makes the following motions while says the lines. She rolls the script into a tube, holds the script half way making the script look shorter, as though it is a tube. Juliet then holds the tube up and looks at it. She smells the top of the tube and then tries to drink some.)**
What's here? A cup, closed in my true love's hand?
Poison, I see, hath been his timeless end.
Drunk all, and left no friendly drop
To help me after? I will kiss thy lips.
**(Juliet stretches her neck leaning forward, closes her eyes and then opens them.)**
Haply some poison yet doth hang on them
To make me die with a restorative.* (* *medicine*)
Thy lips are warm.
**(She rolls the script even tighter making a dagger.)**
O happy dagger! This is thy sheath; there rust and let me die.

**(Juliet stabs herself by thrusting the dagger by her right side and reacting slightly. She slowly sinks to the ground, lying partially on top of Romeo.)**

NARRATOR 1

Romeo and Juliet lay dead in one another's arms on the tomb. The story ends with the Capulet's and Montague's seeing the errors of their ways and offering mutual friendship.

PRINCE

**(FTA)**
For never was a story of more woe

ROMEO & JULIET

**(Stand facing audience)**
Than this of Juliet and her Romeo.

ALL

**(All actors FTA, stand and move downstage beside Romeo and Juliet in a single line facing the audience. All actors grasp hands with the people on either side of them. Lady Capulet leads the bow by raising her hands, all others raise hands at the same time. Led by Lady Capulet, in unison they say…)**
The end.
**Bow still holding hands. After the bow, actors drop hands. Romeo offers his arm and Juliet takes it and they exit together behind the audience. Abrams seeks out Sampson and Gregory. They exchange a brief greeting and exit in a tight clump up right. Tybalt seek out and exits with Mercutio up left. All others exit with someone in a friendly manner up left or up right.**

# Part Four: *Midsummer Night's Dream*

## Chapter 12: *Midsummer Night's Dream* Background

### NUTSHELL

Midsummer's eve, sometime between June 21 and 24 depending on the solstice, is a night that has been celebrated as a time of renewal and repair. For example, picking medicinal flowers on Midsummer's eve is said to increase their ability to heal. The structure of *Midsummer Night's Dream* deals with journeys of rejuvenation: from hate to love, jealousy to trust, tragedy to comedy, single life to married, and barren to fertile.

*Midsummer Night's Dream* is a celebration with three weddings and a triumphant theatrical opening. It has transformations from fairy spells, crossed loves, fruitless squabbles, true love rediscovered, and a blanket happy ending. So even though Puck, who drives much of the play with his misadventures, laughs, "Lord, what fools these mortals be!" we all can laugh at the dream. In the end, the amateur thespians are successful, the King and Queen of the Fairies are reconciled, and the right men fall in love with the right women. *Midsummer Night's Dream* is Shakespeare's luckiest and happiest comedy, as no one gets permanently hurt or punished.

### SYNOPSIS

*A Midsummer Night's Dream* might be described as a series of misadventures ending in harmony and love, involving three Athenian groups: the Lovers, the Mechanicals, and the Fairies. The Lovers include Theseus (the ruler of Athens) and his bride to be, Hippolyta; Lysander and Hermia; and Helena and Demetrius. The Mechanicals are a group of amateur actors led by Peter Quince (the writer and director) and Nick Bottom (the lead actor). The Fairies are led by the King, Oberon, and his wife, Queen Titania.

The play begins with an ominous threat against one of the couples. Hermia's father, Egeus, insists—on pain of death—that Hermia marry Demetrius, the young man of his choice, not hers. Lysander, the young man Hermia has chosen, proposes that they flee Athens, but they get lost in the woods. During the night they encounter the other couple, the scorned Helena and the man she loves, Demetrius.

PART FOUR: MIDSUMMER NIGHT'S DREAM

Puck, although hardworking and able (he can fly around the earth in 40 minutes), gets insufficient information to do his job properly. He is told to anoint the eyes of an Athenian youth with a magic flower. There is more than one Athenian youth in the forest and Puck anoints the eyes of the wrong one, Lysander. When Lysander awakens he falls in love with the wrong woman, Helena. Demetrius also has the potion dropped into his eyes and also falls in love with Helena. Helena goes from having no suitors to having two, who leave to fight one another.

Puck is chastised for his errors and told to take the four young Athenians on a wild goose chase that ends with them all asleep near Titania. Then Oberon makes sure the right eyes are un-enchanted.

Oberon uses the same flower to anoint the eyes of his wife, Queen Titania, to punish her. Titania falls in love with Bottom even though he has been given the head of an ass. Later, Oberon releases his wife from the spell and they reconcile.

Theseus finds the four lovers asleep and wakes them. Demetrius explains that he is now engaged to Helena and no longer loves Hermia. The play culminates with the right woman being married to the right man and everyone forgives everyone else, explaining the bizarre events as just a dream. The play *Pyramus and Thisbe* is performed by the Mechanicals at the wedding festivities. Puck has the final word in an epilogue that asks forgiveness if any offense was taken.

## SOURCES

*Midsummer Night's Dream*, perhaps more than any other of his plays, shows that Shakespeare had talent. It points to a number of Shakespeare gifts including: (1) his range of reading, (2) his ability to weave plots together to a satisfactory end, and (3) his avid imagination.

The plot and various sub-plots can be traced to a number of different sources. Ovid's *Metamorphoses* seems to have been very important, as therein can be found elements of all three subplots. Titania's name, for example, can be found in *Metamorphoses*, as can the story of Theseus and Hippolyta. The plots concerning the Lovers are also found in Ovid's work. It is probably also the inspiration for the Mechanical's play, *Pyramus and Thisbe. Metamorphosis* was translated by Arthur Golding in 1567 but he did not include Titania's name. That Shakespeare used the name Titania suggests that he read Metamorphosis in its original Latin.

Chaucer, who lived in the 14th century, was heralded during the Elizabethan age as the Father of English literature. Shakespeare was very familiar with Chaucer and many plot points came from his work. Chaucer's *Knight's Tale* provided Shakespeare with some aspects of Theseus and Hippolyta's courtship as well as the competition of two men for one woman.

Apuleius wrote *The Golden Ass* in the second century CE in Latin. Both this and a translation by William Adlington, completed in 1566, were available to Shakespeare. An important part of the plot has a noble woman falling in love with a young man who transforms into an ass.

Elements of the plot can also be found in local events, and the traditions and customs of the time; stories that were not written down, but that circulated by word of mouth. Oberon and Puck, for example, could be found in books but they were also common folklore characters.

*Midsummer Night's Dream* shows growth in Shakespeare's technique. Though books by Chaucer and Ovid might be held as sources of the play, it is Shakespeare's imagination and firm grasp of structure that are the real sources of this play. Combining and arranging of the various characters and sub-plots are all Shakespeare. It was his imagination that merged the Fairy subplot and the supernatural with the Lovers and Mechanicals and via Puck changes their direction. It is Puck and Oberon, from Shakespeare's imagination, who change the present and cause confusion, eventually creating the suitable pairings.

*Midsummer Night's Dream* was probably written before 1595 and performed numerous times before its official publication in 1600. It is probable that the play was originally built to celebrate an important person's wedding. Just as the Mechanicals present a play celebrating a wedding at the end of the play, so it was that this was to be a play presented at a wedding. There are a number of possible weddings conducted for high society families. One of the most probable is the wedding of the Lord Chamberlain's granddaughter, Elizabeth Carey to Thomas Berkeley in February 1596. The Lord Chamberlain Players presenting a play for the Lord Chamberlain's granddaughter at her wedding seems to be both logical and romantic.

## PUBLISHING HISTORY

Current versions of *Midsummer Night's Dream* are based on two quartos and the First Folio, printed in 1623. Two quarto versions of Midsummer Night's Dream have as their publishing date the year 1600. Q1 (the First Quarto) has on its title page: "A Midsummer night's dreame. As it hath been sundry times publickly acted by the right honourable, the Lord Chamberlaine his servants. Written by William Shakespeare. Imprinted at London for Thomas Fisher, and are to be souled at his shippe, at the singe of the White Hart, in Fleetstreete. 1600." Q2 has the same title with the name James Roberts instead of Thomas Fisher. Recent research suggests that Q2 was probably published in 1619 to be one of a set of plays.

It seems that Q1 was typeset from Shakespeare's foul (or working) papers, though probably up to date with Shakespeare's revisions. It is generally accepted that Q1 was printed with Shakespeare's intent. Q2 reprints Q1 with additional stage directions and the First Folio is based on Q2.

Interesting is that stage directions in the First Folio as well as the title page of Q2 suggest *Midsummer Night's Dream* was played regularly by The Lord Chamberlain's / King's Men from its inception in the 1590s to the printing of the First Folio in 1623.

The English language was in transition during this period. A passage from Q1 compared to the same passage in the First Folio shows how spelling changed over the quarter century. From Act III Demetrius is spurning Helena, he says in Q1:

> *I will not ftay thy queftionf. Let me goe:*
> *Or if thou followe mee, do not beleeue,*
>
> *But I fhall doe thee mifchiefe, in the wood*

In the First Folio the same passage is much more aligned with modern English:

> *I will not stay thy questions; let me go:*
> *Or, if thou follow me, do not believe,*
>
> *But I shall do thee mischief in the wood.*

## WHY *MIDSUMMER NIGHT'S DREAM* IS EXTRAORDINARY

*Midsummer Night's Dream* is called a dream because it floats above reality. It has one foot in the fantasy realm, with the supernatural powers of Oberon and Puck, and the other foot in romantic comedy. Even in romantic comedies, wrapping up the loose ends with an "oh it was all a dream" is improbable. Hermia does not chastise Lysander for turning on her. She does not even mention that Lysander called her a "cat, thou burr! vile thing." Egeus, who at the top of the play demanded that his daughter marry Demetrius, seems to forget that he had called for his daughter's death if she did not comply.

But the play is so skillfully crafted that, in the end, the audience accepts the conclusion. The use of the wedding as the ending is especially clever as it seems to wrap up and sanction all the incongruent and dissimilar elements. Puck's final speech says in essence, "we may have erred, please forgive us; we like you, please like us."

The three groups (Lovers, Mechanicals, and Fairies) all exist within an ambiguous reality, that is heightened and beautiful. The setting is magical and deliberately vague, so that ultimately, the only explanation for the events is to accept that all is well that ends well, or that the end justifies the means. The logic is circular: this must be a dream because it has odd events that could only happen in a dream. Puck even suggests that the audience "have but slumbered here."

This would be a perfect play to perform for wedding guests. A wedding is carefully crafted to be a celebratory event that sits outside the grind of normal life. It is a song and a dance that has as its purpose joy. So is the *Midsummer Night's Dream* a song and a dance that celebrates marriage.

## IMPORTANT PRODUCTIONS OF *MIDSUMMER NIGHT'S DREAM*

### 1594

It is probable that The Lord Chamberlain's Men toured smaller venues in Southern England during the 1592 to 1594 plague of London, with a version of *Midsummer Night's Dream*. Shakespeare probably acted in it, perhaps playing one of the Mechanicals. There is a tradition of actor-managers playing the character of Bottom.

### 1604

A performance at the court of King James lists the play as, *A Play of Robin Goodfellow*.

### 1692

Henry Purcell adapted *Midsummer Night's Dream* to create an opera titled, *The Fairy Queen*. Thomas Betterton produced the opera that cut and rearranged Shakespeare's text.

**1755**

David Garrick produced *The Fairies* which cut the Mechanicals completely and focused on the Lovers and Fairies. Garrick added songs by John Dryden. Burying the play under spectacle and music became the norm for the next 60 years.

**1826**

Felix Mendelssohn created an overture and incidental music for the play. Ludwig Tieck produced a translated version of *Midsummer Night's Dream* in Berlin using this music the following year.

**1840**

Mendelssohn's music was used in an 1840 English revival at the Covent Garden. Lucia Vestris started the tradition of a woman playing Puck.

**1900**

Herbert Beerbohm Tree produced *Midsummer Night's Dream* and again in 1911. He had elaborate sets and props that included live rabbits scurrying across the stage.

**1909**

This Charles Kent-directed black and white silent film was eight minutes in length. Oberon was replaced by a Penelope for no apparent reason.

**1935**

Max Reinhardt directed *Midsummer Night's Dream* on film in 1935 with Olivia de Haviland (Hermia), James Cagney (Bottom) and Mickey Rooney as Puck. He was chosen to direct based on his *Midsummer Night's Dream* Hollywood Bowl extravaganza the year previous.

**1937**

Tyrone Guthrie production at the Old Vic had Vivian Leigh as Titania and Ralph Richardson as Puck.

**1962**

New York City Ballet produced a George Balanchine full length *Midsummer Night's Dream* ballet on January 17.

**1969**

Peter Hall adapted *Midsummer Night's Dream* for film from his stage production. The film starred Helen Mirren (Hermia), Judi Dench (Titania), Ian Richardson (Oberon), and Ian Holm as Puck.

**1970**

Arguably the most influential recent production was Peter Brook's live 1970 production that was staged in a white box. Brook states, "The aim was to appeal to the imagination through a lively, humourous contact between stage and audience."

**1999**

Michael Hoffman adapted the play and directed Kevin Kline, Michelle Pfeiffer, Christian Bale, Stanley Tucci, and Calista Flockhart in a version that was set in 19th century Italy.

## WRAP-UP

This may be Shakespeare's most perfect play. If his objective was to write a romantic comedy that celebrated love, he did it – marvelously. He wove three sub-plots effortlessly together and terminated with a beautiful wedding.

Puck's epilogue is skillful as it reflects honestly on the experience. He in essence says, we intended to take you away from your daily cares, you have to go back to them now, don't be cranky with us, and let's keep this special moment as a memory.

Puck hopes that the audience will leave as his friends, and by extension, friends with all the performers. It is a gentle good night intended to soften the change from this magical space and time back to reality.

PART FOUR: *MIDSUMMER NIGHT'S DREAM*

# Chapter 13: Midsummer Night's Dream, 45-Minute Readers' Theatre Version

## CASTING SUGGESTIONS

One reader per part

16 readers
Reader 1: Narrator 1
Reader 2: Theseus
Reader 3: Hippolyta
Reader 4: Hermia
Reader 5: Lysander
Reader 6: Demetrius
Reader 7: Egeus
Reader 8: Helena
Reader 9: Quince
Reader 10: Bottom
Reader 11: Flute
Reader 12: Snug
Reader 13: Puck
Reader 14: Oberon
Reader 15: Titania
Reader 16 : Narrator 2

Using nine readers with some double casting
Reader 1: Narrator 1, Narrator 2
Reader 2: Theseus, Oberon
Reader 3: Hippolyta, Titania
Reader 4: Hermia, Snug
Reader 5: Lysander
Reader 6: Demetrius
Reader 7: Egeus, Bottom
Reader 8: Helena, Flute
Reader 9: Quince, Puck

## Midsummer Night's Dream

## 45-Minute Readers' Theatre Version

**ALL**

Midsummer Night's Dream.

**LOVERS**

By William Shakespeare.

**SNUG**

Adapted by John Poulsen.

**NARRATOR 1**

The plot of Midsummer Night's Dream revolves around three intertwined sub-plots. The first sub-plot involves three sets of lovers. The first couple is,

**THESEUS**

Theseus the Duke and lord of Athens, who is engaged to marry,

**HIPPOLYTA**

Hippolyta, Queen of the Amazons.

**THESEUS**

Now, fair Hippolyta, our nuptial* hour*(\* marriage)*
Draws on apace* in four happy days.*(\*quickly)*

**HIPPOLYTA**

Four days will quickly steep* themselves in night *(\*turn, change)*
Four nights will quickly dream away the time.

**THESEUS**

Hippolyta, I wooed thee with my sword
But I will wed thee in another key,*
*(\*Theseus and Hippolyta fought in the past but now they will marry)*
With pomp, with triumph, and with reveling.

**NARRATOR 2**

The Lovers also include:

**HERMIA**

Hermia, who loves

**LYSANDER**

Lysander, dashingly handsome and beloved of Hermia.

**HERMIA**

But I am promised by my father to,

**DEMETRIUS**

Demetrius, dashingly handsome and promised to Hermia.

**NARRATOR 1**

Hermia's father, Egeus, demands that Hermia marry Demetrius.

**EGEUS**

As Hermia is mine, I may dispose of her:
Which shall be either to this gentleman
Or to her death, according to our law.

**NARRATOR 2**

He makes Hermia stand before the Duke of Athens, Theseus. Hermia explains.

**HERMIA**

I would my father looked but with my eyes.
I beseech what is the worst that may befall* me in this case.
(*what is the worst that will happen)
If I refuse to wed Demetrius?

**THESEUS**

Either to die the death or to abjure* (*avoid)
Forever the society of men.
And endure the livery of a nun.* (*suffer in the clothes of a nun)
To live a barren sister all your life
Chanting faint hymns to the cold fruitless moon.
Take time to pause and by my wedding day
Either prepare to die or wed Demetrius.

**DEMETRIUS**

Relent, sweet Hermia and Lysander yield.

**LYSANDER**

You have her father's love, Demetrius
Let me have Hermia's; do you marry him.

**NARRATOR 1**

Theseus is the law in Athens and his proclamation that Hermia must obey her father is considered harsh by Hermia and Lysander. They plan their future.

**LYSANDER**

How now my love? why is your cheek so pale?
The course of true love never did run smooth.

**HERMIA**

O spite! To choose love by another's eyes.

**LYSANDER**

Love
Swift as a shadow, short as any dream;
Brief as the lightning in the collied* night. (*thick and dark)

**HERMIA**

If then true lovers have been ever crossed* (*if lovers have ever met difficulty)
Let us teach our trial patience.

**LYSANDER**

Hear me Hermia.
I have a widow aunt, that hath no child.
She respects me as her only son.
From Athens is her house remote seven leagues,
There, gentle Hermia, may I marry thee
And to that place the sharp Athenian law
Cannot pursue us.
Steal forth thy father's house tomorrow night
And in the wood, will I stay for thee.

**HERMIA**

I swear to thee by Cupid's strongest bow
Tomorrow truly will I meet with thee.

**NARRATOR 2**

Helena, is Hermia's best friend and in love with Demetrius. Helena
asks Hermia what she does to capture Demetrius's heart.

**HELENA**

Teach me how you look and with what art
You sway the motion of Demetrius' heart.

**HERMIA**

I frown upon him; yet he loves me still.

**HELENA**

O that your frowns would teach my smiles such skill!

**HERMIA**

The more I hate, the more he follows me.

**HELENA**

The more I love, the more he hateth me.

**HELENA**

Take comfort, he no more shall see my face.
Lysander and myself will fly this place.

**LYSANDER**

To you our minds we will unfold:
Through Athens' gates have we devised to steal.

**HERMIA**

And in the wood, where often you and I
Upon faint primrose-beds were wont to lie,
Emptying our bosoms of their counsel sweet,
There my Lysander and myself shall meet;
And thence from Athens turn away our eyes,
To seek new friends and stranger companies.

**NARRATOR 1**

Hermia and Lysander exit. Helena schemes to gain Demetrius's favour.

**HELENA**

Love looks not with the eyes, but with the mind,
And therefore is winged Cupid painted blind.
I will go tell Demetrius of fair Hermia's flight
Then to the wood will he tomorrow night.

**NARRATOR 2**

The second plot involves a group of workers or Mechanicals who are preparing to put on a play for the Duke Theseus on his wedding day, four days hence. They are led by Quince.

**QUINCE**

Is all our company here?

**NARRATOR 1**

And Nick Bottom.

**BOTTOM**

Your were best to call them man by man, according to the script. Masters spread yourselves.

**QUINCE**

Our play is, 'The most lamentable comedy and most cruel death of Pyramus and Thisby.' Nick Bottom, the weaver.

**BOTTOM**

Ready. Name what part I am for.

**QUINCE**

You, Nick Bottom, are set down for Pyramus.

**BOTTOM**

What is Pyramus? A lover or a tyrant?

**QUINCE**

A lover that kills himself, most gallant, for love.

**BOTTOM**

That will ask some tears in the performing of it. Let the audience look to their eyes. I will move storms.*
(*my acting will be so good that the audience will weep as though it is raining)

**QUINCE**

Francis Flute, the bellows maker, you must take Thisby on you.

**FLUTE**

What is Thisby? A wandering knight?

**QUINCE**

It is the lady that Pyramus must love.

**FLUTE**

Nay, faith, let me not play a woman. I have a beard coming.

**BOTTOM**

Let me play Thisby too.
I'll speak in a monstrous little voice. "Thisne, Thisne!"

**QUINCE**

No, no; you must play Pyramus, and you Flute, you Thisby.
Snug, the joiner, you the lion's part.

**SNUG**

Have you the lion's part written? Pray you, if it be, give it me, for I am slow of study.

**QUINCE**

You may do it extempore*, for it is nothing but roaring.(*improvise)

**BOTTOM**

Let me play the lion too. I will roar that I will make the Duke say, 'Let him roar again.'

**QUINCE**

A lion among ladies is a most dreadful thing. And you would fright the Duchess and the ladies and were enough to hang us all.

**MECHANICALS**

That would hang us, every mother's son.

**BOTTOM**

I will aggravate my voice so that I will roar as gently as any suckling dove; I will roar you as 'twere any nightingale.*

*(*bottom will roar gently as a baby pigeon or a sweet sounding bird)*

**QUINCE**

Bottom, you can play no part but Pyramus for
Pyramus is a sweet-faced man; a proper
Man as one shall see on a summer's day.

**NARRATOR 2**

The mechanicals resolve to meet to rehearse in the same part of the forest to which Hermia, Lysander, Helena, and Demetrius are going.

**NARRATOR 1**

The third plot revolves around the Fairies. Puck is the primary agent of change in this play.

**PUCK**

I am the mischievous Puck. I am that merry wanderer of the night.

**NARRATOR 2**

The King of the Fairies, Oberon, and his wife the Queen of the Fairies, Titania, meet in the wood. They are quarreling.

**OBERON**

Ill met by moonlight, proud Titania.

**TITANIA**

What, jealous Oberon! Fairies, skip hence:
I have forsworn* his bed and company. *(*rejected)*

**OBERON**

Tarry, rash wanton*; am not I thy lord? *(*wait you impulsive and cruel woman)*

**TITANIA**

Then I must be thy lady.
We shall chide* downright, if I longer stay. *(*fight)*

**NARRATOR 1**

Titania and her servants leave, but Oberon wants to make his wife suffer, so he summons Puck.

**OBERON**

Well, go thy way: thou shalt not from this grove**(*forest)*

Till I torment thee for this injury.
My gentle Puck, come hither.
Know you where the bolt of Cupid fell?
It fell upon a little western flower,
Fetch me that flower;
The juice of it on sleeping eye-lids laid
Will make man or woman madly dote
Upon the next live creature that it sees.*

(*find me a specific little flower that has magical love inducing powers)

### PUCK

I'll put a girdle round about the earth
In forty minutes.* (*Puck can fly around the world in 40 minutes)

### NARRATOR 2

Puck leaves to find the flower. Oberon plans his torment of his
wife, Titania.

### OBERON

Having once this juice,
I'll watch Titania when she is asleep,
And drop the liquor of it in her eyes.
But who comes here? I am invisible;
And I will overhear their conference.

### NARRATOR 1

Oberon is interrupted and observes unseen the entrance of Demetrius
followed by the love sick Helena.

### DEMETRIUS

I love thee not, therefore pursue me not.
Where is Lysander and fair Hermia?
The one I'll slay, the other slayeth me.*
(*I will kill Lysander and Hermia kills me for want of her love)
Thou told'st me they were stolen unto this wood;
Hence, get thee gone, and follow me no more.

### HELENA

You draw me, you hard-hearted adamant;
But yet you draw real iron, for my heart
Is true as steel: leave you your power to draw,
And I shall have no power to follow you.*
(*my heart is steel, you are a magnet. Stop being a magnet and I will stop following you)

### DEMETRIUS

Do I entice you? Do I speak you fair?
Or, rather, do I not in plainest truth

Tell you, I do not, nor cannot love you?

**HELENA**

And even for that do I love you the more.
Neglect me, lose me; only give me leave,
Unworthy as I am, to follow you.

**DEMETRIUS**

Tempt not too much the hatred of my spirit;
For I am sick when I do look on thee

**HELENA**

And I am sick when I look not on you.

**DEMETRIUS**

You do impeach your modesty too much,* *(*you put yourself in danger)*
To trust the opportunity of night
And the ill counsel of a desert place
With the rich worth of your virginity.

**HELENA**

How can it be said I am alone,
When all the world is here to look on me?

**DEMETRIUS**

I'll run from thee and hide me in the brakes,* *(*bushes)*
And leave thee to the mercy of wild beasts.

**HELENA**

The wildest hath not such a heart as you.
Run when you will, the story shall be changed:
The dove pursues the griffin; the mild deer
Makes speed to catch the tiger.

**DEMETRIUS**

I will not stay thy questions; let me go:
Or, if thou follow me, do not believe
But I shall do thee mischief in the wood.

**HELENA**

We cannot fight for love, as men may do;
We should be woo'd and were not made to woo.
I'll follow thee and make a heaven of hell,
To die upon the hand I love so well.

**NARRATOR 2**

Oberon feels pity for Helena and promises to help her.

**OBERON**

Fare thee well, maid: ere he do leave this grove,
Thou shalt fly and he shall seek thy love.

**NARRATOR 1**

Puck reenters with the flower.

**OBERON**

Hast thou the flower there? Welcome, wanderer.

**PUCK**

Ay, there it is.

**OBERON**

I pray thee, give it me.
I know a bank where the wild thyme blows,
Where oxlips and the nodding violet grows,
Quite over-canopied with luscious woodbine,
With sweet musk-roses and with eglantine:
There sleeps Titania, I'll streak her eyes.
And make her full of hateful fantasies.
Take thou some of it, and seek through this grove:
A sweet Athenian lady is in love
With a disdainful youth, anoint his eyes;
But do it when the next thing he espies
May be the lady: thou shalt know the man
By the Athenian garments he hath on.

**PUCK**

Fear not, my lord, your servant shall do so.

**NARRATOR 2**

Puck exits to drop some of the magic into Demetrius's eyes. It is now
dark. Lysander and Hermia enter. They are lost.

**LYSANDER**

Fair love, you faint with wandering in the wood;
And to speak truth, I have forgot our way:
We'll rest us, Hermia, if you think it good,
And tarry* for the comfort of the day. (*wait*)

**HERMIA**

Be it so, Lysander: find you out a bed;
For I upon this bank will rest my head.

**LYSANDER**

One turf shall serve as pillow for us both;
One heart, one bed, two bosoms and one troth.* (*love*)

**HERMIA**

Nay, good Lysander; for my sake, my dear,
Lie further off yet, do not lie so near.

**LYSANDER**

Here is my bed: sleep give thee all his rest!

**NARRATOR 1**

Lysander and Hermia sleep. Enter Puck looking for the Athenian youth
into whose eyes he was instructed to drop some of the magic potion.

**PUCK**

Through the forest have I gone.
But Athenian found I none,
Who is here?
Weeds* of Athens he doth wear. *(*clothes)*
Upon thy eyes I throw
All the power this charm doth owe.
So awake when I am gone;
For I must now to Oberon.

**NARRATOR 2**

Pucks leaves to report to Oberon that he has dripped some drops in the
Athenian Youth's eyes. Enter Helena trying to find Demetrius.

**HELENA**

But who is here? Lysander! on the ground!
Dead? or asleep? I see no blood, no wound.
Lysander if you live, good sir, awake.

**LYSANDER**

And run through fire I will for thy sweet sake.

**NARRATOR 1**

The magic potion has made Lysander fall madly in love with the first
person he saw upon waking: Helena.

**HELENA**

Do not say so, Lysander; say not so
What though you love your Hermia? Lord, what though?
Yet Hermia still loves you: then be content.

**LYSANDER**

Content with Hermia! No; I do repent
The tedious minutes I with her have spent.
Not Hermia but Helena I love:
Who will not change a raven for a dove?

**HELENA**

Wherefore was I to this keen mockery born?
When at your hands did I deserve this scorn?
Good troth, you do me wrong, good sooth,* you do, *(*truly)*
In such disdainful manner me to woo.

**NARRATOR 2**

Helena flees Lysander, seeking Demtrius. Lysander follows newly in love with Helena. Hermia awakens from a nightmare to find Lysander gone.

**HERMIA**

Help me, Lysander, help me! do thy best
To pluck this crawling serpent from my breast!
Lysander! what, removed? Lysander! lord!
What, out of hearing? gone? no sound, no word?
I well perceive you all not nigh
Either death or you I'll find immediately.

**NARRATOR 1**

Hermia runs to find Lysander. Titania goes to sleep in the forest glade and Oberon drops some of the potion into her eyes.

**OBERON**

What thou seest when thou dost wake,
Do it for thy true-love take,
When thou wakest, it is thy dear:
Wake when some vile thing is near.

**NARRATOR 2**

Enter the mechanicals, looking for a place to rehearse their play, Pyramus and Thisby. Bottom has been convinced to play only Pyramus and Flute, a young man, has agreed to play Thisby.

**BOTTOM**

Are we all met?

**QUINCE**

Here's a marvelous convenient place
for our rehearsal. This green plot shall be our stage, and we will do it in action as we will do it before the duke.

**BOTTOM**

Peter Quince,—

**QUNICE**

What sayest thou, bully* Bottom? *(*approval, as in 'bully for you')*

**BOTTOM**

We must have a wall in the great
chamber; for Pyramus and Thisby says the story, did
talk through the chink of a wall.

**FLUTE**

You can never bring in a wall. What say you, Bottom?

**BOTTOM**

Some man or other must present Wall; and let him
have some plaster, about him, to signify wall; and let him hold his
fingers thus, and through that cranny shall Pyramus
and Thisby whisper.

**NARRATOR 1**

Puck enters. He speaks an aside to the audience.

**PUCK**

What hempen home-spuns* have we swaggering here,
(*rude and uncouth oafs)
So near the cradle of the fairy queen?

**NARRATOR 2**

Quince, the director, tries to get his troupe to focus.

**QUINCE**

Speak, Pyramus. Thisby, stand forth.

**BOTTOM**

Thisby, the flowers of odious* savours sweet,— (*revolting)

**QUINCE**

Odours, odours.

**BOTTOM**

Odours savours sweet:
So hath thy breath, my dearest Thisby dear.
But hark, a voice! stay thou but here awhile,
And by and by I will to thee appear.

**NARRATOR 1**

Bottom exits into the forest and Puck changes Bottom to resemble a
donkey. Bottom enters with an Ass's head.

**BOTTOM**

If I were fair, Thisby, I were only thine.

**QUNICE**

O monstrous! O strange! we are haunted. Pray,

masters! fly, masters! Help!

**NARRATOR 2**

The actors all flee

**QUINCE**

Bless thee, Bottom! bless thee! Thou art translated.*
(*= Quince means transformed)

**NARRATOR 2**

leaving Bottom alone.

**BOTTOM**

I see their knavery: this is to make an ass of me;
to fright me, if they could. But I will not stir
from this place, do what they can: I will walk up
and down here, and I will sing, that they shall hear
I am not afraid.

**NARRATOR 1**

Bottom singing is actually the braying of a donkey. Titania wakes and
sees Bottom. The magic potion makes her fall in love with the first
thing she sees, the Ass-headed Bottom.

**TITANIA**

What angel wakes me from my flowery bed?
I pray thee, gentle mortal, sing again.

**BOTTOM**

Methinks, mistress, you should have little reason
for that: and yet, reason and
love keep little company together now-a-days.

**TITANIA**

Thou art as wise as thou art beautiful.
Out of this wood do not desire to go:
Thou shalt remain here, whether thou wilt or no.
And I do love thee: therefore, go with me;
I'll give thee fairies to attend on thee.

**NARRATOR 2**

Titania takes Bottom with the Ass's head away. Meanwhile Puck
reports to Oberon.

**OBERON**

Here comes my messenger.
How now, mad spirit!
I wonder if Titania be awaked;

Then, what it was that next came in her eye.

**PUCK**

My mistress with a monster is in love.
Near to her close and consecrated bower,
So it came to pass,
Titania waked and straightway loved an ass.

**OBERON**

This falls out better than I could devise.
But hast thou yet latched* the Athenian's eyes (*locked)
With the love-juice, as I did bid thee do?

**NARRATOR 1**

Hermia and Demetrius enter. Oberon and Puck watch unseen.

**OBERON**

Stand close: this is the same Athenian.

**PUCK**

This is the woman, but not this the man.

**DEMETRIUS**

O, why rebuke you him that loves you so?

**HERMIA**

For thou, I fear, hast given me cause to curse,
If thou hast slain Lysander in his sleep.

**DEMETRIUS**

I am not guilty of Lysander's blood;
Nor is he dead, for aught that I can tell.

**HERMIA**

I pray thee, tell me then that he is well.

**DEMETRIUS**

An if I could, what should I get therefore?

**HERMIA**

A privilege never to see me more.
And from thy hated presence part I so:
See me no more, whether he be dead or no.

**DEMETRIUS**

There is no following her in this fierce vein:
Here therefore for a while I will remain.

PART FOUR: *MIDSUMMER NIGHT'S DREAM*

**NARRATOR 2**

Hermia leaves and Demetrius, exhausted, lies down and sleeps. Oberon chastises Puck for the error.

**OBERON**

What hast thou done? Thou hast mistaken quite
And laid the love-juice on some true-love's sight:
About the wood go swifter than the wind,
And Helena of Athens look thou find:
By some illusion see thou bring her here:
I'll charm his eyes against she do appear.

**PUCK**

I go, I go; look how I go,
Swifter than arrow from the Tartar's bow.

**NARRATOR 1**

Puck leaves to find Helena and to bring her to the sleeping Demetrius. Oberon drops the magic potion into Demetrius's eyes.

**OBERON**

Flower of this purple dye,
Hit with Cupid's archery,
Sink in apple of his eye.
When his love he doth espy.

**NARRATOR 2**

Puck re-enters followed by Helena and Lysander.

**PUCK**

Captain of our fairy band,
Helena is here at hand;
And the youth, mistook by me,
Pleading for a lover's fee.
Shall we their fond pageant see?
Lord, what fools these mortals be!

**OBERON**

Stand aside: the noise they make
Will cause Demetrius to awake.

**LYSANDER**

Why should you think that I woo in scorn?

**HELENA**

These vows are Hermia's: will you give her over?

**LYSANDER**

I had no judgment when to her I swore.

**NARRATOR 1**

Suddenly Demetrius wakes, sees Helena, and falls madly in love.

**DEMETRIUS**

O Helena, goddess, nymph, perfect, divine!
To what, my love, shall I compare thine eyne?* *(*eye)*

**HELENA**

O spite! I see you all are bent
To set against me for your merriment:
If you were men, as men you are in show,
You would not use a gentle lady so.

**LYSANDER**

You are unkind, Demetrius; be not so;
For you love Hermia; this you know I know.

**DEMETRIUS**

Lysander, keep thy Hermia; I will none:
If ever I loved her, all that love is gone.

**NARRATOR 2**

Hermia enters.

**HERMIA**

Mine ear, I thank it, brought me to thy sound
But why unkindly didst thou leave me so?

**LYSANDER**

Why should he stay, whom love doth press to go?

**HERMIA**

What love could press Lysander from my side?

**LYSANDER**

Fair Helena.

**HERMIA**

You speak not as you think: it cannot be.

**HELENA**

Lo, she is one of this confederacy!
Now I perceive they have joined all three
To fashion this false sport, in spite of me.
So we grew together,

Like to a double cherry, seeming parted,
Two lovely berries moulded on one stem;
So, with two seeming bodies, but one heart;
And will you join with men in scorning your poor friend?
It is not friendly, 'tis not maidenly:
Our sex, as well as I, may chide* you for it. *(scold)*

**HERMIA**

I am amazed at your passionate words.
I scorn you not: it seems that you scorn me.

**HELENA**

Have you not set Lysander, as in scorn,
To follow me and praise my eyes and face?

**HERMIA**

I understand not what you mean by this.

**HELENA**

O excellent!

**DEMETRIUS**

I say I love thee more than he can do.

**LYSANDER**

If thou say so, withdraw, and prove it too.

**DEMETRIUS**

Quick, come!

**HERMIA**

Lysander, whereto tends all this?

**LYSANDER**

Away, you! Hang off, thou cat, thou burr! vile thing, let loose,
Or I will shake thee from me like a serpent!

**HERMIA**

Do you not jest?

**HELENA**

Yes, sooth; and so do you.

**LYSANDER**

What, should I hurt Hermia, strike her, kill her dead?
Although I hate her, I'll not harm her so.

**HERMIA**

What, can you do me greater harm than hate?
Hate me! wherefore? O me! what news, my love!
Am not I Hermia? Are not you Lysander?
I am as fair now as I was erewhile.* *(*before)*
Since night you loved me; yet since night you left me.

**LYSANDER**

Ay, by my life;
And never did desire to see thee more.
'Tis no jest
That I do hate thee and love Helena.

**HERMIA**

O me! you juggler! you canker-blossom!* *(*cold sore)*
You thief of love! What, have you come by night
And stolen my love's heart from him?

**HELENA**

Have you no modesty, no maiden shame,
No touch of bashfulness? What, will you tear
Impatient answers from my gentle tongue?
Fie, fie! you puppet, you!

**HERMIA**

Puppet? why so? ay, that way goes the game.
Now I perceive that she hath made compare
Between our statures; she hath urged her height;
And are you grown so high in his esteem;
Because I am so dwarfish and so low?
How low am I, thou painted maypole? speak;
How low am I? I am not yet so low
But that my nails can reach unto thine eyes.

**HELENA**

I pray you, though you mock me, gentlemen,
Let her not hurt me
Let her not strike me. You perhaps may think,
Because she is something lower than myself,
That I can match her.

**HERMIA**

Lower! hark, again.

**HELENA**

Good Hermia, do not be so bitter with me.

I evermore did love you, Hermia.

**HERMIA**

Why, get you gone: who is it that hinders you?

**HELENA**

O, when she's angry, she is keen and shrewd!
She was a vixen when she went to school;
And though she be but little, she is fierce.

**HERMIA**

Little' again! nothing but 'low' and 'little'!
Why will you suffer her to flout* me thus? *(*insult*)

**LYSANDER**

Get you gone, you dwarf;
You minimus, You bead, you acorn.

**HERMIA**

Let me come to her.

**LYSANDER**

Now Demetrius, follow, if thou darest, to try whose right,
Of thine or mine, is most in Helena.

**DEMETRIUS**

Follow! nay, I'll go with thee, cheek by jowl.

**NARRATOR 1**

Demetrius and Lysander leave to fight. Helena though taller is
frightened of Hermia and runs away.

**HELENA**

I will not trust you, I,
Nor longer stay in your curst company.
Your hands than mine are quicker for a fray,
My legs are longer though, to run away.

**HERMIA**

I am amazed, and know not what to say.

**NARRATOR 2**

Hermia leaves following Helena. Oberon, having seen the quarrel,
turns to Puck for explanation.

**OBERON**

This is thy negligence: still thou mistakest,
Or else committ'st thy knaveries wilfully.

**PUCK**

Believe me, king of shadows, I mistook.

**OBERON**

Lead these testy rivals so astray
As one come not within another's way.
Till over their brows death-counterfeiting sleep
With leaden legs and batty wings doth creep:
Then crush this herb into Lysander's eye.

**PUCK**

My fairy lord, this must be done with haste,
For night's swift dragons cut the clouds full fast,
And yonder shines Aurora's harbinger;*
(*there shines the suns forerunner, the morning star )
At whose approach, ghosts, wandering here and there,
Troop home to churchyards.

**OBERON**

Make haste; make no delay:
We may effect this business yet ere day.

**NARRATOR 1**

In the dark, Puck now taunts Demetrius and Lysander leading them
through the forest till they are so exhausted they fall to the ground and
sleep. Helena enters and also sleeps.

**PUCK**

Yet but three? Come one more;
Two of both kinds make up four.
Here she comes, curst and sad:
Cupid is a knavish lad,
Thus to make poor females mad.

**HERMIA**

Never so weary, never so in woe,
Bedabbled* with the dew and torn with briers, (*soaked)
I can no further crawl, no further go;
My legs can keep no pace with my desires.
Here will I rest me till the break of day.

**NARRATOR 2**

All four are sleeping soundly. Puck squeezes the magic potion into
Lysander's eyes.

**PUCK**

On the ground sleep sound:

I'll apply to your eye,
Gentle lover, remedy
When thou wakest, thou takest
True delight in the sight
Of thy former lady's eye: and the country proverb known,
That every man should take his own,
In your waking shall be shown:
Jack shall have Jill; nought shall go ill;
The man shall have his mare again, and all shall be well.

**NARRATOR 1**

Act four begins with Titania fawning over Bottom who still has an ass's
head. Oberon has made himself invisible and watches.

**TITANIA**

Come, sit thee down upon this flowery bed,
While I thy amiable cheeks do coy, (*I will stroke your cheery cheeks)
And stick musk-roses in thy sleek smooth head,
And kiss thy fair large ears, my gentle joy.

**BOTTOM**

Scratch my head Peaseblossom. I must to the barber's, monsieur;
for methinks I am marvellous hairy about the face; and I am such a
tender ass, if my hair do but tickle me, I must scratch.

**TITANIA**

Say, sweet love, what thou desirest to eat.

**BOTTOM**

Truly, I could munch your good dry oats. Methinks I have a great
desire to hay: good hay, sweet hay, hath no fellow.* (*equal)

**TITANIA**

I have a venturous fairy that shall seek
The squirrel's hoard, and fetch thee new nuts.

**BOTTOM**

I had rather have a handful or two of dried peas.
But, I pray you, let none of your people stir me: I have an exposition
of sleep come upon me.

**TITANIA**

Sleep thou, and I will wind thee in my arms.
O, how I love thee! how I dote on thee!

**NARRATOR 2**

Bottom and Titania fall asleep entwined in one another's arms. Oberon
and Puck enter.

**OBERON**

See'st thou this sweet sight?
Her dotage now I do begin to pity:
I will release the fairy queen.
Be as thou was wont to be;
See as thou was wont to see:
Now, my Titania; wake you, my sweet queen.

**TITANIA**

My Oberon! what visions have I seen!
Methought I was enamoured of an ass.*
(*I thought I was in love with a donkey)

**OBERON**

There lies your love.

**TITANIA**

How came these things to pass?
O, how mine eyes do loathe his visage* now! (*hate his face)

**OBERON**

Silence awhile. Robin*, take off this head.
(*Puck is also called Robin Goodfellow)

**PUCK**

Now, when thou wakest, with thine own fool's eyes peep.

**OBERON**

Come, my queen, take hands with me,
And leave the ground whereon these sleepers be.

**PUCK**

Fairy king, attend, and mark: I do hear the morning lark.

**TITANIA**

Come, my lord, and in our flight
Tell me how it came this night
That I sleeping here was found
With these mortals on the ground.

**NARRATOR**

Titania, Oberon and Puck exit. The Duke of Athens, Theseus, his
bride, Hippolyta, and Egeus enter.

**EGEUS**

My lord, this is my daughter here asleep;
And this, Lysander; this Demetrius is;
This Helena, I wonder of their being here together.

PART FOUR: *MIDSUMMER NIGHT'S DREAM*

**THESEUS**

No doubt they rose up early to observe
The rite of May, and hearing our intent,
but speak, Egeus; is not this the day
That Hermia should give answer of her choice?

**EGEUS**

It is, my lord.

**NARRATOR 1**

Helena, Hermia, Lysander, and Demetrius wake up. Theseus speaks to
the rivals Lysander and Demetrius.

**THESEUS**

I pray you all, stand up.
I know you two are rival enemies:
How comes this gentle concord in the world,
That hatred is so far from jealousy,
To sleep by hate, and fear no enmity?* (*hate)

**LYSANDER**

I came with Hermia hither: our intent
Was to be gone from Athens, where we might,
Without the peril of the Athenian law.

**EGEUS**

Enough, enough, my lord; you have enough:
I beg the law, the law, upon his head.
They would have stolen away; they would.

**DEMETRIUS**

My good lord, I know not by what power,—
But by some power it is,—my love to Hermia,
Melted as the snow, seems to me now
Is only Helena. To her, my lord, am I betrothed.

**THESEUS**

Fair lovers, you are fortunately met:
Egeus, I will overbear your will;
For in the temple by and by with us
These couples shall eternally be knit:
Away with us to Athens; three and three,
We'll hold a feast in great solemnity.

**NARRATOR 2**

The royal couple and Egeus exit, leaving the four young lovers.

**DEMETRIUS**

Are you sure that we are awake? It seems to me that yet we sleep,
we dream. Do not you think the duke was here, and bid us follow him?

**HERMIA**

Yea; and my father.

**LYSANDER**

And he did bid us follow to the temple.

**DEMETRIUS**

Why, then, we are awake: let's follow him
And by the way let us recount our dreams.

**NARRATOR 1**

The Lovers walk back to Athens. Bottom, without the ass's head, wakes.

**BOTTOM**

Heigh-ho! They left me asleep! I have had a most rare vision. I have
had a dream, past the wit of man to say what dream it was: man is but
an ass. The eye of man hath not heard, the ear of man hath not seen,
man's hand is not able to taste, his tongue to conceive, nor his heart to
report, what my dream was.

**NARRATOR 2**

Bottom goes to Quince's house where the other Mechanicals are
waiting.

**BOTTOM**

Where are these lads? where are these hearts?

**QUINCE**

Bottom! O most courageous day! O most happy hour!

**BOTTOM**

Masters, I will tell you every thing, right as it fell out.

**QUINCE**

Let us hear, sweet Bottom.

**BOTTOM**

Not a word of me. All that I will tell you is, that the duke hath dined.
Get your apparel together and meet presently at the palace; every man
look o'er his part; for the short and the long is, our play is preferred.

**NARRATOR 1**

The last act, Act Five, takes place in Theseus's palace. Enter Theseus,
and his wife Hippolyta.

**HIPPOLYTA**

'Tis strange my Theseus, that these lovers speak of.

**THESEUS**

More strange than true: I never may believe
These antique fables, nor these fairy toys.
Lovers and madmen have such seething* brains. *(*muddled)*

**NARRATOR 2**

Enter Lysander, Demetrius, Hermia, and Helena.

**THESEUS**

Joy, gentle friends! joy and fresh days of love
Accompany your hearts!

**HIPPOLYTA**

Come now; what masques, what dances shall we have,
To wear away this long age of three hours
Between our after-supper and bed-time?

**THESEUS**

'A tedious brief scene of young Pyramus
And his love Thisbe; very tragical mirth.'
Merry and tragical! tedious and brief!
That is, hot ice. Let them approach.

**NARRATOR 1**

The Mechanicals enter to a flourish of trumpets to perform Pyramus
and Thisby. Enter Bottom, Flute, and Snug.

**BOTTOM**

O grim-looked night! O night with hue so black!
O night, which ever art when day is not!
O night, O night! alack, alack, alack,
I fear my Thisby's promise is forgot!
And thou, O wall, O sweet, O lovely wall,
That stand'st between her father's ground and mine!
Thou wall, O wall, O sweet and lovely wall,
Show me thy chink, to blink through with mine eyne!

**NARRATOR 2**

The Wall holds up two fingers.

**BOTTOM**

Thanks, courteous wall: Jove shield thee well* for this!
*(*may the god Jove protect you)*
But what see I? No Thisby do I see.
O wicked wall, through whom I see no bliss!

Cursed be thy stones for thus deceiving me!

**NARRATOR 1**

Enter Thisbe.

**FLUTE**

O wall, full often hast thou heard my moans,
For parting my fair Pyramus and me!
My cherry lips have often kiss'd thy stones,
Thy stones with lime and hair knit up in thee.

**BOTTOM**

Wilt thou at Ninny's tomb meet me straightway?

**FLUTE**

I come without delay.

**NARRATOR 2**

Pyramus and Thisby agree to meet at a tomb.

**SNUG**

Thus have I, Wall, my part discharged so;
And, being done, thus Wall away doth go.

**HIPPLOYTA**

This is the silliest stuff that ever I heard.

**THESEUS**

The best in this kind are but shadows: and the worst are no worse, if
imagination amend them.

**HIPPLOYTA**

It must be your imagination then and not theirs.

**THESEUS**

Here comes a lion.

**SNUG**

You, ladies, you, whose gentle hearts do fear
The smallest monstrous mouse that creeps on floor,
May now perchance both quake and tremble here,
When lion rough in wildest rage doth roar.
Then know that I, one Snug the joiner, am.

**THESEUS**

A very gentle beast, of a good conscience.

**NARRATOR 1**

Enter Thisby.

**FLUTE**

This is old Ninny's tomb. Where is my love?

**SNUG**

Roar Oh.

**NARRATOR 2**

Thisby runs off, dropping her coat.

**DEMETRIUS**

Well roared, Lion.

**THESEUS**

Well run, Thisbe.

**NARRATOR 1**

The Lion shakes Thisbe's coat and exits.

**LYSANDER**

And so the lion vanished.

**DEMETRIUS**

And then came Pyramus.

**HIPPOLYTA**

I pity the man.

**PYRAMUS (BOTTOM)**

O wherefore, Nature, didst thou lions frame?
Since lion vile hath here deflower'd my dear:
Which is—no, no—which was the fairest dame
That lived, that loved, that liked, that look'd with cheer.
Come, tears, confound;
Out, sword, and wound
Where heart doth hop.

**NARRATOR 2**

Pyramus stabs himself.

**PYRAMUS (BOTTOM)**

Thus die I, thus, thus, thus.
Now am I dead,
Now am I fled;
My soul is in the sky:
Tongue, lose thy light;
Moon take thy flight:
Now die, die, die, die, die.

**NARRATOR 1**

> Pyramus dies. Re-enter Thisby.

**THISBE (FLUTE)**

> Asleep, my love? What, dead, my dove?
> O Pyramus, arise!
> Speak, speak. Quite dumb? Dead, dead? A tomb
> Tongue, not a word: Come, trusty sword;
> Come, blade.

**NARRATOR 2**

> Thisby stabs herself.

**THISBE (FLUTE)**

> And, farewell, friends; Thus Thisby ends:
> Adieu, adieu, adieu.

**NARRATOR 1**

> And Thisby dies.

**THESEUS**

> The iron tongue of midnight hath told twelve:
> Lovers, to bed; 'tis almost fairy time.

**NARRATOR 2**

> The Lovers, Mechanicals and Fairies exit. Puck remains to deliver the epilogue.

**PUCK**

> If we shadows have offended,
> Think but this, and all is mended,
> That you have but slumber'd here
> While these visions did appear.
> And this weak and idle theme,
> No more yielding but a dream,
> Gentles, do not reprehend:
> if you pardon, we will mend:
> Else the Puck a liar call;
> So, good night unto you all.
> Give me your hands, if we be friends,
> And Robin shall restore amends.

**ALL**

> The end.

PART FOUR: *MIDSUMMER NIGHT'S DREAM*

## Chapter 14: *Midsummer Night's Dream*, 20-Minute Readers' Theatre Version

### CASTING SUGGESTIONS

<u>One reader per part</u>

<u>16 readers</u>
    Reader 1: Narrator 1
    Reader 2: Theseus
    Reader 3: Hippolyta
    Reader 4: Hermia
    Reader 5: Lysander
    Reader 6: Demetrius
    Reader 7: Egeus
    Reader 8: Helena
    Reader 9: Quince
    Reader 10: Bottom
    Reader 11: Flute
    Reader 12: Snug
    Reader 13: Puck
    Reader 14: Oberon
    Reader 15: Titania
    Reader 16 : Narrator 2

<u>Using nine readers with some double casting</u>
    Reader 1 : Narrator 1, Narrator 2
    Reader 2 : Theseus, Oberon
    Reader 3: Hippolyta, Titania
    Reader 4: Hermia, Snug
    Reader 5: Lysander
    Reader 6: Demetrius
    Reader 7: Egeus, Bottom
    Reader 8: Helena, Flute
    Reader 9: Quince, Puck

*Midsummer Night's Dream*

## 20-Minute Readers' Theatre Version

| | |
|---|---|
| \ALL | |
| | Midsummer Night's Dream. |
| SNUG | |
| | By William Shakespeare. |
| QUINCE | |
| | Adapted by John Poulsen. |
| NARRATOR 1 | |
| | The plot of Midsummer Night's Dream revolves around three intertwined sub-plots. The first sub-plot revolves around three sets of lovers. The first couple is, |
| THESEUS | |
| | Theseus the Duke and lord of Athens, who is engaged to marry, |
| HIPPOLYTA | |
| | Hippolyta. Queen of the Amazons. |
| NARRATOR 2 | |
| | The Lovers also include: |
| \HERMIA | |
| | Hermia, who loves |
| LYSANDER | |
| | Lysander, dashingly handsome and beloved of Hermia. |
| HERMIA | |
| | But I am promised by my father to, |
| DEMETRIUS | |
| | Demetrius, dashingly handsome and promised to Hermia. |
| NARRATOR 1 | |
| | Hermia's father, Egeus, demands that Hermia marry Demetrius. |
| EGEUS | |
| | As Hermia is mine, I may dispose of her: Which shall be either to this gentleman Or to her death, according to our law. |

**NARRATOR 2**

He makes Hermia stand before the Duke of Athens, Theseus. Hermia explains.

**HERMIA**

I would my father looked but with my eyes.
I beseech what is the worst that may befall me in this case.
If I refuse to wed Demetrius?

**THESEUS**

Either to die the death or to abjure* (*avoid)
Forever the society of men.

**DEMETRIUS**

Relent, sweet Hermia and Lysander yield.

**LYSANDER**

You have her father's love, Demetrius
Let me have Hermia's; do you marry him.

**NARRATOR 1**

Theseus is the law in Athens and his proclamation that Hermia must obey her father is considered harsh by Hermia and Lysander. They plan their future.

**LYSANDER**

How now my love? why is your cheek so pale?
The course of true love never did run smooth.

**HERMIA**

O spite! To choose love by another's eyes.

**LYSANDER**

Love
Swift as a shadow, short as any dream.

**HERMIA**

If then true lovers have been ever crossed* (*if lovers have ever met difficulty)
Let us teach our trial patience.

**LYSANDER**

I have a widow aunt, that hath no child.
She respects me as her only son.
From Athens is her house remote seven leagues,
There, gentle Hermia, may I marry thee
And to that place the sharp Athenian law
Cannot pursue us.
Steal forth thy father's house tomorrow night

And in the wood, will I stay for thee.

**HERMIA**

I swear to thee by Cupid's strongest bow
Tomorrow truly will I meet with thee.

**NARRATOR 2**

Helena, is Hermia's best friend and in love with Demetrius. Helena
asks Hermia what she does to capture Demetrius's heart.

**HELENA**

Teach me how you look and with what art
You sway the motion of Demetrius' heart.

**HERMIA**

Take comfort, he no more shall see my face.
Lysander and myself will fly this place.

**LYSANDER**

To you our minds we will unfold:
Through Athens' gates have we devised to steal.

**NARRATOR 1**

Hermia and Lysander leave, planning their reunion in the forest.
Helena schemes to gain Demetrius's favour.

**HELENA**

I will go tell Demetrius of fair Hermia's flight
Then to the wood will he tomorrow night.

**NARRATOR 2**

The second sub-plot involves a group of workers or mechanicals who
are preparing to put on a play for the Duke Theseus on his wedding day
four days hence. They are led by Quince.

**QUINCE**

Our play is, 'The most lamentable comedy and most cruel death of
Pyramus and Thisby.' Nick Bottom, the weaver.

**BOTTOM**

Ready. Name what part I am for.

**QUINCE**

You, Nick Bottom, are set down for Pyramus.

**BOTTOM**

What is Pyramus? A lover or a tyrant?

**QUINCE**

A lover that kills himself, most gallant, for love.
Francis Flute, the bellows maker, you must take Thisby on you.

**FLUTE**

What is Thisby? A wandering knight?

**QUINCE**

It is the lady that Pyramus must love.

**FLUTE**

Nay, faith, let me not play a woman. I have a beard coming.

**QUINCE**

Snug, the joiner, you the lion's part.

**SNUG**

Have you the lion's part written? Pray you, if it be, give it me, for I am slow of study.

**QUINCE**

You may do it extempore*, for it is nothing but roaring. *(*improvise)*

**BOTTOM**

Let me play the lion too. I will roar that I will make the Duke say, 'Let him roar again.'

**QUINCE**

A lion among ladies is a most dreadful thing. And you would fright the Duchess and the ladies and were enough to hang us all.

**MECHANICALS**

That would hang us, every mother's son.

**NARRATOR 1**

The mechanicals resolve to meet to rehearse in the same part of the forest to which Hermia, Lysander, Helena, and Demetrius are going.

**NARRATOR 2**

The third plot revolves around the Fairies. Puck is the primary agent of change in this play.

**PUCK**

I am the mischievous Puck. I am that merry wanderer of the night.

**NARRATOR 1**

The King of the Fairies, Oberon and his wife the Queen of the Fairies, Titania, meet in the wood. They are quarreling.

**OBERON**

Ill met by moonlight, proud Titania.

**TITANIA**

What, jealous Oberon! Fairies, skip hence:
I have forsworn* his bed and company. *(*rejected)*

**OBERON**

Am not I thy lord?

**TITANIA**

We shall chide* downright, if I longer stay. *(*fight)*

**NARRATOR 2**

Titania and her servants leave, but Oberon wants to makes his wife
suffer, so he calls Puck.

**OBERON**

My gentle Puck, come hither.
Fetch me that flower;
The juice of it on sleeping eye-lids laid
Will make man or woman madly dote
Upon the next live creature that it sees.*
*(*find me a specific little flower that has magical love inducing powers)*

**PUCK**

I'll put a girdle round about the earth
In forty minutes.*
*(*Puck can fly around the world in 40 minutes)*

**NARRATOR 1**

Puck leaves to find the flower. Oberon plans his torment of his
wife, Titania.

**OBERON**

Having once this juice,
I'll watch Titania when she is asleep,
And drop the liquor of it in her eyes.
But who comes here? I am invisible;
And I will overhear their conference.

**NARRATOR 2**

Oberon is interrupted and observes unseen the entrance of Demetrius
followed by the love sick Helena.

**DEMETRIUS**

I love thee not, therefore pursue me not.
Thou told'st me they were stolen unto this wood;

PART FOUR: *MIDSUMMER NIGHT'S DREAM*

Hence, get thee gone, and follow me no more.

**HELENA**

You draw me, leave you your power to draw,
And I shall have no power to follow you.

**DEMETRIUS**

Tempt not too much the hatred of my spirit;
For I am sick when I do look on thee.

**HELENA**

And I am sick when I look not on you.

**DEMETRIUS**

I'll run from thee and hide me in the brakes,* *(*bushes)*
And leave thee to the mercy of wild beasts.

**HELENA**

The wildest hath not such a heart as you.
Run when you will, the story shall be changed:
The dove pursues the griffin; the mild deer
Makes speed to catch the tiger.

**NARRATOR 1**

Demetrius runs away and Helena follows. Oberon feels pity for Helena
and promises to help her.

**OBERON**

Fare thee well, maid: ere he do leave this grove,
Thou shalt fly and he shall seek thy love.

**NARRATOR 2**

Puck reenters with the flower.

**OBERON**

Hast thou the flower there? Welcome, wanderer.

**PUCK**

Ay, there it is.

**OBERON**

I pray thee, give it me.

**NARRATOR 1**

Oberon decides to drop some of the love potion into Titania's eyes.

**NARRATOR 2**

Puck is instructed to drop some of the love potion into Demetrius's eyes when he sleeps. It is now dark. Lysander and Hermia enter. They are lost.

**LYSANDER**

We'll rest us, Hermia, if you think it good.

**HERMIA**

Good Lysander; for my sake, my dear,
Lie further off yet, do not lie so near.

**NARRATOR 1**

Lysander and Hermia sleep. Puck enters looking for the Athenianyouth into whose eyes he was instructed to drop some of the magic potion.

**PUCK**

Who is here?
Weeds* of Athens he doth wear: (*clothes)
Upon thy eyes I throw
All the power this charm doth owe.
So awake when I am gone;
For I must now to Oberon.

**NARRATOR 2**

Pucks leaves to report to Oberon that he has dripped some drops in the Athenian Youth's eyes. Enter Helena running after Demetrius.

**HELENA**

Who is here? Lysander! on the ground!
Dead? or asleep? I see no blood, no wound.
Lysander if you live, good sir, awake.

**LYSANDER**

And run through fire I will for thy sweet sake.

**NARRATOR 1**

The magic potion has made Lysander fall madly in love with the first person he saw upon waking: Helena.

**HELENA**

Do not say so, Lysander; say not so
What though you love your Hermia? Lord, what though?
Yet Hermia still loves you: then be content.

**LYSANDER**

Content with Hermia! No; I do repent
The tedious minutes I with her have spent.

**HELENA**

Wherefore was I to this keen mockery born?
When at your hands did I deserve this scorn?

**NARRATOR 2**

Helena flees Lysander, seeking Demtrius. Lysander follows.

**NARRATOR 1**

In another part of the forest, Titania goes to sleep and Oberon drops some of the potion into her eyes.

**OBERON**

What thou seest when thou dost wake,
Do it for thy true-love take,
When thou wakest, it is thy dear:
Wake when some vile thing is near.

**NARRATOR 2**

Enter the mechanicals, looking for a place to rehearse their play, *Pyramus and Thisby.*

**BOTTOM**

Are we all met?

**NARRATOR 1**

Puck enters. He speaks an aside to the audience.

**PUCK**

What hempen home-spuns* have we swaggering here, *(*rude and uncouth oafs)*
So near the cradle of the fairy queen?

**NARRATOR 2**

Bottom exits into the forest and Puck changes Bottom to resemble a donkey. Bottom enters with an Ass's-head.

**NARRATOR 2**

The Mechanicals are rehearsing their play, *Pyramus and Thisby,* in another part of the same woods. Bottom has wandered off and is discovered by Puck.

**NARRATOR 1**

Puck changes Bottom to resemble a donkey. Bottom enters with an Ass's head.

**QUNICE**

O monstrous! O strange! we are haunted. Pray, masters! fly, masters! Help!

**NARRATOR 2**

The actors all flee

**QUINCE**

Bless thee, Bottom! bless thee! Thou art translated.*
(*Quince means transformed)

**NARRATOR 2**

leaving Bottom alone.

**BOTTOM**

Why do they run away? This is a knavery of them to make me afeard.

**NARRATOR 2**

Titania wakes and sees Bottom. The magic potion makes her fall in love with the first thing she sees, the Ass-headed Bottom.

**TITANIA**

What angel wakes me from my flowery bed?
I pray thee, gentle mortal, sing again.

**BOTTOM**

Methinks, mistress, you should have little reason
for that: and yet, reason and
love keep little company together now-a-days.

**NARRATOR 1**

Titania takes Bottom with the Ass's head away.

**NARRATOR 2**

Hermia and Demetrius enter.

**DEMETRIUS**

O, why rebuke you him that loves you so?

**HERMIA**

For thou, I fear, hast given me cause to curse,
If thou hast slain Lysander in his sleep.

**DEMETRIUS**

An if I could, what should I get therefore?

**HERMIA**

A privilege never to see me more.

**DEMETRIUS**

There is no following her in this fierce vein:
Here therefore for a while I will remain.

PART FOUR: *MIDSUMMER NIGHT'S DREAM*

**NARRATOR 1**

Hermia leaves and Demetrius, exhausted, lies down and sleeps. Oberon chastises Puck for the error.

**OBERON**

What hast thou done? Thou hast mistaken quite
And laid the love-juice on some true-love's sight.

**PUCK**

I go, I go; look how I go,
Swifter than arrow from the Tartar's bow.

**NARRATOR 2**

Oberon drops the magic potion into Demetrius's eyes.

**NARRATOR 1**

Puck re-enters followed by Helena and Lysander.

**PUCK**

Captain of our fairy band,
Helena is here at hand;
Shall we their fond pageant see?
Lord, what fools these mortals be!

**OBERON**

Stand aside
the noise they make
Will cause Demetrius to awake.

**HELENA**

These vows are Hermia's: will you give her over?

**LYSANDER**

I had no judgment when to her I swore.

**NARRATOR 2**

Suddenly Demetrius wakes, sees Helena, and falls madly in love.

**DEMETRIUS**

O Helena, goddess, nymph, perfect, divine!
To what, my love, shall I compare thine eyne?

**HELENA**

O spite! I see you all are bent
To set against me for your merriment.

**NARRATOR 1**

Hermia enters.

**HERMIA**

What love could press Lysander from my side?

**LYSANDER**

Fair Helena.

**HERMIA**

You speak not as you think it cannot be.

**HELENA**

Lo, she is one of this confederacy!
Now I perceive they have conjoin'd all three
To fashion this false sport, in spite of me.

**HERMIA**

I am amazed at your passionate words.
I scorn you not
it seems that you scorn me.

**LYSANDER**

Away, you! Hang off, thou cat, thou burr! vile thing, let loose,
Or I will shake thee from me like a serpent!

**DEMETRIUS**

Lysander, keep thy Hermia: I will none.
If ever I love her, all that love is gone.

**LYSANDER**

Now Demetrius, follow, if thou darest, to try whose right,
Of thine or mine, is most in Helena.

**DEMETRIUS**

Follow! nay, I'll go with thee, cheek by jowl.

**NARRATOR 2**

Demetrius and Lysander leave to fight. Helena though taller is
frightened of Hermia and runs away.

**HELENA**

I will not trust you, I,
Nor longer stay in your curst company.
Your hands than mine are quicker for a fray,
My legs are longer though, to run away.

**HERMIA**

I am amazed, and know not what to say.

PART FOUR: *MIDSUMMER NIGHT'S DREAM*

**NARRATOR 1**

Hermia leaves following Helena. Oberon, having seen the quarrel, turns to Puck for explanation.

**OBERON**

This is thy negligence
Lead these testy rivals so astray
As one come not within another's way.
Till sleep doth creep:
Then crush this herb into Lysander's eye.

**NARRATOR 2**

In the dark, Puck now taunts Demetrius and Lysander leading them through the forest till they are so exhausted they fall to the ground and sleep. Helena enters and also sleeps.

**PUCK**

Here she comes, curst and sad:
Cupid is a knavish lad,
Thus to make poor females mad.

**HERMIA**

Here will I rest me till the break of day.

**NARRATOR 1**

All four are sleeping soundly. Puck squeezes the magic potion into Lysander's eyes.

**PUCK**

On the ground sleep sound:
I'll apply to your eye,
Gentle lover, remedy
Jack shall have Jill; nought shall go ill.

**NARRATOR 2**

Oberon regrets his cruelty to his wife and resolves to remove the spell.

**OBERON**

I will release the fairy queen.
Be as thou wast wont to be;
See as thou wast wont to see:
Now, my Titania; wake you, my sweet queen.

**TITANIA**

My Oberon! what visions have I seen!
Methought I was enamour'd of an ass.

**OBERON**

Silence awhile. Robin*, take off this head.
*(*Puck is also called Robin Goodfellow)*

**NARRATOR 1**

Puck removes the Ass's head from Bottom.

**PUCK**

Now, when thou wakest, with thine own fool's eyes peep.

**NARRATOR 2**

Titania, Oberon and Puck exit. The Duke of Athens, Theseus enters.

**THESEUS**

I pray you all, stand up.
How comes this gentle concord in the world,

**DEMETRIUS**

My good lord, I know not by what power,—
But by some power it is,—my love to Hermia,
Melted as the snow, Is only Helena.
To her, my lord, am I betrothed.

**THESEUS**

Fair lovers, you are fortunately met:
Away with us to Athens; three and three,
We'll hold a feast in great solemnity.

**NARRATOR 1**

The Lovers leave for the Duke's palace.

**NARRATOR 2**

Bottom without the ass's head, awakes and goes to Quince's house where the other Mechanicals are waiting.

**QUINCE**

Bottom! O most courageous day! O most happy hour!

**BOTTOM**

Get your apparel together, for the short and the long is, our play is preferred.

**NARRATOR 1**

The last act takes place in Theseus's palace. Enter The Lovers.

**THESEUS**

Joy, gentle friends! joy and fresh days of love
Accompany your hearts!

**NARRATOR 2**

The Mechanicals perform Pyramus and Thisbe.

**FLUTE**

Where is my love?

**THESEUS**

Here comes a lion.

**SNUG**

You, ladies, you, whose gentle hearts do fear
The smallest monstrous mouse that creeps on floor,
May now perchance both quake and tremble here,
When lion rough in wildest rage doth roar.
Then know that I, one Snug the joiner, am.

**THESEUS**

A very gentle beast, of a good conscience.

**SNUG**

Roar Oh.

**NARRATOR 1**

Thisby runs off dropping her coat.

**DEMETRIUS**

Well roared, Lion.

**THESEUS**

Well run, Thisbe.

**NARRATOR 2**

The Lion shakes Thisbe's coat,, and exits.

**DEMETRIUS**

And then came Pyramus.

**HIPPOLYTA**

I pity the man.

**PYRAMUS (BOTTOM)**

O wherefore, Nature, didst thou lions frame?
Since lion vile hath here deflower'd my dear:
Which is—no, no—which was the fairest dame
That lived, that loved, that liked, that look'd with cheer.
Come, tears, confound;
Out, sword, and wound Pyramus.

**NARRATOR 1**

Pyramus stabs himself.

**PYRAMUS (BOTTOM)**

Thus die I, thus, thus, thus.
Now am I dead,
Now am I fled.

**NARRATOR 2**

Pyramus dies. Re-enter Thisby.

**THISBE (FLUTE)**

Asleep, my love? What, dead, my dove?
Speak, speak. Quite dumb? Dead, dead? A tomb
Come, trusty sword;
Come, blade.

**NARRATOR 1**

Thisby stabs herself.

**THISBE (FLUTE)**

And, farewell, friends; Thus Thisby ends:
Adieu, adieu, adieu.

**NARRATOR 2**

And Thisby dies.

**THESEUS**

The iron tongue of midnight hath told twelve:
Lovers, to bed; 'tis almost fairy time.

**NARRATOR 1**

The Lovers, Mechanicals and Fairies exit. Puck remains to deliver the epilogue.

**PUCK**

If we shadows have offended,
Think but this, and all is mended,
That you have but slumbered here
While these visions did appear.
Give me your hands, if we be friends,
And Robin shall restore amends.

**ALL**

The end.

## Chapter 15: *Midsummer Night's Dream:* Readers' Theatre Director's Script

This *Director's Script* has suggestions for directing the following abridged Readers' Theatre production of *Midsummer Night's Dream*. The suggestions correspond with the *Midsummer Night's Dream Readers' Theatre 20-Minute Version*. The 20-minute version of *Midsummer Night's Dream* has a running time of about 20 minutes — from the time the actors start their entrance to when they walk off stage.

### INTRODUCTION

Bold indicates suggested direction. If there is no bold directorial suggestion connected to the line, the actors should briefly freeze while others say their lines and interpret their own lines as they see fit. They should use off stage focus, by delivering the line straight ahead.

Text without bold or italics are the words to be spoken. Print a copy of the script *(Midsummer Night's Dream Readers' Theatre 20-Minute Version)* for each reader. The first rehearsal should be a read through where actors read their assigned parts. After the read through, performers should highlight or underline their lines. If an actor has more than one character, lines for each should be highlighted in a different colour. Have readers write in pencil directorial notes (such as when to stand, sit, and move forward), as well as clarification of line meaning or line intention.

Italics in smaller font indicate meaning. Sometimes a specific word is defined, other times the phrase is clarified. The asterisk follows the word or phrase. Left justified on the next line is the clarification.

The casting suggestions below require as few as nine and as many as 16 actors. If you have 16 performers there are parts for all. Using double casting as few as nine performers can be accommodated.

### DIRECTORIAL PARAMETERS

Actors use off-stage focus for this presentation until the very end. They assume that all action takes place toward the audience. If they are speaking to someone they pretend the person is standing in front of them.

The performing area is pre-set. Before the audience arrives the performers' chairs and stools are arranged in a straight line. Put about one meter between each seat. The characters enter and sit on chairs set sideways with the chair-backs towards stage left. Narrators sit at the ends of the line, farthest stage right and left, on stools that are slightly higher than the performers sitting on chairs. If double casting, the minimal costume pieces needed to clarify a character change are arranged under the appropriate chairs.

If the audience is sitting on the floor, stretch a rope or lay some tape to indicate where the audience is to sit. If using chairs, all audience seats will be set out.

The actors' seating is pre-arranged with the primary consideration having the Lovers sit with the Lovers, Mechanicals sit with the Mechanicals, and the Fairies sit with the Fairies.

Narrators will not use Back to Audience (BTA) for exits or Front to Audience (FTA) for entrances. They usually use the Freeze convention, so that when they finish saying a line they will stop moving until their next line. The direction to "freeze" in practical terms means that there will be some minimum movement as the actors check their scripts.

As much as possible the actors should say their lines directly to the audience. Reading is acceptable but speaking directly forward using offstage focus can improve the production by making actors easier to see and hear.

Front to Audience (FTA) direction requires that actors spin to face the audience before their line. Generally actors should be spinning and breathing in as the previous speaker is saying the last words of their line. For example, Helena is the first to spin FTA She should spin as the Narrator is saying "...to capture...". She should also be taking in air so she can start her line loudly and slowly as the Narrator finishes saying "... Demetrius's heart."

Drop Head (DH) and Raise Head (RH) direction is used when the performer will be needed shortly. The actors drop their heads at the end of their line and bring their heads up as the final words in the previous line are being said. The raising of the head should be accompanied with an intake of breath so that the next line can be said immediately and loudly. Oberon is one of the first to use DH/RH convention for entering. He is about to reprimand Puck and has been DH for more than a page but the pace at this point in the script is fast and a BTA/FTA will probably be too distracting. His RH is motivated by at least annoyance, perhaps even anger. Oberon should breathe in and raise his head briskly as the Narrator says,

"...chastises Puck for...". He needs to be "in character" with the motivation of anger and the objective of reprimanding Puck as he raises his head. This should draw audience attention. Oberon then starts speaking sharply as the Narrator finishes saying "...the error."

However, in this script the RH convention is often used to bring a character on stage to listen to instructions. In these cases the character should RH with energy and a movement. For example, Oberon commands, "My gentle Puck, come hither." Puck should turn and be ready for instruction by cocking his head or even bringing his hand to his ear.

## CASTING SUGGESTIONS

Casting can be fluid up until performance. At performance, should you have fewer than the actors originally cast, consider using some or all of the following double casting suggestions. It is important that the actors taking on extra parts highlight their new lines in a different and distinctive manner.

<u>One reader per part</u>

<u>16 readers</u>
    Reader 1: Narrator
    Reader 2: Theseus
    Reader 3: Hippolyta
    Reader 4: Hermia
    Reader 5: Lysander
    Reader 6: Demetrius
    Reader 7: Egeus
    Reader 8: Helena
    Reader 9: Quince
    Reader 10: Bottom
    Reader 11: Flute
    Reader 12: Snug
    Reader 13: Puck
    Reader 14: Oberon
    Reader 15: Titania
    Reader 16 : Narrator 2

<u>Using nine readers with some double casting</u>

Reader 1: Narrator 1, Narrator 2

Reader 2: Theseus, Oberon

Reader 3: Hippolyta, Titania

Reader 4: Hermia, Snug

Reader 5: Lysander, Wall

Reader 6: Demetrius

Reader 7: Egeus, Bottom

Reader 8: Helena, Flute

Reader 9: Quince, Puck

## ENTRANCE

Actors enter as themselves chatting about the day's events. They enter in small groups of two or three. As soon as they arrive at the chair or stool designated for them they stop talking and wait. Hippolyta will wave her script forward as the signal to sit and turn. She will then wave her script forward again to signal the saying of the title in unison.

**Bold = suggested direction.**

Regular = text to be spoken by the actor.

*Italics = *definition or clarification of line meaning.*

## *MIDSUMMER NIGHT'S DREAM* READERS' THEATRE DIRECTOR'S SCRIPT

**ALL**

Midsummer Night's Dream.
**(All but Snug, Quince, Theseus, Hippolyta, Narrators, Hermia, Lysander, Demetrius and Egeus turn to face upstage and then sit still, BTA)**

**SNUG**

By William Shakespeare.
**(BTA)**

**QUINCE**

Adapted by John Poulsen.
**(BTA)**

**NARRATOR 1**

The plot of Midsummer Night's Dream revolves around three intertwined sub-plots. The first sub-plot revolves around three sets of lovers. The first couple is,
**(Freeze. Narrators freeze after each line unless instructed otherwise.)**

**THESEUS**

Theseus the Duke and lord of Athens, who is engaged to marry,

**HIPPOLYTA**

Hippolyta. Queen of the Amazons.
**(BTA)**

**NARRATOR 2**

The Lovers also include:

**HERMIA**

Hermia, who loves

**LYSANDER**

**(Stands, nods head)**
Lysander, dashingly handsome and beloved of Hermia.
**(Sits)**

**HERMIA**

But I am promised by my father to,

**DEMETRIUS**

(Stands, nods head)
Demetrius, dashingly handsome and promised to Hermia.
(Sits)

**NARRATOR 1**

Hermia's father, Egeus, demands that Hermia marry Demetrius.

**EGEUS**

As Hermia is mine, I may dispose of her;
Which shall be either to this gentleman
Or to her death, according to our law.
(BTA)

**NARRATOR 2**

He makes Hermia stand before the Duke of Athens, Theseus. Hermia
explains.

**HERMIA**

I would my father looked but with my eyes.
I beseech what is the worst that may befall me in this case.
If I refuse to wed Demetrius?

**THESEUS**

Either to die the death or to abjure* (*avoid)
Forever the society of men.
(BTA)

**DEMETRIUS**

Relent, sweet Hermia and Lysander yield.
(BTA)

**LYSANDER**

You have her father's love, Demetrius
Let me have Hermia's; do you marry him.

**NARRATOR 1**

Theseus is the law in Athens and his proclamation that Hermia must
obey her father is considered harsh by Hermia and Lysander. They plan
their future.

**LYSANDER**

How now my love? why is your cheek so pale?
The course of true love never did run smooth.

**HERMIA**

O spite! To choose love by another's eyes.

**Lysander**

Love
Swift as a shadow, short as any dream.

**Hermia**

If then true lovers have been ever crossed* (*if lovers have ever met difficulty)
Let us teach our trial patience.

**Lysander**

I have a widow aunt, that hath no child.
She respects me as her only son.
From Athens is her house remote seven leagues,
There, gentle Hermia, may I marry thee
And to that place the sharp Athenian law
Cannot pursue us.
Steal forth thy father's house tomorrow night
And in the wood, will I stay for thee.

**Hermia**

I swear to thee by Cupid's strongest bow
Tomorrow truly will I meet with thee.

**Narrator 2**

Helena, is Hermia's best friend and in love with Demetrius. Helena
asks Hermia what she does to capture Demetrius's heart.

**Helena**

**(FTA: spin to Face the Audience, deliver the first words clearly.)**
Teach me how you look and with what art
You sway the motion of Demetrius' heart.

**Hemia**

Take comfort, he no more shall see my face.
Lysander and myself will fly this place.

**Lysander**

To you our minds we will unfold:
Through Athens' gates have we devised to steal.
**(Lysander and Hermia BTA)**

**Narrator 1**

Hermia and Lysander leave, planning their reunion in the forest.
Helena schemes to gain Demetrius's favour.

**Helena**

I will go tell Demetrius of fair Hermia's flight
Then to the wood will he tomorrow night.
**(BTA)**

**NARRATOR 2**

The second sub-plot involves a group of workers or Mechanicals who are preparing to put on a play for the Duke Theseus on his wedding day, four days hence. They are led by Quince.

**QUINCE**

(FTA)
Our play is, 'The most lamentable comedy and most cruel death of Pyramus and Thisby.' Nick Bottom, the weaver.

**BOTTOM**

(FTA)
Ready. Name what part I am for.

**QUINCE**

You, Nick Bottom, are set down for Pyramus.

**BOTTOM**

What is Pyramus? A lover or a tyrant?

**QUINCE**

A lover that kills himself, most gallant, for love.
Francis Flute, the bellows maker, you must take Thisby on you.

**FLUTE**

(FTA)
What is Thisby? A wandering knight?

**QUINCE**

It is the lady that Pyramus must love.

**FLUTE**

Nay, faith, let me not play a woman. I have a beard coming.

**QUINCE**

Snug, the joiner, you the lion's part.

**SNUG**

(FTA)
Have you the lion's part written? Pray you, if it be, give it me, for I am slow of study.

**QUINCE**

You may do it extempore*, for it is nothing but roaring. (*improvise)

**BOTTOM**

Let me play the lion too. I will roar that I will make the Duke say, 'Let him roar again.'

**QUINCE**

A lion among ladies is a most dreadful thing. And you would fright the Duchess and the ladies and were enough to hang us all.

**MECHANICALS**

That would hang us, every mother's son.
**(Mechanicals BTA)**

**NARRATOR 1**

The Mechanicals resolve to meet to rehearse in the same part of the forest to which Hermia, Lysander, Helena, and Demetrius are going.

**NARRATOR 2**

The third plot revolves around the Fairies. Puck is the primary agent of change in this play.

**PUCK**

**(FTA)**
I am the mischievous Puck. I am that merry wanderer of the night.
**(DH: Drop Head and freeze.)**

**NARRATOR 1**

The King of the Fairies, Oberon and his wife the Queen of the Fairies, Titania, meet in the wood. They are quarreling.

**OBERON**

**(FTA)**
Ill met by moonlight, proud Titania.

**TITANIA**

**(FTA)**
What, jealous Oberon! Fairies, skip hence:
I have forsworn* his bed and company. (*rejected)

**OBERON**

Am not I thy lord?

**TITANIA**

We shall chide* downright, if I longer stay. (*fight)
**(BTA)**

**NARRATOR 2**

Titania and her servants leave, but Oberon wants to make his wife suffer, so he calls Puck.

**OBERON**

My gentle Puck, come hither.
**(RH: Puck raises head and listens.)**

Fetch me that flower;
The juice of it on sleeping eye-lids laid
Will make or man or woman madly dote
Upon the next live creature that it sees.

**PUCK**

I'll put a girdle round about the earth
In forty minutes.*
**(DH)**
*(*Puck can fly around the world in 40 minutes)*

**NARRATOR 1**

Puck leaves to find the flower. Oberon plans his torment of his wife,
Titania.

**OBERON**

Having once this juice,
I'll watch Titania when she is asleep,
And drop the liquor of it in her eyes.
But who comes here? I am invisible;
And I will overhear their conference.
**(Freeze)**

**NARRATOR 2**

Oberon is interrupted and observes unseen the entrance of Demetrius
followed by the love sick Helena.

**DEMETRIUS**

**(FTA)**
I love thee not, therefore pursue me not.
Thou told'st me they were stolen unto this wood;
Hence, get thee gone, and follow me no more.

**HELENA**

**(FTA)**
You draw me, leave you your power to draw,
And I shall have no power to follow you.

**DEMETRIUS**

Tempt not too much the hatred of my spirit;
For I am sick when I do look on thee.

**HELENA**

And I am sick when I look not on you.

**DEMETRIUS**

I'll run from thee and hide me in the brakes,* *(*bushes)*
And leave thee to the mercy of wild beasts.

PART FOUR: MIDSUMMER NIGHT'S DREAM

**(BTA)**

**HELENA**

The wildest hath not such a heart as you.
Run when you will, the story shall be changed:
The dove pursues the griffin; the mild deer
Makes speed to catch the tiger.
**(BTA)**

**NARRATOR 1**

Demetrius runs away and Helena follows. Oberon feels pity for Helena
and promises to help her.

**OBERON**

Fare thee well, maid: ere he do leave this grove,
Thou shalt fly and he shall seek thy love.

**NARRATOR 2**

Puck reenters with the flower.
**(Puck RH)**

**OBERON**

Hast thou the flower there? Welcome, wanderer.

**PUCK**

Ay, there it is.

**OBERON**

I pray thee, give it me.
**(BTA)**

**NARRATOR 1**

Oberon decides to drop some of the love potion into Titania's eyes.

**NARRATOR 2**

Puck is instructed to drop some of the love potion into Demetrius's
eyes when he sleeps. It is now dark. Lysander and Hermia enter. They
are lost.

**LYSANDER**

**(FTA)**
We'll rest us, Hermia, if you think it good.

**HERMIA**

**(FTA)**
Good Lysander; for my sake, my dear,
Lie further off yet, do not lie so near.
**(Hermia BTA)**

**NARRATOR 1**

Lysander and Hermia sleep. Puck enters looking for the Athenian youth into whose eyes, he was instructed to drop some of the magic potion.
**(Lysander lies back in his chair with eyes almost closed.)**

**PUCK**

Who is here?
Weeds* of Athens he doth wear: *(*clothes*)* Upon thy eyes I throw
All the power this charm doth owe
**(Puck stands, stretches forward, and mimes dropping some drops into Lysander's eyes. Lysander should react as though in his sleep.)**
So awake when I am gone;
For I must now to Oberon.
**(Sits and DH)**

**NARRATOR 2**

Pucks leaves to report to Oberon that he has dripped some drops in the Athenian Youth's eyes. Enter Helena running after Demetrius.

**HELENA**

**(FTA)**
Who is here? Lysander! on the ground!
**(Stand and kneel forward. Mime shaking Lysander.)**
Dead? or asleep? I see no blood, no wound.
Lysander if you live, good sir, awake.

**LYSANDER**

**(Sits up.)**
And run through fire I will for thy sweet sake.

**NARRATOR 1**

The magic potion has made Lysander fall madly in love with the first person he saw upon waking: Helena.

**HELENA**

**(Stand facing forward.)**
Do not say so, Lysander; say not so
What though you love your Hermia? Lord, what though?
Yet Hermia still loves you: then be content.

**LYSANDER**

**(Stand and kneel with hand outstretched.)**
Content with Hermia! No; I do repent
The tedious minutes I with her have spent.

*PART FOUR: MIDSUMMER NIGHT'S DREAM*

**HELENA**

Wherefore was I to this keen mockery born?
When at your hands did I deserve this scorn?
**(Helena and Lysander sit and BTA)**

**NARRATOR 2**

Helena flees Lysander, seeking Demtrius. Lysander follows.

**NARRATOR 1**

In another part of the forest, Titania
**(Titania FTA, stretches and sleeps by dropping head back and closing eyes. Reacts as though asleep to drops in eyes.)**
goes to sleep and Oberon drops some of the potion into her eyes.

**OBERON**

**(FTA stand and reach forward as though dropping potion in Titania's eyes.)**
What thou seest when thou dost wake,
Do it for thy true-love take,
When thou wakest, it is thy dear:
Wake when some vile thing is near.
**(Oberon sits DH Titania remains stretched on chair with head back)**

**NARRATOR 2**

The Mechanicals are rehearsing their play, *Pyramus and Thisby,* in another part of the same woods. Bottom has wandered off and is discovered by Puck.
**(Bottom FTA)**

**NARRATOR 1**

Puck changes Bottom to resemble a donkey. Bottom enters with an Ass's head.

**QUNICE**

**(FTA)**
O monstrous! O strange! we are haunted. Pray,
masters! fly, masters! Help!

**NARRATOR 2**

The actors all flee

**QUINCE**

Bless thee, Bottom! bless thee! Thou art translated.*
(*= Quince means transformed)
**(BTA)**

**NARRATOR 2**

leaving Bottom alone.

**BOTTOM**

Why do they run away? This is a knavery of them to make me afeard.
**(Bottom has been turned into an ass and should make some of his words sound as though he is braying. He ends his sentence with Hee Haw, Hee Haw, Hee Haw.)**

**NARRATOR 2**

Titania wakes and sees Bottom. The magic potion makes her fall in love with the first thing she sees, the Ass-headed Bottom.

**TITANIA**

**(Sits up.)**
What angel wakes me from my flowery bed?
I pray thee, gentle mortal, sing again.

**BOTTOM**

Methinks, mistress, you should have little reason
for that: and yet, reason and love keep little company together
now-a-days.

**NARRATOR 1**

Titania takes Bottom with the Ass's head away.
**(Titania and Bottom — BTA)**

**NARRATOR 2**

Hermia and Demetrius enter.

**DEMETRIUS**

**(FTA)**
O, why rebuke you him that loves you so?

**HERMIA**

**(FTA)**
For thou, I fear, hast given me cause to curse,
If thou hast slain Lysander in his sleep.

**DEMETRIUS**

An if I could, what should I get therefore?

**HERMIA**

A privilege never to see me more.
**(DH)**

**DEMETRIUS**

There is no following her in this fierce vein:

Here therefore for a while I will remain.
**(Stretches on chair and mimes going to sleep.)**

**NARRATOR 1**

Hermia leaves and Demetrius, exhausted, lies down and sleeps. Oberon chastises Puck for the error.

**OBERON**

**(RH)**
What hast thou done? Thou hast mistaken quite
And laid the love-juice on some true-love's sight.

**PUCK**

**(RH)**
I go, I go; look how I go,
Swifter than arrow from the Tartar's bow.
**(Oberon reaches forward and mimes dripping potion into Demetrius's eyes.)**

**NARRATOR 2**

Oberon drips the magic potion into Demetrius's eyes.

**NARRATOR 1**

Puck re-enters followed by Helena and Lysander.

**PUCK**

Captain of our fairy band,
Helena is here at hand;
Shall we their fond pageant see?
Lord, what fools these mortals be!

**OBERON**

Stand aside
the noise they make
Will cause Demetrius to awake.
**(DH)**

**HELENA**

**(FTA)**
These vows are Hermia's: will you give her over?

**LYSANDER**

**(FTA)**
I had no judgment when to her I swore.

**NARRATOR 2**

Suddenly Demetrius wakes, sees Helena, and falls madly in love.

**DEMETRIUS**

(Wakes and sits forward.)
O Helena, goddess, nymph, perfect, divine!
To what, my love, shall I compare thine eyne?

**HELENA**

O spite! I see you all are bent
To set against me for your merriment.

**NARRATOR 1**

Hermia enters.

**HERMIA**

(RH)
What love could press Lysander from my side?

**LYSANDER**

Fair Helena.

**HERMIA**

You speak not as you think: it cannot be.

**HELENA**

(Stand as though to get away from the other three.)
Lo, she is one of this confederacy!
Now I perceive they have conjoin'd all three
To fashion this false sport, in spite of me.

**HERMIA**

(Stand as though to explain.)
I am amazed at your passionate words.
I scorn you not: it seems that you scorn me.

**LYSANDER**

(Stand as though to protect Helena.)
Away, you! Hang off, thou cat, thou burr! vile thing, let loose,
Or I will shake thee from me like a serpent!

**DEMETRIUS**

(Stand as though to confront Lysander.))
Lysander, keep thy Hermia
I will none.
If ever I love her, all that love is gone.

**LYSANDER**

Now Demetrius, follow, if thou darest, to try whose right,
Of thine or mine, is most in Helena.

**DEMETRIUS**

Follow! nay, I'll go with thee, cheek by jowl.
**(Lysander and Demetrius stare straight ahead in anger, then with a snort they turn, sit and freeze.)**

**NARRATOR 2**

Demetrius and Lysander leave to fight. Helena though taller is frightened of Hermia and runs away.

**HELENA**

**(Step forward)**
I will not trust you, I,
Nor longer stay in your curst company.
Your hands than mine are quicker for a fray,
My legs are longer though, to run away.
**(Pivot, walk to chair, sit and freeze.)**

**HERMIA**

I am amazed, and know not what to say.
**(Hermia pivots, walks to chair, sits and freezes.)**

**NARRATOR 1**

Hermia leaves following Helena. Oberon, having seen the quarrel, turns to Puck for explanation.

**OBERON**

**(Puck and Oberon — RH)**
This is thy negligence
Lead these testy rivals so astray
As one come not within another's way.
Till sleep doth creep:
Then crush this herb into Lysander's eye.

**NARRATOR 2**

In the dark, Puck now taunts Demetrius and Lysander
**(Demetrius and Lysander stand. They step forward as though exhausted and then fall slowly to the ground.)**
leading them through the forest till they are so exhausted they fall to the ground and sleep.
**(Helena stands. She is tired and stumbles forward and sinks slowly to the ground.)**
Helena enters and also sleeps.

**PUCK**

Here she comes, curst and sad:
Cupid is a knavish lad,
Thus to make poor females mad.

**HERMIA**

**(Stands, stumbles forward, and sinks to the ground.)**
Here will I rest me till the break of day.

**NARRATOR 1**

All four are sleeping soundly. Puck squeezes the magic potion into Lysander's eyes.

**PUCK**

**(Puck stands, reaches forward and mimes dropping some potion into Lysander's eyes. Freeze.)**
On the ground sleep sound:
I'll apply to your eye,
Gentle lover, remedy
Jack shall have Jill; nought shall go ill.

**NARRATOR 2**

Oberon regrets his cruelty to his wife and resolves to remove the spell.

**OBERON**

I will release the fairy queen.
Be as thou wast wont to be;
See as thou wast wont to see:
Now, my Titania; wake you, my sweet queen.

**TITANIA**

**(Titania FTA)**
My Oberon! what visions have I seen!
Methought I was enamour'd of an ass.
**(DH)**

**OBERON**

Silence awhile. Robin*, take off this head.
*(*Puck is also called Robin Goodfellow)*

**NARRATOR 1**

Puck removes the Ass's head from Bottom.

**PUCK**

**(Bottom FTA Closes eyes. Puck, still standing, mimes removing a head from Bottom.)**
Now, when thou wakest, with thine own fool's eyes peep.
**(Sits. Puck, Oberon, Titania BTA)**

**NARRATOR 2**

Titania, Oberon and Puck exit. The Duke of Athens, Theseus enters.

**THESEUS**

**(FTA)**
I pray you all, stand up.
How comes this gentle concord in the world?

**DEMETRIUS**

**(Demetrius, Helena, Lysander and Hermia kneel facing audience.)**
My good lord, I know not by what power,—
But by some power it is,—my love to Hermia,
Melted as the snow, Is only Helena.
To her, my lord, am I betrothed.
Theseus
Fair lovers, you are fortunately met:
Away with us to Athens; three and three,
We'll hold a feast in great solemnity.
**(Demetrius, Helena, Lysander and Hermia turn and sit where they are facing upstage with their backs to the audience.)**

**NARRATOR 1**

The Lovers leave for the Duke's palace.

**NARRATOR 2**

Bottom without the ass's head, awakes and goes to Quince's house where the other Mechanicals are waiting.

**QUINCE**

**(FTA)**
Bottom! O most courageous day! O most happy hour!
**(Freeze)**

**BOTTOM**

**(FTA)**
Get your apparel together, for the short and the long is, our play is preferred.
**(Freeze)**

**NARRATOR 1**

The last act takes place in Theseus's palace. Enter The Lovers.

**THESEUS**

**(Hippolyta FTA Theseus and Hippolyta stand.)**
Joy, gentle friends! joy and fresh days of love
Accompany your hearts!
**(Theseus and Hippolyta sit with the other lovers facing upstage.)**

**NARRATOR 2**

The Mechanicals perform Pyramus and Thisbe.

**FLUTE**

(FTA Stands.)
Where is my love?

**THESEUS**

(The Lovers whose backs are now to the audience will have lines in between the Mechanicals' performance. The convention of offstage focus is removed for them until the end. When they speak they should turn their head and speak to the other Lovers.)
Here comes a lion.

**SNUG**

(FTA Stands.)
You, ladies, you, whose gentle hearts do fear
The smallest monstrous mouse that creeps on floor,
May now perchance both quake and tremble here,
When lion rough in wildest rage doth roar.
Then know that I, one Snug the joiner, am.

**THESEUS**

A very gentle beast, of a good conscience.

**SNUG**

Roar Oh.

**NARRATOR 1**

Thisby runs off dropping her coat.

**DEMETRIUS**

Well roared, Lion.

**THESEUS**

(Loudly)
Well run, Thisbe.

**NARRATOR 2**

The Lion shakes Thisbe's coat, and exits.
(Snug mimes chewing a coat. Sits. DH)

**DEMETRIUS**

And then came Pyramus.

**HIPPOLYTA**

I pity the man.

**BOTTOM**

**(RH Stands.)**
O wherefore, Nature, didst thou lions frame?
Since lion vile hath here deflower'd my dear:
Which is—no, no—which was the fairest dame
That lived, that loved, that liked, that look'd with cheer.
Come, tears, confound;
Out, sword, and wound Pyramus.

**NARRATOR 1**

Pyramus stabs himself.

**BOTTOM**

Thus die I, thus, thus, thus.
Now am I dead,
Now am I fled.
**(Dies, slowly falling to the ground.)**

**NARRATOR 2**

Pyramus dies. Re-enter Thisby.

**FLUTE**

Asleep, my love? What, dead, my dove?
Speak, speak. Quite dumb? Dead, dead? A tomb
Come, trusty sword;
Come, blade.

**NARRATOR 1**

Thisby stabs herself.

**FLUTE**

And, farewell, friends; Thus Thisby ends:
Adieu, adieu, adieu.
**(Dies, slowly falling to the ground.)**

**NARRATOR 2**

And Thisby dies.

**THESEUS**

The iron tongue of midnight hath told twelve:
Lovers, to bed; 'tis almost fairy time.

**NARRATOR 1**

The Lovers, Mechanicals and Fairies exit. Puck remains to deliver the epilogue.

PUCK

(Lovers turn to face the audience still sitting. Puck walks forward toward the audience. Stopping just before the Lovers sitting on the floor. Bottom and Flute sit up on the floor and face audience. All other performers FTA.)
If we shadows have offended,
Think but this, and all is mended,
That you have but slumber'd here
While these visions did appear.
Give me your hands, if we be friends,
And Robin shall restore amends.

ALL

(All stand in a single line. Grasp hands and in unison say…)
The end.
(In unison raise hands together and bow. Exit stage right and left in small groups, chatting as though good friends.)

## Epilogue

Shakespeare wrote about human experience that included the extremes of love and hate, joy and sadness, life and death. The plays all deal with the emotions and conundrums that face us every day. We may not have to deal, like Hamlet, with the murder of a father and a visit by a ghost, but we do have to examine our lives and determine our future.

The essence of this book is contained in Miranda's speech from *The Tempest*. She has been marooned on an island with very few other beings. Her loneliness and reduced world is about to be opened. She has just met new people and her optimism concerning what is about to come is sketched by Shakespeare in a few strokes of the pen:

**MIRANDA**

O, wonder!
How many goodly creatures are there here!
How beauteous mankind is! O brave new world,
That has such people in't!

# Bibliography

Barnet, Sylvan. "Introduction" in Wolfgang Clemen, ed. *A Midsummer Night's Dream,* Toronto: Signet Classic Shakespeare, 1963.

Bealey, Betty "The Sources of Hamlet" in *Hamlet* Toronto: Longmans Canada Limited, 1963.

Boyce, Charles. *The Wordsworth Dictionary of Shakespeare.* Hertfordshire, England: Wordsworth Reference, 1990.

Boyce, Charles. *Shakespeare A to Z: The Essential Reference to his Plays, his Poems, his Life and Times, and More.* New York: Roundtable Press, 1990.

Brockett, Oscar. *History of the Theatre.* 4th ed. Toronto: Allyn and Bacon, 1982.

Brooks, Keith, Eugene Bahn, and LaMont Okey. *The Communicative Act of Oral Interpretation.* Boston: Allyn and Bacon,1967.

Bryson, Bill. *Shakespeare: The Illustrated and Updated Edition.* New York: Atlas Books, 2009.

Bullough, G., ed. *Narrative and Dramatic Sources of Shakespeare, Vol. 1: Early Comedies, Poems, Romeo and Juliet.* New York: Columbia University Press, 1964.

Calderwood, James. *Twayne's New Critical Introductions to Shakespeare.* New York: Twayne Publishers, 1992.

Coger, Leslie Irene and Melvin R. White. *Readers Theatre Handbook: a Dramatic Approach to Literature,* rev. ed. Glenview, IL: Scott, Foresman and Company, 1973.

Dalby, Andrew. *Rediscovering Homer.* New York: Norton, 2006.

Deighton, Kenneth. "Introduction and Notes" in *Romeo and Juliet.* London: Macmillan, 1947.

Dobson, Michael and Stanley Wells, eds. *The Oxford Companion to Shakespeare.* Oxford University Press, 2001.

Erne, Lukas, ed. *The First Quarto of Romeo and Juliet.* Cambridge University Press, 2007.

Evans, Bertrand. *Shakespeare's Tragic Practice*. Oxford: Clarendon Press, 1979.

Fairchild, Arthur. *Shakespeare and the Tragic Theme*. Folcroft, PA: Folcroft Press, 1969.

Shakespeare, William. *Romeo and Juliet*. First and Second Quartos. British Library Board, http://special-1.bl.uk/treasures/SiqDiscovery/ui/record2.aspx?Source=text&LHCopy=79&LHPage=1&RHCopy=80&RHPage=1

Frye, Roland. *Shakespeare's Life and Times: A Pictorial Record*. Princeton University Press, 1967.

Gibbons, Brian, ed. *The Arden Edition of the Works of William Shakespeare: Romeo and Juliet*. London: Methuen, 1980.

Gurr, Andrew. *William Shakespeare: The Extraordinary Life of the Most Successful Writer of All Time*. London: Harper Collins Publishers, 1995.

Halio, Jay. *Romeo and Juliet: A Guide to the Play*. Westport CT: Greenwood Press, 1998.

Harbage, Alfred, ed. *William Shakespeare: The Complete Works*. New York: Viking Press, 1969.

Harrison, G. B. *Introducing Shakespeare*. 3rd.ed. Harmondsworth, England: Penguin Books, 1966.

Homan, Sidney. *A Midsummer Night's Dream William Shakespeare*. Dubuque, IA: WM. C. Brown, 1970.

'KJ', "Peter Brook's 1970 *Midsummer Night's Dream*", *Bardfilm: The Shakespeare and Film Microblog* Feb. 9, 2009. http://bardfilm.blogspot.jp/2009/02/peter-brooks-1970-midsummer-nights.html.

Lamb, Sidney. *Hamlet: Complete Study Edition*. Lincoln, NE: Cliffs Notes, 1967.

Painter, William. *The Palace of Pleasure* Volume 3 Project Gutenberg. http://www.gutenberg.org/files/34840/34840-h/34840-h.htm

Papp, Joesph. "Forward" in David Bevington, ed. *A Midsummer Night's Dream*, Toronto: Signet Classic Shakespeare, 1963

Selbourne, David. *The Making of A Midsummer Night's Dream: An eye-witness account of Peter Brook's production from first rehearsal to first night.* London: Methuen, 1982.

Shakespeare, William. *Hamlet.* Edited by Betty Bealey. Toronto: Longmans Canada, 1963.

Shakespeare, William. *Hamlet.* Edited by W. F. Langford. Don Mills, Ont: Academic Press, 1961.

Shakespeare, William. *Hamlet.* Quarto 1 (1603) University of Victoria: Internet Shakespeare Editions. http://internetshakespeare.uvic.ca/Annex/Texts/Ham/Q1/

Shakespeare, William. *A Midsummer Night's Dream.* Edited by David Bevington. Forward by Joseph Papp. Toronto: Bantam Books, 1988.

Shakespeare, William *A Midsummer Night's Dream.* Edited by Wolfgang Clemen. Toronto: Signet Classic Shakespeare,1963.

Shakespeare, William. *Oxford School Shakespeare: Hamlet.* Edited by Roma Gill. Oxford University Press, 1992.

Shakespeare, William. *Romeo and Juliet.* London: Macmillan, 1947.

Shakespeare, William. *Romeo and Juliet.* First and Second Quartos. Internet Archive. http://archive.org/stream/romeojulietparal00shakuoft#page/n19/mode/2up

Shakespeare, William. *Shakespeare's Comedy of A Midsummer Night's Dream.* Preface by Israel Gollancz. London: J. M. Dent & Sons, 1910.

Wells, Stanley. *Shakespeare: An Illustrated Dictionary.* Oxford University Press, 1978.

## About the Author

John Poulsen BEd, PhD (University of Calgary) & MA (University of London, England).

John is an academic, performer, director and writer. As a specialist in Drama Education, his research examines diverse fields such as affective attunement, teacher as performer, theatre direction, history of Drama Education, and Shakespeare. John is a founding member of two performing companies: masQuirx and Loose Moose Theatre Company (from which came Theatre Sports). He has directed over 50 productions, with a focus on classics, including Shakespeare and Theatre for Young Audiences collective creation.

## BOOKS BY FIVE RIVERS

### NON-FICTION

*Al Capone: Chicago's King of Crime,* by Nate Hendley

*Crystal Death: North America's Most Dangerous Drug,* by Nate Hendley

*Dutch Schultz: Brazen Beer Baron of New York,* by Nate Hendley

*Motivate to Create: a guide for writers,* by Nate Hendley

*The Organic Home Gardener,* by Patrick Lima and John Scanlan

*Elephant's Breath & London Smoke: historic colour names, definitions & uses,* Deb Salisbury, editor

*Stonehouse Cooks,* by Lorina Stephens

*John Lennon: a biography,* by Nate Hendley

*Shakespeare & Readers' Theatre: Hamlet, Romeo & Juliet, Midsummer Night's Dream,* by John Poulson

*Stephen Truscott,* by Nate Hendley

### FICTION

*Immunity to Strange Tales,* by Susan J. Forest

*Growing Up Bronx,* by H.A. Hargreaves

*North by 2000+, a collection of short, speculative fiction,* by H.A. Hargreaves

*A Subtle Thing,* Alicia Hendley

*Kingmaker's Sword, Book 1: Rune Blades of Celi,* by Ann Marston

*Things Falling Apart,* by J.W. Schnarr

*And the Angels Sang: a collection of short speculative fiction,* by Lorina Stephens

*From Mountains of Ice,* by Lorina Stephens

*Memories, Mother and a Christmas Addiction,* by Lorina Stephens

*Shadow Song,* by Lorina Stephens

### YA FICTION

*Mik Murdoch: Boy-Superhero,* by Michell Plested

EPILOGUE, BIBLIOGRAPHY, ET CETERA

## FICTION COMING SOON

*The Runner and the Wizard,* by Dave Duncan

*Cat's Pawn,* by Leslie Gadallah

*Cat's Gambit,* by Leslie Gadallah

*The Loremasters,* by Leslie Gadallah

*Old Growth,* by Matt Hughes

*88,* by M.E. Fletcher

*Stitching Butterflies,* by Shermin Nahid Kruse

*Western King, Book 2: The Rune Blades of Celi,* by Ann Marston

*Broken Blade, Book 3: The Rune Blades of Celi,* by Ann Marston

*Cloudbearer's Shadow, Book 4: The Rune Blades of Celi,* by Ann Marston

*King of Shadows, Book 5: The Rune Blades of Celi,* by Ann Marston

*Sword and Shadow, Book 6: The Rune Blades of Celi,* by Ann Marston

*Bane's Choice, Book 7: The Rune Blades of Celi,* by Ann Marston

*A Still and Bitter Grave,* by Ann Marston

*Diamonds in Black Sand,* by Ann Marston

*A Method to Madness: A Guide to the Super Evil,* edited by Michell Plested and Jeffery A. Hite

*A Quiet Place,* by J.W. Schnarr

*5000 Mile Journey,* by Kelly Stephens

*Forevering,* by Peter Such

## YA FICTION COMING SOON

*My Life as a Troll,* by Susan Bohnet

*Type,* by Alicia Hendley

*A Touch of Poison,* by Aaron Kite

*Out of Time,* by David Laderoute

*Mik Murdoch: The Power Within,* by Michell Plested

## NON-FICTION COMING SOON

*China: the New Superpower,* by Nate Hendley

CPSIA information can be obtained at www.ICGtesting.com
Printed in the USA
LVOW11s1226140913

352382LV00003B/8/P